Contents

6 chapters

The reciprocal nature of the partnership – References – Acknowledgements

Introduction – Working with parents as clients or partners – Special educational needs and parental involvement – Behavioural problems: involving parents in a whole-school approach – Evolving strategies – Applications: practice and possibilities – Further reading – References – Appendix: Parental Profile

Education as negotiation – Open files: a basis for partnership – The open class: a truancy project – The analysis of a problematic situation – Attempting partnership: an example – Conclusions – References

The Contributors

ROGER BURLAND is an educational psychologist and Director of the Chelfham Group of Schools, which were acknowledged by Bridgeland as pioneers of the behavioural approach in residential education in the UK. He established the Association of Behavioural Approaches with Children and has published widely in this area.

ROBERT CAMERON is Tutor for Continuing Professional Development in Educational Psychology at Southampton University. He is also joint author (with E. V. Westmacott) of *Behaviour Can Change*, which has proved a popular book on behavioural management for parents and teachers.

LEE CANTER, President of Lee Canter and Associates, Inc., Santa Monica, California, USA, is the developer of 'Assertive Discipline', and is considered one of the leading experts on school discipline in the USA. He has written over 20 books and produced 25 videos on his programme.

NEIL FRUDE trained as a clinical psychologist at the Institute of Psychiatry, London. Dr Frude is now Senior Lecturer in the School of Psychology at the University of Wales College of Cardiff. He has written and edited a number of books in the fields of aggression, human relations and computers. With Hugh Gault, he has edited *Disruptive Behaviour in Schools* (1984).

LYN FRY trained as a teacher and educational psychologist in New Zealand, and she has been Staff Tutor at Lea Green School and Deputy Principal Educational Psychologist in Waltham Forest. She has published numerous articles and chapters on educational topics but is now mainly interested in behaviour management of young children. She is in private practice in London.

IRVINE GERSCH has worked as a teacher, educational psychologist and Open University tutor. He has published in the areas of behaviour management, pupil involvement, teacher support groups and systems work in schools. He is currently Principal Educational Psychologist in the London Borough of Waltham Forest.

FIONA GREEN is Divisional Coordinator for Support Services in

Southwark and Honorary Lecturer at the Institute of Education. For ten years she worked in partnership with David Lane at the Islington Educational Guidance Centre, and with him, she is the recipient of an award (1986) from the Campaign for Freedom of Information, for their policy of allowing children complete access to all information on their files.

PETER GURNEY is Senior Administrator, School of Education, Exeter University, and lectures part-time. He has been senior tutor to a full-time course in special educational needs, is a chartered psychologist and has published articles on educational psychology and special needs.

DON HILLS has taught for seven years in the London area and worked as an educational psychologist in Leeds, Coventry (senior), Birmingham (senior), Brent (principal) and Wolverhampton (principal). For the last six years he has gone back to his primary interest of full-time field-work in north Devon.

DAVID LANE has taught in a variety of settings over twenty years. He is particularly known for his writing on the 'Impossible Child', but has also published widely on diverse topics in education. He was for several years the Director of the Islington Educational Guidance Centre and is currently the Director of the Professional Development Foundation, a trust providing research and training support to individual practitioners and organisations, and an Adjunct Professor of Psychology at Syracuse University (London Centre).

JEAN LAWRENCE was formerly head of a Croydon secondary modern and an ILEA comprehensive school. She has held an SSRC Fellowship in Educational Psychology and for many years combined a Principal Lectureship at Goldsmiths' College, University of London, with research into disruptive behaviour. Her books include co-authorship of *Norwood Was a Difficult School* (1988). She is currently a research officer in the Department of Education, London Borough of Harrow.

MARTIN SCHERER became a headteacher at Chelfham Mill School after teaching in mainstream and special education in ILEA, including the secure unit of a regional resource centre. He has published a number of articles about disruptive behaviour.

COLIN J. SMITH is Lecturer in Education, University of Birmingham, and tutor to courses for teachers of children with difficulties in learning and behaviour. He has co-authored *Effective Classroom Management: A Teacher's Guide* (1984), and edited *New Directions in Remedial Education* (1985). He is editor of *Maladjustment and Therapeutic Education*, the journal of the Association of Workers for Maladjusted Children.

DAVID STEED is a senior lecturer at the University of London Post-graduate Department, Goldsmiths College. He is co-author of *Disruptive Children – Disruptive Schools?*, with Jean Lawrence and Pamela Young, and a number of other articles in this area. His present interest is the behaviour of children in primary schools.

KEITH TOPPING is an educational psychologist who is known for research, dissemination and in-service training concerning children whose behaviour is problematic. He has authored three books and co-edited a fourth, and published more than 80 chapters, articles and training packages. His specialisms also include systems for non-professional tutoring via parents, peers and others.

SHEILA WOLFENDALE has been a primary school remedial teacher and educational psychologist in several LEAs and is currently Professor in the Psychology Department of the Polytechnic of East London, in charge of a postgraduate training course for educational psychologists. She has published extensively, most recently *Primary Schools and Special Needs: Policy, Planning and Provision*; and *The Parental Contribution to Assessment*, and in 1989 an edited text on parental involvement.

Acknowledgements

We should like to express our particular
gratitude to Barbara Gersch, for her support
and help throughout, and to our publishers,
and especially Miranda Carter and Lynne
McFarland, for their patience and guidance.

Editors

Introduction

Martin Scherer

Readers often omit to read the introduction to books. This is unfortunate, for the introduction – as in this case – may give an explanation of the book's emergence and some outline of its main principles.

Why this book?

Today in the UK education is experiencing radical and widespread change, particularly in the area of the curriculum, appraisal of pupil and teacher performance, assessment and provision of special needs, involvement of parents, management of schools and the role of support services. The speed of that change is rapid, placing great demands on teachers to understand and to implement new methods and procedures. While these may take time to consolidate, nevertheless the majority constitute substantive changes. One issue, namely disruptive behaviour, seems to re-emerge biennially, and the names ascribed to that issue (and its causes, context and solution) changes with an equal rapidity, yet the problem persists. The subject of this book is the management of such pupil behaviour, whether it be called 'maladjusted' or 'disruptive' or 'disaffected'.

This book emerged from symposia presented to the British Psychological Society, the Association of Educational Psychologists and the Association for Behavioural Approaches with Children. These were organised by the first editor (Scherer), who as a teacher, wanted to know about current developments that were applicable in the classroom. In addition, we present chapters by authors who have something pertinent to say about the management of disruptive behaviour. All the authors of this volume have direct, practical experience in the topics of their chapters; and most are practising teachers, lecturers involved in teacher training or educational psychologists.

The structure of the book

This book is divided into four sections: approaches, assessment, intervention and partnerships; and the chapters within each section are interrelated.

The main themes running throughout this book reflect those principles in meeting disruptive behaviour which have emerged in education over the past 30 years. With their growing use, we believe we may now see practical solutions to the problem of misbehaviour.

An historical perspective of approaches to disruptive behaviour

All change, however radical or revolutionary, occurs within an historical context. In Section A we look at the various labels (Chapter 1), causes and solutions, as applied to disruptive behaviour. While no single approach is claimed as sufficient, one in particular does appear to be emerging as prominent (Chapter 3). That approach is a recurring theme throughout the book, but we hesitate to label it, for such a label may prompt misunderstanding before the approach is clearly understood. First, we shall identify the key elements.

Methods of assessing behaviour

Our approach is based on the rigorous assessment of pupils' individual needs, beginning with the precise description of the behaviour in question (Chapters 4 and 5). We seek objectively to observe that behaviour on several occasions in the context in which it occurs (Chapter 4), and taking into account the participants' description. Finally, this approach seeks accurately to evaluate the proposed method of influencing the attitude and behaviour of the pupils (Chapters 5 and 6).

The method described here has been widely used over the past decade, as may be witnessed by texts in other fields of nursing, social work, industrial and commercial management, and in the disciplines of clinical and occupational psychology. Practitioners are offered an objective and scientific basis which may be readily applied in their practice. In the classroom teachers have the opportunity to test the validity of professional advice and academic theories. The method may be used to evaluate curriculum development and pupil performance, and to appraise the procedures and performance of teachers and their managers. Importantly, it offers teachers a model for self-appraisal.

The method as outlined in Section B is termed 'single-subject, steady-state methodology', or 'single subject' or 'baselining'. It is also known as 'repeated measures design' as validity rests not on a single measurement of behaviour or performance, but involves repeated observation. Single-subject methods attend to an actual individual rather than the mean performance of a group of individuals.

Rigorous evaluation of practice

A secondary theme of this book is the rigorous evaluation of practice. The single-subject method is used in both the assessment of the problem and evaluation of provision to meet that problem.

Practical procedures for use in classrooms and schools

Third, a major problem in education is that most research has occurred outside the classroom. Consequently, the methods advanced are often highly complex, demanding resources and specialist knowledge that goes beyond the training of teachers. In contrast, single-subject methods are directly applicable to the classroom and may be adapted for use by the teacher while teaching, or the manager while managing. For clarity we illustrate the methods and procedures with examples that originate in the classroom, remembering the demanding role of the teacher and the busy and stressful life of school.

A second limitation of some of the current literature is that what seems to have emerged is a set of golden and immutable rules of practice. We do not accept this as valid. Every pupil, every teacher, every classroom and every school is different, unique. Every teacher has his or her own style, and the content of their teaching varies from subject to subject and age-group to age-group. Hence we believe that each application of a method or procedure should be evaluated rigorously in the classroom by the teacher who uses it. It is *not* sufficient to 'trust to faith' and use a procedure because it has worked elsewhere. We all need to discover our own solutions which may be influenced by the advice of others but are adapted to fit our own circumstances.

The methods and procedures that we have chosen have each emerged from the classroom, and we hope that the reader will view these as potentially useful, while requiring adaptation and rigorous evaluation for own use; the single-subject method of evaluation we present (Chapter 6) is just that, a potentially useful method. We favour the growth of 'action research' in schools and conclude that for any reader trying out new ideas the real test is its usefulness to that teacher. This can only be discovered by applying ideas and objectively evaluating outcomes.

Behavioural analysis

From the single-subject method certain basic principles have emerged about behaviour. It is difficult to refer to these principles as a unified theory; many practitioners deny that it is. This may be a brave admission for those with a felt need for a unified and complete explanation before having the confidence to proceed. However, this approach does recognise the infinite variability and complexity of human behaviour.

Two basic principles emerge: first, that behaviour is maintained or suppressed by its consequences; changing the consequences may influence the behaviour (Chapters 9–11). Second, events that are antecedent to the behaviour may reliably indicate what the consequences of it will be and thereby come to exercise control over that behaviour. Changing the antecedents, then, may be a method of changing behaviour through such factors as behavioural rules (Chapters 8 and 9), classroom organisation (Chapter 8) and contracts (Chapter 11). This view of behaviour, known as 'behavioural' or 'functional analysis', emphasises the function of behaviour in producing or avoiding certain behaviour and the function of consequences in maintenance or suppression of behaviour. All such behaviour should be understood in the context within which it occurs.

Behavioural analysis may be classed as 'interactionist', emphasising that behaviour is the product of the interaction between the behaviour and events in the environment, and that the behaviour of one individual is, in turn, influenced by his/her interaction with others. In the classroom the key roles are those of the pupil, the teacher and other pupils; others, including non-teaching staff, parents (Chapters 8, 13 and 14), peers, managers and other professionals (Chapters 14 and 16) and politicians, have a less direct influence. Nevertheless, they do play an important secondary role (Section D).

Pupils may arrive in a new class or school with previously learnt behaviour (Chapter 3), but whether or not that behaviour is maintained will depend on what happens in the new setting. A behavioural approach does not make social judgements, attributing cause, credit or blame to any one individual; the emphasis is on teaching and maintaining appropriate behaviour (Chapters 8–13) and not expecting it to occur by chance. Rather than punishing misbehaviour, emphasis is placed on teaching and the maintenance of appropriate behaviour.

This analysis is therefore complementary to the view that the school system serves to control and maintain behaviour (Chapter 13); and both antecedents and consequences may be used in conjunction, as in contracts (Chapter 11). Indeed, behavioural analysis demystifies behaviour, in its assumption that what disruptive pupils need to learn are specific skills that are required and maintained by schools (Chapters 5, 6, 9 and 12).

Partnerships in changing behaviour

Another theme of this book emphasises the necessary participation by all those involved. Pupils are seen as participants in the procedures of assessment, behaviour change (Chapters 7, 11 and 16) and the procedures devised to meet their disruptive behaviour (Chapters 7 and 16). Involvement and participation increase the probability both of consensus and achievement. This is reflected in the participation of parents (Chapter 15) and the changing role of educational psychologists from consultant diagnosticians of child-focused problems to supporters and advocates of the needs of pupils, parents and teachers (Chapter 14).

Integration

The theme of integration in this book is substantially supported by a behavioural analysis, where behaviour is seen as influenced by consequences and antecedents. Hence there are considerable difficulties in removal of a disruptive child in the hope that 'segregated treatment' in a specialised context will resolve the problem. Indeed the only reason for removal may be when the behaviour is potentially dangerous to the pupil or others or is damaging to the education of that pupil or others, or if that provision cannot otherwise occur. This is in line with the integration principle advanced by the Warnock Committee (1978) and the Education Act (1981). Before pupils are segregated, they have a right to rigorous definition of the offending behaviour, and objective evidence of its occurrence (Chapters 1, 4, 6, 7 and 16), rather than subjective assumptions and anecdotal accounts. Teachers have a duty to attempt to maintain appropriate behaviour in class and, where necessary, to establish appropriate individual programmes (Chapter 16; for methods see Chapters 8–11). To do this, overall classroom management is important (Chapter 8).

What is contemporary behaviourism?

Contemporary behaviourism (Chapter 3) has been defined as an approach that uses an objective, single-subject method from which certain principles of behavioural analysis have emerged and avoids hypothetical guessing about unobservable causes of behaviour. However rigorous, objective observation may not always be possible. The pupil may then be a valid observer of his/her own behaviour. Hence procedures which involve pupils are often more accurate and, in the long term, more successful. Contemporary behaviourism views behaviour as influenced and maintained by its environment. Segregating a pupil from that environment may not teach pupils to behave appropriately when they return (Chapters 1 and 2).

Behaviourism has changed; and perhaps that is why this approach is labelled contemporary. This book is *not* about 'behaviour modification', a nebulous term today often misperceived as including the short, sharp shock, ECT, aversion therapy, chemotherapy and lobotomy. Contemporary behaviourists would not wish to be associated with these procedures, nor to view people as passive responders to be modified. Rather we perceive individuals as active participants with a role to play, whatever their ability, age or developmental level.

How to use this book

We hope that this book may be used as a sourcebook of potentially useful procedures that may be adapted by the reader for his/her context. Authors have recommended texts for further reading. The procedures discussed in this book may be most useful with children aged between seven and fourteen years; however, they may be adapted for use with any age-group.

We would encourage rigorous evaluation of each application and sharing of results with a group of colleagues – as the authors of this book are doing. Once you have been successful in adapting and applying one of the procedures described here, you may be encouraged to examine the other applications outlined.

Conclusions

In identifying the causes of disruptive behaviour (Chapters 1-3), it has been fashionable to blame the pupil (Chapter 1), or more recently the pupil's background (Chapter 2). Today it is becoming fashionable to blame the teacher. However, teachers are not the sole determinants of what happens inside the classroom. For decades teachers have carried out instructions, guidance and advice of trainers, managers, consultants, advisers and politicians. Further, it should be understood that blaming teachers can disaffect the profession – in the same way that it has demoralised and disaffected pupils and parents. 'Faults' lie in a system that fails to keep pace with the rate of change, and the isolation of training, research and evaluation from the classroom.

It is surely time for teachers to take an active role in deciding what procedures may be applicable in their classrooms by rigorously evaluating the application of their procedures and reporting upon the outcome to colleagues. The various authors in the present book essentially take this approach. For teachers to take on this professional role, we need both a method that enables the rigorous definition and assessment of the problem and objective evaluation of practice. One approach that uses an objective method and is gaining increasing acceptance is contemporary behaviourism (Chapter 3).

SECTION A

Approaches to Disruptive Behaviour

Chapter 1

Perspectives on Disruptive Behaviour

Neil Frude

There are a number of reasons why classroom aggression causes concern, and why it is important to develop effective strategies for managing and containing it. Many pupils suffer emotionally from the aggression directed towards them by school bullies. Classroom aggression can seriously disrupt the education process, thereby affecting the educational attainment of many pupils. It can even lead to physical injury.

Schools are complex social institutions in which, by and large, pupils are educated successfully and socialized positively. Pupils generally learn to appreciate the needs of others and to behave within certain restrictions imposed by legitimate authority. Teachers convey the standards of the wider society by example and by the application of rules, and their authority is backed by their power to invoke certain positive and negative sanctions. Thus the school, like the family, is a powerful agent of socialization. The pupil who continually exhibits aggressive behaviour and opposes the influence of the school is also likely later to reject the legal constraints of the wider society. Children judged to be aggressive by their teachers tend to be involved in criminal activity in later life (Farrington, 1978; West, 1982). Serious aggression in the school can therefore be seen as a danger signal, indicating that a 'window of opportunity' for positive socialization is being missed.

Disruption at school also merits concern because of the effect that it can have on teachers. Several of the teachers' unions have called attention to the problem in recent years, and evidence that antisocial, uncooperative and aggressive behaviour are common sources of stress for teachers has come from a number of studies. Dierenfield (1982) found among a large sample of teachers in England that one in three regard classroom disruption as a severe problem. Surveys by Kyriacou and Sutcliffe (1978), Dunham (1977) and others have shown that for many teachers disruptive and aggressive behaviour is the most important single source of stress in their professional lives. Dunham (1984) provides evidence that such stress can lead to lack of confidence, depression and various psychosomatic conditions. He reported that stress leads some teachers to take 'sick leave' or to opt for early retirement.

Some degree of aggression is a natural part of school life. The classroom is a 'social laboratory' in which pupils explore different styles of social behaviour and learn the limits of acceptable conduct. Feedback from peers and teachers provides a 'social mirror' which guides behaviour and affects the pupil's confidence and self-perception. Among those aspects of social behaviour likely to be subjected to such experimentation will be many which relate to issues of power, tolerance, justice and retribution. Boisterousness, competition, rivalry, teasing and games-playing can all 'misfire' and lead to aggression. Some of the events that happen within the classroom, as within almost any social situation, will be annoying and frustrating. From time to time pupils will have genuine grievances against teachers and other pupils. Thus a degree of aggression is fully to be expected within the school setting, and we must accept that much of the aggression witnessed will be 'normal' and 'natural', and will not therefore call for an explanation which involves labelling children as 'maladjusted' or 'conduct disordered'.

Yet bullying, and aggressiveness towards teachers, can present a chronic and serious problem, and certain pupils will need specialist treatment. When 'ring-leaders', 'deviant' and 'hostile' pupils are identified, the most appropriate explanation for their disruptive behaviour may be one which focuses on peer influences or the teacher–pupil relationship rather than one which relies on a diagnosis of individual psychopathology. Thus in order to deal most appropriately with a child who is highly disruptive, we need to examine many aspects of the particular social environment. Only by being aware of the nature of 'normal' aggressive incidents within the classroom, and especially of the teacher's response to such events, can we confidently disentangle 'personalogical' factors from 'situational' factors.

Numerous explanations have been advanced to explain the phenomenon of school disruption. It has been identified with the phenomenon of 'mobbing' described by animal ethologists (Heinemann, 1972), it has been seen as a form of pupil protest against over-authoritarian schools, and it has been regarded (by several neo-Marxist analysts – Furlong, 1985, provides a useful review) as a facet of working-class resistance against hegemony. Amongst the variables examined for possible correlations with school aggression have been class size, parental unemployment, IQ, teacher skills, and testosterone level (the last of these – in a study by Olweus *et al.*, 1980 – proved to be only indirectly related to school aggression!). The task of integrating concepts and evidence from studies of hormones and of hegemony will not be an easy one. Information from research by psychologists, sociologists, psychiatrists and educationalists, and based on methodologies as different as micro-ethnographic studies and longitudinal survey studies, can however be represented as reflecting different perspectives or levels of analysis. One such level is the disruption *incident*; another is the disruptive *individual*. Other levels of analysis involve *teacher–pupil relationships*, *classes and peer groups*, *schools* and *the wider context*. Evidence relating to each of these levels will be presented before considering the implications of the various approaches for the 'treatment' and 'prevention' of classroom disruption.

Incidents

One type of study concentrates on analysing specific incidents in detail. The approach taken is generally ethnographic and such studies take as their data accounts of the events as given by the teachers, the pupils or, more usefully, both. Subsequent analyses seek to identify common structural features of incidents. Thus Pik (1981) showed that many incidents could be seen as having four distinct phases – he labelled these 'the build-up', 'the trigger', 'the escalation', and 'the finale'. Marsh, Rosser and Harre (1978) suggest that disruption often takes the form of a pupil's 'retaliation' against a teacher's 'offensive' behaviour.

It is clear that much disruption is a result of the pupils' bid to make life in the classroom more entertaining. Messing about or having a laugh (Woods, 1979; Beynon and Delamont, 1984) is a disruptive classroom sport which has been enjoyed by generations of schoolchildren. By introducing a distraction the flow of the lesson is broken. Boring lessons (and lessons which are taken less seriously, perhaps because they are not part of the examination system) are at most risk of such interruption. Boring teachers (and those who over-react to slight disruption) are also likely targets. Messing about may lead to nothing more than a transitory break from the formal agenda, or it can seed a full-blown classroom crisis.

The teacher's tolerance and skill in handling the situation are the most important determinants of whether or not the situation will escalate. The over-permissive teacher will invite a constant barrage of 'fun' strategies. The over-reactive teacher, however, will provide an exciting entertainment following any slight sign of messing about. The ideal response would seem to be for the teacher to recognize the distraction for what it is and to allow it to run its natural course (often only a matter of a few seconds) before quickly recovering the lesson. It is clear that one of the main strategies used to derive entertainment is to produce a disruptive stimulus as bait for the teacher. It is the teacher's response which promises to provide the fun rather than the initial stimulus itself.

A special form of messing about, employed with new teachers, is known as 'sussing out' (Ball, 1980; Beynon, 1982). New teachers are systematically harassed in order to test their tolerance threshold and their breaking point, and to discover how they will deal with disruptive pupils. A newly trained teacher may lack the necessary confidence and skills for containing distraction and may thus provide a high entertainment pay-off. Systematic harassment of such teachers tests the unknown quantity. Certain pupils see how far they can push the teacher, so indicating to other class members how far they can go.

A common sequence in disruptive classroom incidents is one in which an 'offence' by the teacher leads to 'retribution' by pupils. Marsh, Rosser and Harre (1978) noted that common 'offences' of teachers included being arrogant or distant, administering unjust or inconsistent punishment and forgetting a child's name. It is an offence to be seen as 'picking on' a particular child or to show favouritism. Offences merit retaliation, and Marsh *et al.* showed how such retribution is governed by a set of rules centring on the concepts of 'justice' and 'reciprocity'.

A point of difference between the teacher and the pupil may quickly escalate to a high level of conflict. Operating from different standpoints, the two may appraise an event quite differently. The pupil may feel that the teacher has a biased judgement and is using power unfairly. A protest will commonly take the line that the teacher's behaviour is arrogant and authoritarian and out of line with 'natural justice.'

The teacher who backs down as a result of a pupil's protest may be seen as weak and is likely to face further trouble in future. If, however, the teacher is seen to settle the matter by asserting power or imposing strong sanctions, then the class might well interpret this as a further 'offence'. Teacher and pupil may soon be in a state of serious conflict, and engage in an open row before a class of pupils who are eager to judge which of them will emerge from the 'contest' as the victor.

Incident analyses based on classroom observation, and on reports from teachers and pupils, clearly show how quickly conflict can escalate. Accounts from pupils also indicate that even behaviour which might appear from the outside as spontaneous and random has a logic and reason when interpreted from their perspective. Disruptive pupils will generally explain their behaviour, and will defend it as 'reasonable in the circumstances'. Incident analysis therefore stresses the importance of understanding individuals' perception of the disruption or aggression.

There are several implications of such analysis for prevention and treatment of classroom disruption. Clearly, it is important that the teacher appreciate that much disruption is only messing about and need not be the first sign of serious trouble. It is also essential that teachers be trained in the skills for defusing situations so that escalation is unlikely. It is equally important that the teacher, and any outside professional brought in to help with a disruptive pupil or class, be aware of the fact that disruptive behaviour is likely to have a rationale and a meaning for pupils. One approach, therefore, would be to consider whether the disruption can be treated as a conflict between two parties both of whom are convinced of the legitimacy of their position. This, of course, involves a form of arbitration which may not be to the liking of the teacher. It is hardly surprising that teachers tend to view disruption as a sign of maladjustment or conduct disorder in one or more pupils rather than as the result of the social dynamics between teacher and pupils, or within class.

Individuals

Some pupils are clearly more disruptive than others, and a traditional approach has been to focus on the 'personality defects', 'emotional problems', 'behavioural dysfunctions' or 'psychopathology' of individuals. In recent years, however, there has been some degree of disenchantment with using such disease entities as 'maladjustment' to account for school disruption. The main criticisms levelled against such an approach have been that it ignores the situational context and that it tends to over-estimate the consistency of a pupil's behaviour.

Yet the personality approach to understanding disruption cannot easily be dismissed. There *is* a degree of cross-situational consistency and disruption has been shown to be related to a number of identifiable individual and background characteristics. Some disruption would seem to be related to facets of temperament – 'aggressiveness', for example, and 'excitability' – and among the thousands of children and adolescents identified as antisocial there will undoubtedly be some who are disadvantaged by neurological impairment. Graham and Rutter (1968) are among those who have reported a significant association between behaviour disturbance and neurological damage or dysfunction.

The stability issue is crucial for analysis at the individual level, and the facts present a somewhat complex picture. On the one hand it is clear that some disruptive pupils present as a problem only in particular classes, or with particular teachers. Some children seem to become problems only as a result of peer-group influence. Many children who are aggressive and antisocial at home are well behaved at school, and *vice versa* (Rutter, Tizard and Whitmore, 1970). On the other hand there is a good deal of evidence supporting the idea that children who are seen as presenting management problems in the early years continue to do so into adolescence and beyond. Thus Farrington (1978) found a significant tendency for the same pupils to be described as 'aggressive' at the ages of nine and sixteen.

On the basis of a number of studies of Swedish boys between thirteen and fifteen years old, Olweus (1978, 1984) believes that the most appropriate explanation of bullying is one which centres on the personalities of the bullies and their victims. Olweus found considerable consensus between teachers in their view of which children were bullies and which were targets for aggression, and noted that these identifications remained stable over a three-year period (and despite changes of school, teachers and classmate). Bullies were shown to have a strong need to dominate and were characterized by what Olweus labelled as a 'spirit of violence'. They were physically and verbally aggressive, confident and tough, and lacked empathy for their victims. Thus their aggressive behaviour was reflected in their attitudes and their general behavioural style. Olweus found that the bullies' victims (whom he labels 'whipping boys') were often unpopular, anxious and low in self-esteem.

Interviews conducted with the parents suggested that a mother's treatment of her son in the early years may have been partly responsible for a child's level of aggression. Mothers of bullies had tended to treat their offspring either with indifference and over-permissiveness or with hostility (often expressed by the frequent use of physical punishment). The mothers of 'whipping boys' had tended to be over-anxious and over-protective.

The importance of the early treatment of the child is indicated in another series of studies by Margaret Manning and her colleagues. From observations of nursery school behaviour, Manning and Sluckin (1984) were able to show a considerable variation in the amount and type of aggression practised at the age of three years. Manning and Hermann (1981) found that children described by their nursery teachers as 'aggressive' were attention-seeking, hostile, dominating and boastful while another group – 'demanding' children – were dependent, difficult and unpopular. Manning and Sluckin (1984) also report a 'remarkable stability' in aggressiveness over two years of nursery schooling. Because the individual differences were apparent when nursery schooling commenced these authors, like Olweus, suggest that factors in the homes of the children may be responsible for the differences in level and type of aggression.

Thus stability would seem to have been established for one personality feature – 'aggressiveness' – which is likely to be related to which pupils are disruptive in school. Reviewing longitudinal studies of aggressiveness, Olweus (1979) reports a consensus indicating a degree of stability: '. . . not much lower than that found in the intelligence domain.' Certain studies in the field of school disruption support the stability hypothesis. The same children are likely to be regarded as aggressive and disruptive by their (different) teachers between eight years and sixteen years, and those identified as aggressive as early as eight are likely to have criminal records in their adult life (Farrington, 1978). From the results of his twenty-year study West (1982) found that being involved in disruption and aggression at school as an eight or ten year old was the *best* predictor, among the many variables included at that stage of the study, of whether the child would later become delinquent.

Although the evident stability in aggressiveness is consistent with the view that there might be a genetic basis for such individual differences, attempts to test this directly have not yielded positive results. Twin studies and adoption studies on child and criminal populations have failed to find evidence supporting the genetic transmission of aggressiveness or violent criminality (Plomin, Foch and Rowe, 1981; Mednick et al., 1982). On the other hand, evidence does support the view that family factors during the early years may be of key importance in determining the child's level and style of aggression. There is a significant association between parental coldness and rejection of the child and high aggressiveness as shown at school. Children from this type of family background tend to react angrily and are unable or unwilling to exercise restraint. Such children frequently act in a hostile fashion and seem, from quite an early age, to view violence positively.

Many of the studies which support the stability hypothesis, however, focus on aggression expressed towards peers. Bullying, in which the target is a fellow pupil 'selected' as weak, unpopular and defenceless, may be a very different phenomenon from that of classroom disruption. Some bullies confine their aggressiveness to the playground and do not show hostility towards or in the presence of teachers. Thus care should be exercised in assessing the relevance of studies of bullies to the issue of general classroom disruption. However, it is clear that some children are boisterous and hostile towards both teachers and peers. Teachers, too, may become 'whipping boys'.

Thus despite the tendency in recent decades to analyse disruption as an 'interactive', 'transactional' or 'social group' phenomenon, rather than as the manifestation of the personality of individual pupils, the potential contribution of children's personality characteristics should not be dismissed. It is likely that in some cases of disruption the most useful focus for analysis and treatment might be the individual pupil. This, however, is something which needs to be carefully *assessed* rather than *assumed*.

By the same token, consideration of the individual characteristics of the teacher might provide a useful focus for case analysis. Teachers differ markedly in the extent to which they seem to attract disruption. Various teacher typologies have been suggested, and Hargreaves *et al.* (1975) have provided an 'ideal typology' which bears directly on the disruption issue, with categories of 'deviance-provocative' and 'deviance-insulative' teachers. It is clear that pupils also use schemes for categorizing teachers. Teachers are classified in terms of their teaching ability, the level of interest of their lessons, their tolerance, their fairness and their ability to keep control. March *et al.* (1978) found that children distinguished 'good teachers', who merited respect and were not frequently disrupted, 'soft teachers' who provided an easy target for playful disruption, and some teachers, those who merited a hostile and retributive response, who were regarded as 'a load of rubbish'.

Teacher–pupil relationships

Some disruption would seem to be the result of a long-standing feud between a teacher and a particular pupil. Thus in a study of children who had been suspended from school, Galloway *et al.* (1982) found that a large proportion had experienced what they described as a 'long-standing personality clash' with a teacher. The researchers formed the impression that this intense mutual dislike was sometimes at the root of the child's problems at school. Classroom arguments between teachers and pupils can become quite vicious, and even physically violent, and once such an incident has occurred the relationship between the two may be permanently damaged. Each will have a lowered threshold for judging the other's subsequent behaviour as 'offensive'. The pupil is likely to seek consensus from his or her peers that the teacher is 'mad' or 'bad' while the teacher is likely to seek confirmation within the staff-room, or to broadcast the 'fact', that the pupil is 'maladjusted' or 'conduct disordered'.

Teacher–pupil conflict is not conflict between equals. The teacher may find that the class is loyal to the pupil, regarding the child as a victim who has been unfairly picked on by the teacher. Thus the teacher may have to face the resentment not just of the one pupil but of the class as a whole. On the other hand the teacher has the power to apply sanctions, to punish, and has much more power to define the situation. Thus the teacher can characterize the pupil, by word or deed, as 'deviant' in the public arena of the classroom. This process by which teachers 'label' deviant pupils has been given considerable attention (Hargreaves, 1976). Labelling may produce a 'self-fulfilling prophecy', with a pupil having once been perceived as deviant more likely to attract the label on future occasions. Pupils considered to be deviant will be regarded with suspicion and their behaviour closely monitored.

A child who is aware that the 'deviant' label has been applied may behave especially well, in order to have the label removed, or may accept the label and behave accordingly. Hargreaves (1976) has suggested that the degree to which a child accepts the teacher's judgement of deviancy will depend on how frequently, consistently and publicly the label is applied. If the judgement appears to be shared by many teachers then, in the face of such consensus, the child may incorporate the view into his or her self-image. A child thus 'stigmatized' is likely to live up to others' expectations.

Labelling theory represents a powerful combination of two familiar psychological concepts – cognitive consistency and 'mirroring'. Once a person has formed a view of another there will be a tendency for that person to interpret future behaviour of the other in line with the original view. Thus if a teacher has formed the impression that a child is aggressive, future actions are likely to be interpreted as signs of aggression rather than more charitably as boisterousness or playfulness. There are individual differences in how open teachers will be to changing impressions on the basis of evidence which could be taken as disconfirmatory. 'Mirroring' refers to the process by which people tend to accept as part of their self-image a view of them which is presented by powerful others. People then have expectations of their own behaviour and tend to behave accordingly. Teacher expectation has of course been suggested as a powerful determinant of pupils' academic performance as well as of the level of disruptive or deviant behaviour.

There is a tendency for those who favour a 'labelling' explanation of disruption, however, to de-emphasize the first stage of the process, that by which the individual initially attracts the label. This will hardly be a random process, and it is likely that it will be disruptive pupils who attract the 'disruptive' label. Thus although labelling theory has been widely used to explain deviant behaviour at school it may be more relevant for explaining how relationships between teachers and particular pupils develop, and of how pupils respond to teachers' actions, rather than of how some pupils come to be disruptive.

Classes and peer groups

Classes have different 'personalities' or 'atmospheres' and, like individual pupils, may acquire staff-room reputations. To some extent, all pupils within a class may be tarred with the same brush, and classes may be addressed, congratulated or blamed collectively. Poor relationships tend to develop between teachers and classes as well as between teachers and individual pupils (Finlayson and Loughran, 1976). But teachers and pupils also appreciate that within the single class there is a sociometric structure. Each class evolves as a mini-society with its key figures, its heroes, its scapegoats, its stars and its isolates. The presence of sub-groups can lead to strong inter-group rivalries and in-group solidarities. For a number of reasons, therefore, an appreciation of the social structure within the class may be fundamental to an understanding of much classroom disruption.

Individual pupils may belong to one or more groups or gangs within the class and will be highly influenced by membership of such peer-groups. Membership depends on a number of characteristics such as ability, interests, and attitude to authority, and once a pupil identifies with a group there will be strong pressures on him or her to adopt the consensus attitudes and the behavioural norms of the group. Classroom sub-groups can often be sharply differentiated by their general orientation to school and to the authority of the teacher (Meyenn, 1980; Pollard,

1980; Willis, 1977). Some groups have a positive attitude towards school, authority, teachers and work, while others have decidedly negative attitudes. Inter-group rivalries and intra-group processes lead to polarization around this pro- or anti-school orientation. Willis found that pupils distinguished between the anti-school 'lads' and the pro-school 'ear 'oles', and Pollard found that conforming pupils were referred to by rebel groups as 'puffs', 'goody-goodies' and 'teacher's pets'.

The existence of such groupings may clearly promote aggressive behaviour in the classroom. A defiant act by one member of a gang or rebel group may be regarded by other members of the group as heroic or brave. They may goad one of their number to retaliate against a teacher's offence, or members might effectively take turns to disrupt the lesson. By encouraging bravado, and by promising and giving support for disruption, therefore, certain peer groups will facilitate the rebellious behaviour of a member. A group leader, or 'hero', may 'represent' and 'act for' the group as a whole. A peripheral member of a 'rebel' group, as yet unsure of his acceptance by his peers, may exhibit defiance towards the teacher in a bid to gain approval by the group.

Some pupils will be left out of all groups and so feel isolated and unpopular. They may make desperate bids for recognition and acceptance, or their frustration and loneliness may produce withdrawn or disturbed behaviour. A proportion of those who cause trouble are of this type, and Galloway *et al.* (1982) found that a third of a sample of suspended pupils were isolates.

Schools

At another level, there is convincing evidence to show that aspects of school organization and ethos can contribute markedly to the frequency of disruptive acts. Polk and Shafer (1972) put forward the view that: 'Underachievement, misbehaviour and early school leaving are properly and most usefully to be seen as adverse school–pupil interactions, and not simply as individual acts carried out by students as natural responses to damaged psyches or defective homes.'

Within any school, however, there will be major differences between individuals in the frequency with which they disrupt lessons, and thus an analysis at the level of the school clearly cannot tell the whole story about disruption. But a number of impressive studies have indicated that schools vary markedly in the frequency of disruptive acts (Power *et al.*, 1967; Rutter *et al.*, 1979; Galloway, 1980). Such studies indicate that physical provision (size of buildings, class size, teacher-to-pupil ratio, etc.) are not as important as the less tangible aspects, or ethos, of the school. Rutter *et al.* (1979) found that among the most important factors were an emphasis on reward rather than punishment, the immediacy of action on indiscipline, and the democratic organization of the teaching staff.

Reynolds and Sullivan (1979) found higher rates of disruption in 'coercive schools' than in what they term 'incorporative schools' (i.e. those which consult with pupils in making rules and which encourage pupils and parents to participate in the running of the school). A number of studies have indicated that a key factor contributing to the school ethos is the attitude of the headteacher, particularly with respect to the less academically successful pupils. In some way the rather global variable of school ethos would seem to be represented in the classroom environment such that it influences the behaviour of individual pupils. The matter may be rather complex, however, for the atmosphere of a school is likely to reflect, as well as to help determine, the behaviour of its pupils. The results of one recent study (West, 1982) suggest that differences between schools in 'contributing' delinquents is largely a reflection of differences in the pupil uptake.

The wider context

Finally, influences beyond those of the individual school have also been suggested as contributing to school disruption. High-level decisions regarding school planning, the curriculum, the structure of examinations, etc., however causally distant from individual antisocial acts within the classroom, can all be expected to have some eventual impact on this aspect of school life.

Many school problems, including disruption and truancy, increase in frequency with age. The fact that older boys, in particular, are often involved in the most serious disruptive acts has led some writers to suggest that, particularly for the less academically gifted teenager, the school is an 'unnatural' environment. The biological fact of the earlier onset of puberty, and the social fact of the emergence of a teenage culture mean that young adults are now confined within a type of social organization originally designed to contain and educate young children.

Older pupils may exercise considerable personal power and independence in their lives outside school and have to suspend many of their 'adult powers and privileges' while in school. Much disruptive behaviour can be seen as a bid to be 'adult' (to heckle, to choose to be uncooperative, to smoke, to dress unconventionally, etc.) in a context in which such 'normal' behaviour for 15 year olds is judged to be innappropriate. There is also strong evidence that many secondary school pupils, especially those of lower ability levels, find much of their school work boring and pointless (Raven, 1978). They may express their frustration through acts of aggression and vandalism and use disruption to make life more entertaining. There may also be some impact of the perceived difficulties in finding later employment. More able pupils may be made more instrumental in their pursuit of high-level qualifications while those of less ability may regard striving for the meagre certificates they are likely to obtain as simply not worthwhile.

The analysis of school disruption in such global terms does not stand *instead* of closer analyses, but rather highlights some additional factors. Wider social factors (such as the increased rate of unemployment or changes in social policy) trickle down through long causal pathways to make their impact on individuals and to affect their behaviour and experience.

Multiple phenomena, multiple levels, multiple factors

Many analyses have been provided for classroom disruption and useful evidence has come from studies of many kinds. Whatever the focus or level of investigation it has proved possible to identify certain factors which seem to add to the overall risk of disruption. Although some studies may hardly seem to touch upon the issues raised by other work, it is possible to integrate findings from studies as different as the ethnographic micro-studies and the longitudinal epidemiological work.

Classroom disruption is not a simple or indeed a single phenomenon. Sometimes it represents a planned rebellion against a teacher who is judged as guilty of a serious offence against pupils. Sometimes it begins as 'messing about' and escalates as a result of a teacher's mishandling of the situation. Sometimes a bully's victimisation of another pupil spills over into the more public arena of the classroom. Sometimes it is the result of a rivalry or long-term feud between groups or gangs of pupils.

Incidents are influenced by historical factors (the teacher's reputation, previous incidents, etc.) and each incident leaves its own legacy. Disruption may be part of an on-going story with pupils often deriving much pleasure from the 'soap opera' aspects of the classroom drama. When faced with a boring lesson or teacher, they may be pleased when one of their number adds a degree of social spice to the proceedings. Stars may emerge who can be counted on to start the fun, and they may be reinforced by their classmates. If being disruptive brings social rewards to one pupil, others may be keen to imitate and join in.

The teacher's response to baiting is all-important, and an ill-phrased accusation or a misjudged comment may turn a fun incident into a crisis. But things are more likely to turn sour if the rapport between the teacher and the class has been poor. Many factors condition the quality of the atmosphere, the social backdrop which colours the meaning of the pupils' behaviour. The lesson content, the organization of the curriculum, the attitude of the school towards its less gifted pupils all affect the risk of disruption. Moreover, the general quality and content of the educational provision is important. If pupils see a particular lesson, or the whole curriculum, as pointless then since little is to be gained by attending to the lesson, some alternative and disruptive activity is to be preferred. The classroom is also an arena in which individuals may assert themselves, show off, gain kudos from misbehaviour, and challenge the system. If the morale of teachers is low, then they are more vulnerable to disruption.

Implications for treatment

A number of guidelines for preventing and treating classroom disruption can be drawn from the analyses presented in this chapter. It is important not to *assume* that school aggression indicates that one or more children has a 'behaviour disorder'. Much disruption emerges as the result of social interaction and the cause may lie not within a pupil but in the relationship between the pupil and the school or between a pupil and teacher. Schools are complex social institutions in which some degree of aggression and disruption is to be expected. An incident of 'normal' disruption, however, can quickly escalate to crisis level, and if incidents are handled badly, then disruption can become the norm. Disruption threatens the teacher's professional role and status and may be source of considerable stress. Teachers, therefore, are not dispassionate witnesses to classroom aggression but are often heavily emotionally involved.

A teacher who asks for help from the headteacher or from an outside agent may, in effect, be seeking confirmation of their own version of events. A referral may include the implicit message – 'either they're abnormal . . . or I am'. Colourful accounts by teachers of the misdeeds of a particular child may reflect processes of labelling and stereotyping and indicate the extent to which the relationship between pupil and teacher has broken down. A psychologist or psychiatrist may be brought in to support the teacher's version of events, and it is all too easy for an innocent professional to become entangled in the power politics of the classroom and the school.

The child is likely to regard the professional helper as a confederate of the teacher, and therefore as a threat. Given the opportunity, however, a child will often cite grievances against the teacher and be able to provide a convincing rationale for apparently irrational behaviour. It is therefore important that the child's account of incidents be heard sympathetically (Bolger, 1986). In some cases the evidence will reveal a dysfunction not of an individual child but of the general pattern of relationships within the class or between pupils and one or more teachers. Intervention on a 'systems' level may bring about a positive effect on the dynamics of the teacher–class relationship (Steinberg, 1986). Advice might be given on changing aspects of the curriculum, the seating arrangements, or the rules which operate within the school. Gillham (1984) has advocated an 'organizational' approach to dealing with disruption and has provided several useful examples of how changes in school practices (time-tabling, use of work-sheets, etc.) can be implemented to help prevent disruptive incidents.

If a case analysis reveals a specific incompatibility between the child and a teacher, or where things have developed to such a state that a 'normal' relationship is unlikely to be regained, it might be recommended that the child change to another class or another school. Radical improvement in behaviour may follow such a fresh start, especially if the change is presented to the child as an 'opportunity' rather than a 'punishment'.

Much of the foregoing analysis places emphasis on the importance of social 'ecological' factors in determining when and where disruption will occur, and which children are likely to be involved. Awareness of such issues is likely to prevent the easy assumption that disruption represents only the behavioural manifestation of a 'disruptive personality'. The 'clinical' analysis of a case should not be restricted to an exploration of the personality and behavioural characteristics of a child who has been reported by a teacher as disruptive, but should consider – at

least as part of an initial exploration – an assessment of the social setting. Sometimes the result of such an assessment will make it clear that
the modification of an individual's behaviour is not likely to yield the
desired results.

Despite the more sociological approaches to disruption favoured in
recent years, however, there is strong evidence supporting the view that
the behaviour of *some* children does merit special and individual attention. When such a child is recognized there are many ways in which the
professional (teacher, psychologist or psychiatrist) can attempt to help.
Approaches which have been recommended by various therapists
include psychodynamically based psychotherapy (Boston and Szur,
1983), rational-emotive therapy (DiGuiseppe, 1983), and various programmes of behaviour modification. Peers may prove the most effective
therapeutic agents, providing ideal models and shaping the behaviour
of their disruptive classmates by the manner in which they treat the
aggressive outbursts.

In recent years increased provision has been made in many countries
for special units for dealing with children whose behaviour has proved,
in the longer term, unacceptable to schools (Tattum, 1982; Lawrence,
Steed and Young, 1986). By virtue of their smaller classes and the
increased availability of specially trained personnel, such units – often
dubbed 'sin bins' – are able to provide a therapeutic input in addition
to the closer monitoring and containment of children. Whether
attempts at prevention and treatment take place in the school or in a
special unit, however, the most effective interventions are likely to be
those which focus on the child's *social* behaviour and outlook.

It is clear that much more could be done to equip teachers for coping with the difficulties which may arise in the management of classes,
and a number of initiatives in this direction have been published.
Marland's book 'The Craft of the Classroom: a Survival Guide'
(Marland, 1975) describes a number of useful class management
strategies. Following Hall (1971), Yule, Berger and Wigley (1984) have
recently described an action research project in which teachers were
trained to implement behaviour change programmes in the classroom.
Bernard, Joyce and Rosewarne (1983) have described a programme
based on rational-emotive therapy which aims at helping teachers to
cope with stress. This includes sessions in which teachers are trained to
overcome their irrational beliefs, to be more tolerant of individual differences, to think more positively about pupils who lack academic
prowess, and to feel less threatened as a result of classroom
harassment.

The multi-perspective analysis of disruption suggests that many variable factors act together to precipitate disruptive behaviour, and that these influence individual cases and particular incidents in many different ways. It argues for a case-based approach and indicates that many alternative strategies of intervention may be effective. It acknowledges the relevance and importance of social policy decisions while supporting the view that a clinical and individual approach is likely to be effective in many cases.

The analyses outlined above clearly indicate that while wider social factors do have an impact, much can be done to prevent classroom disruption, at the school level, the classroom level, in teacher training and selection, and in dealing with individual pupils. Two metaphors may be presented to illustrate how the multi-perspective analysis may be used to generate intervention strategies. The first is the chain metaphor. Breaking or removing any link in a chain is sufficient to break it. Disruption can be seen as the endpoint of a causal chain which includes links of many different kinds. We may effectively prevent disruption by working with a peer group that is reinforcing an individual's antisocial attitudes, we may counsel the individual in an attempt to change those attitudes, or we may work behaviourally to break the link between the attitudes and the behaviour.

The other metaphor is that of the straw and the camel's back. Removing any of the multitude of straws may be sufficient to reduce the load below breaking threshold. Thus if a particular pupil's disruption reflects his poor academic performance, combined with his isolation from his peers and his enrolment in the class of an insensitive teacher, then 'treatment' might consist of moving him to another class, of training him in social skills, or of teaching him to read more effectively. The optimal strategy may also be one which approaches the problem simultaneously on several different fronts.

In deciding between different approaches to treatment or prevention, many factors will need to be taken into consideration. Pursuing the metaphors, some links will be easier to break than others, some straws easier to lift. Generally, those elements which bear directly on the inappropriate behaviour will be more effective than those which are causally distant. It may be easier to change an individual's behaviour than to change a school organization. Of course, if many individuals are similarly affected by a particularly poor school ethos, then it would make more sense to try to change this than to work with each individual separately. It should also be acknowledged that effective treatment does not *necessarily* depend on an adequate understanding of the contributory factors. Excessive and inappropriate behaviour might be 'trimmed' without extensive causal analysis.

Thus there are, to introduce a final metaphor, more ways than one to skin the cat. It is likely that the most effective intervention will be one which, mindful of the heterogeneity of different cases, is case-based and takes into account factors operating not only at the level of the individual but also – more *micro*scopically – at the level of the incident – and more *macro*scopically – at levels involving relationships, the social context and the wider societal background.

References

BALL, S.J. (1980) 'Initial encounters in the classroom' in : Woods, P. (ed.), *Pupil Strategies* (London: Croom Helm).

BERNARD, M.E., JOYCE, M.R. and ROSEWARNE, P.M. (1983) 'Helping teachers cope with stress: a rational-emotive approach' in: Ellis, A. and Bernard, M.E. (eds.), *Rational Emotive Approaches to the Problems of Childhood* (New York: Plenum).

BEYNON, J. (1982) 'Ways in and staying in' in: Hammersley, M. (ed.), *The Ethnography of Schooling* (Driffield: Nafferton).

BEYNON, J. and DELAMONT, S. (1984) 'The sound and the fury: pupil perceptions of school violence' in: Frude, N. and Gault, H. (eds.), *Disruptive Behaviour in Schools* (Chichester: Wiley).

BOLGER, A. (1986) 'Counselling in the treatment of disruptive pupils' in : Tattum, D. (ed.), *Management of Disruptive Pupil Behaviour in Schools* (Chichester: Wiley).

BOSTON, M. and SZUR, R. (1983) *Psychotherapy with Severely Deprived Children* (London: Routledge and Kegan Paul).

DIERENFIELD, R. (1982) 'All you need to know about disruption' *T.E.S.*, 29 January.

DiGUISEPPE, R. (1983) 'Rational-emotive therapy and conduct disorders' in: Ellis, A. and Bernard, M.E. (eds.), *Rational Emotive Approaches to the Problems of Childhood* (New York: Plenum).

DUNHAM, J. (1977) 'The effects of disruptive behaviour on teachers' *Educational Review*, 29, 181–7.

DUNHAM, J. (1984) *Stress in Teaching* (London: Croom Helm).

FARRINGTON, D. (1978) 'The family backgrounds of aggressive youths' in: *Behaviour in Childhood and Adolescence* (Oxford: Pergamon).

FINLAYSON, D.S. and LOUGHRAN, J.L. (1976) 'Pupils' perceptions in high and low delinquency schools' *Educational Research*, 18, 138–145.

FURLONG, V.J. (1985) *The Deviant Pupil: Sociological Perspectives* (Milton Keynes: Open University Press).

GALLOWAY, D.M. (1980) 'Exclusions and suspension from school' *Trends in Education*, 2, 33–38.

GALLOWAY, D.M., BALL, T., BLOMFIELD, D., and SEYD, R. (1982) *Schools and Disruptive Behaviour* (London: Longman).

GILLHAM, B. (1984) 'School organization and the control of disruptive incidents' in: Frude, N. and Gault, H. (eds.), *Disruptive Behaviour in Schools* (Chichester: Wiley).

GRAHAM, P. and RUTTER, M. (1968) 'Organic brain dysfunction and ·child psychiatric disorder' *British Medical Journal*, 3, 695–700.

HALL, I. (1971) *Managing Behaviour, Parts I, II, III* (Lawrence, Kansas: H. & H. Enterprises).

HARGREAVES, D. H. (1976) 'Reactions to labelling' in: Hammersley, M. and Woods, P. (eds.), *The Process of Schooling* (Oxford/London: O.U.P./Routledge and Kegan Paul).

HARGREAVES, D.H., HESTER, S.K. and MELLOR, F.J. (1975) *Deviance in Classrooms* (London: Routledge and Kegan Paul).

HEINEMANN, P.-P. (1972) 'Mobbning-gruppvald bland barn och vuxna' (Stockholm: Natur og Kultur).

KYRIACOU, C. and SUTCLIFFE, J. (1978) 'Teacher stress: prevalance, sources and symptoms' *British Journal of Educational Psychology*, 48, 159–167.

LAWRENCE, J., STEED, D. and YOUNG, P. (1986) 'The management of disruptive behaviour in Western Europe' in: Tattum, D. (ed.), *Management of Disruptive Pupil Behaviour in Schools* (Chichester: Wiley).

MANNING, M. and HERMANN, J. (1981) 'The relationships of problem children in nursery schools' in: Duck, S. and Gilmour, R. (eds.), *Personal Relationships 3: Personal Relationships in Disorder* (Brighton: Harvester).

MANNING, M. and SLUCKIN, A. (1984) 'The function of aggression in the pre-school and primary school years' in: Frude, N. and Gault, H. (eds.), *Disruptive Behaviour in Schools* (Chichester: Wiley).

MARLAND, M. (1975) *The Craft of the Classroom: A Survival Guide* (London: Heinemann Educational).

MARSH, P., ROSSER, E. and HARRE, R. (1978) *The Rules of Disorder* (London: Routledge and Kegan Paul).

MEDNICK, S.A., POLLOCK, V., VOLAVKA, J. and GABRIELLI, W.F., Jr. (1982) 'Biology and violence'. in: Wolfgang, M.E. and

Weiner, N.A. (eds.), *Criminal Violence* (Beverly Hills, Calif.: Sage).

MEYENN, R.J. (1980) 'School girls' peer groups' in: Woods, P. (ed.), *Pupil Strategies: Explorations in the Sociology of the School* (London: Croom Helm).

OLWEUS; D. (1978) *Aggression in the Schools: Bullies and Whipping Boys* (Washington, D.C.: Hemisphere).

OLWEUS, D. (1979) 'The stability of aggressive reactions in males: a review' *Psychological Bulletin*, 86, 852–75.

OLWEUS, D. (1984) 'Aggressors and their victims: bullying at school' in: Frude, N. and Gault, H. (eds.), *Disruptive Behaviour in Schools* (Chichester: Wiley).

OLWEUS, D., MATTSON, A., SCHALLING, D. and LÖW (1980) 'Testosterone, aggression, physical and personality dimensions in normal adolescent males' *Psychosomatic Medicine*, 42, 253–269.

PIK, R. (1981) 'Confrontation situations and teacher support systems' in: Gillham, B. (ed.), *Problem Behaviour in the Secondary School* (London: Croom Helm).

PLOMIN, R., FOCH, T. T. and ROWE, D.C. (1981) 'Bobo clown aggression in childhood: environment not genes' *Journal of Research in Personality*, 15, 331–342.

POLK, K. and SHAFER, W.E. (1972) *Schools and Delinquency* (Englewood Cliffs, New Jersey: Prentice-Hall).

POLLARD, A. (1980) 'Teacher interests and changing situations of survival threat in primary school classrooms' in: Woods, P. (ed.), *Pupil Strategies: Explorations in the Sociology of the School* (London: Croom Helm).

POWER, M.J., ALDERSON, M.R., PHILLIPSON, C.M., SCHOENBERG, E. and MORRIS, J.M. (1967) 'Delinquent schools?' *New Society*, 19 October.

RAVEN, J. (1978) 'School rejection and its amelioration' *Educational Research*, 20, 3–9.

REYNOLDS, D. and SULLIVAN, M. (1979) 'Bringing schools back in' in: Barton, L. and Meighan, R. (eds.), *Schools, Pupils and Deviance* (Driffield: Nafferton).

RUTTER, M., MAUGHAN, B., MORTIMORE, P. and OUSTON, J. (1979) *Fifteen Thousand Hours: Secondary Schools and their Effects on Children* (London: Open Books).

RUTTER, M., TIZZARD, J. and WHITMORE, K. (1970) *Education, Health and Behaviour* (London: Longman).

STEINBERG, D. (1986) 'Psychiatric aspects of problem behaviour: a consultative approach' in: Tattum, D. (ed.) *Management of Disruptive*

Pupil Behaviour in Schools (Chichester: Wiley).

TATTUM, D. (1982) *Disruptive Pupils in Schools and Units* (Chichester: Wiley).

WEST, D. J. (1982) *Delinquency, its Roots, Careers and Prospects* (London: Heinemann).

WILLIS, P. (1977) *Learning to Labour* (Farnborough: Saxon House).

WOODS, P. (1979) *The Divided School* (London: Routledge and Kegan Paul).

YULE, W., BERGER, M. and WIGLEY, V. (1984) 'Behaviour-modification and classroom management' in: Frude, N. and Gault, H. (eds.), *Disruptive Behaviour in Schools* (Chichester: Wiley).

Chapter 2

Disruptive Pupils: Changes in Perception and Provision

K. J. Topping

Introduction: the problems of definition

The term 'maladjustment' is incapable of agreed definition, and the equally vague term 'disruptive' has become more popular, having the advantage of sounding neither pseudo-scientific nor immutably fixed.

In the absence of agreed definition, estimating incidence is problematic, and figures cited have ranged from 4 to 49 per cent. In recent years attention has increasingly turned from individual to environmental factors and from historical to current elements in causation.

Segregated special provision for pupils presenting problematic behaviour expanded greatly after the Second World War, first, in the form of special schools, and later in 'off-site' units. In parallel there were increased numbers of Child Guidance Workers and psychologists providing consultative 'out-patient' services. In the 1980s it became clear that the effectiveness of such provision was in doubt, and government reports and subsequent legislation placed increased emphasis on the integration of children with special needs into ordinary schools. However, this shift of emphasis was over-bureaucratised and not satisfactorily funded, and increases in integration have been very slow.

Research evidence on the relative effectiveness and cost-effectiveness of different systems for educating disruptive pupils is now available, and local authorities are increasingly considering the establishment of a flexible and co-ordinated resource continuum to meet the needs of such children. The next decade should see the development and application of more practical strategies orientated towards supporting the child presenting problematic behaviour in the ordinary school.

For some decades past, thinking about children whose behaviour is problematic has been dominated by the concept of 'maladjustment'. Burt traces the origin of this term to the writings of Sully in the late nineteenth century (Sully, 1894). Sully himself emphasised that his use of the term was meant to stress the fact that the child presenting problematic behaviour was not to be considered in isolation, but as an individual personality interacting with and reacting to the historical and immediate environment. Burt himself, in 1952, re-emphasised the environmental aspects in his definition of the 'maladjusted' child, 'one whose adjustment to the recurrent situations of every day life are less adequate than might reasonably be expected from a child of that mental age, whose *conditions and circumstances* therefore require special study and treatment'. In later years, however, partly because of the interest in problematic children by the psychiatric profession, the term began to acquire overtones of 'psychiatric disorder'.

The medical model of understanding commonly involves ascribing a 'diagnostic' label to assorted phenomena often found together. Unfortunately, for children whose behaviour was problematic the application of this kind of label tended to carry the implication that the 'disease' was inherently within the child rather than the environment, and was also a condition for which there was no known cure.

This labelling process was inherently unreasonable in the case of children with problematic behaviour, since their behaviour was usually problematic in a great variety of different ways. As Whitmore (1975) later put it, the 'only thing which maladjusted children have in common is that they are children'. In time, a more educational view of the nature and needs of children who presented problematic behaviour came to hold greater sway. As early as 1955, the Underwood Committee (HMSO, 1955) accepted that the term 'maladjustment' was useful only as an administrative label. The report stated 'a child may be regarded as maladjusted who is developing ways which have a bad effect upon himself or his fellows that cannot without help be remedied by his parents, teachers and other adults in ordinary contact with him'. The circularity of this definition was repeated in the Handicapped Pupils and Special Schools Regulations (1959): maladjusted pupils are 'pupils who show evidence of emotional instability or psychological disturbance and require special educational treatment in order to effect their personal, social or educational re-adjustment'. In other words, the behaviour of some children can be taken as a sign that they need extra, special help.

Some workers made efforts to refine the vague concept of 'maladjustment' by going on to divide it into subtypes of behaviour, differentiated as 'withdrawn vs acting-out' or 'neurotic vs conduct disorder'. Although educationists found some of these labels more in tune with the reality of the classroom they remained essentially labels – or pseudo-explanatory fictions. They did little to provide teachers with clues as to how to manage the problematic behaviour presented by the child.

The term 'maladjustment' was already beginning to fade into disuse in the mid-1970s when the report of the Warnock Committee (HMSO, 1978) proposed the abolition of the existing categories of handicap, a recommendation which was later embodied in the Education Act (1981). Subsequently the adjective 'disruptive' has gained widespread currency in the teaching profession.

To call a pupil 'disruptive' is meaningful, up to a point, for most teachers. It implies that the pupil is disrupting either his/her own efficient learning or the efficient learning of other pupils. Although it is a relative concept subject to a variety of different usages, this is at least self-evident from the nature of the term, which is not laden with pseudo-scientific overtones. When teachers speak of a pupil's outbursts of 'disruptive behaviour', the phrase carries no intimation that the behaviour was other than transient and situational.

Most teachers are aware of the substantial research evidence showing that many children behave differently out of school than in school, that many ordinary children have difficulties adjusting to a new school and that many pupils whose behaviour is problematic in time demonstrate the phenomenon of 'spontaneous remission' – they 'get better'.

Although 'disruptive' is the word currently most commonly used for pupils presenting problematic behaviour, other words creep into the literature from time to time. These often display even greater vagueness, such as 'disaffection', which seems roughly to equate to disruption plus truancy plus under-achievement. Terms change over time, and it remains important that whenever we use words that are relatively meaningless we acknowledge the fact.

In the USA workers have referred to the 'emotionally handicapped' child as a category within the general body of 'exceptional children' (children with special educational needs). Before the term 'maladjustment' perhaps disappears forever, and teachers focus entirely on the 'disruptive' child, it is salutary to remember that many children who might previously have been described as 'neurotic and withdrawn' are presenting behavioural problems which are handicapping to themselves, even if they do not impinge upon the education of other children. It would be a pity if teachers became preoccupied with acting-out, aggressive children, while overlooking others who may be quietly, stoically, failing to adjust to school life.

Incidence and causation

If there is no clear definition of 'maladjustment' or 'disruption' (or whatever phrase we choose to use), it should not be surprising if our attempts to measure the incidence of this type of problem is fraught with difficulty. In a number of large surveys, for example, the Isle of Wight study (Rutter *et al.*, 1970), checklists of behaviour were used, owing much to the medical model. Other workers have used measures like the Bristol Social Adjustment Guide, a multiple-choice checklist of pupil behaviours. Other surveys have taken data from interviews with parents. In the final analysis, all of these are loose and subjective, the answers depending largely on the framing of the questions.

In the early study of Burt and Howard (1952) the authors studied the correlations between 24 conditions reported among 273 'maladjusted' children. Only a small general factor was found, and it was concluded that 'cases of maladjustment can hardly be regarded as forming a single, relatively homogeneous group'. There were considerable variations according to age, locality and social class. In the Isle of Wight study it was deemed that 6.8 per cent of the sample of nine- to twelve-year-olds could be described as having 'clinically significant psychiatric conditions' implying maladjustment. In the National Child Development Study (Davie *et al.*, 1972), 18 per cent of a representative sample of seven-year-old boys were deemed to be maladjusted on the basis of information provided by teachers on the Bristol Social Adjustment Guide, as were 9.9 per cent of girls.

Wall (1973) summarized data from epidemiological studies in several countries, including France, New Zealand and the USA. In these studies children considered to be 'seriously disturbed' ranged from 4 to 14 per cent of the total sample, while the number of children considered to be *in any way* 'maladjusted' ranged from 6.8 to 49 per cent. The studies summarized by Wall covered the years 1920 to 1971, and he comments: 'perhaps the most striking point to emerge is that, if we take the figures for the "seriously maladjusted", there seems to be no significant increase in fifty years'. Wall notes marked cultural differences in acceptability of different behaviours, and this may underlie the frequent finding of variations in problematic behaviour by social class and sex difference.

Whatever the definition of 'disruption' might be, its causation provides an arena for even more vigorous debate. In the past factors 'within the child' were emphasized, and much interest has been paid to temperamental and congenital factors, early developmental difficulties, physical factors and basic intellectual endowment. Attention has increasingly turned to environmental factors, particularly social, economic and psychological factors in the home. Apart from the obvious disadvantages of poverty, the effects of parental rejection, models of unsocialized aggression and excessive or inadequate discipline were investigated. Unfortunately, at the time, remarkably few of these supposed causative factors seemed to be amenable to direct intervention.

In recent years more attention has been paid to such factors as poor school attendance, disturbed patterns of schooling, ineffective instruction in the basic skills, difficulties in the teacher–pupil and in peer relationships and other factors within the school. While it would be naïve to assume that intervention from and within the school could improve more than a tiny proportion of in-school disruptive behaviour, nevertheless the school is an environment which is, in principle, more immediately under control than the wider community. Furthermore, a consideration of historical causative factors is of doubtful worth for practising teachers, except perhaps to render them more sympathetic to and tolerant of the disruptive pupil. Recent work with children presenting problematic behaviour tends to focus much more on the here-and-now of current behaviour, and current causation from the immediate environment, since this has much more practical implications for management. (Readers will note this emphasis in subsequent chapters of this book.)

Policy and legislation

It is difficult to know where to begin an historical perspective. Of course, there have always been badly behaved children. Specialist facilities in the twentieth century for children with special needs were not put on a consistent footing until the pioneering work between the wars of Cyril Burt. With respect to children presenting behavioural difficulties, the Underwood Committee focused attention on this group and began to place them in the context of children with 'special needs' rather than children who were 'bad'. The Underwood Report (1955) carried out surveys of incidence (of doubtful reliability and validity) in three areas of the UK and recommended substantial increases in the number of psychologists and psychiatrists working in Child Guidance Clinics. In the following years many more residential and special schools for maladjusted children were established.

Segregated educational provision for children identified as having special educational needs on account of behavioural difficulties was the order of the day until the 1970s. At this point, teachers began to become less tolerant and/or pupils became more disruptive, and more pressure began to be placed upon local education authorities (LEAs) to 'do something' about the problem of disruptive pupils. For a while, some LEAs tried to maintain a distinction between the supposedly 'maladjusted' and the obviously 'disruptive', leading to the setting up of the first 'off-site units' for disruptives. The Warnock Committee was to foreshadow the beginning of the end of the ensuing boom in this provision.

The Warnock Report (1978) recommended the abolition of 'categories of handicap', and proposed the individualised assessment of children with a view to determination of their personal 'special educational needs', with the purpose of avoiding self-fulfilling labelling and presumptions in advance about appropriate facilities. The Report strongly espoused the principle of integrating children with special needs into ordinary classes in ordinary schools. Furthermore, it was propounded that parents should be more intimately involved in the assessment of the difficulties their children were presenting, and given much fuller advice about their rights and responsibilities with respect to action outcomes of the procedures. Help for parents was to be available from 'the earliest years', and peripatetic teaching services should be available to support children in mainstream education. Nursery education should be provided for children with special needs.

Within schools teachers with day-to-day responsibility for children with special needs were to be involved in formulating individual educational plans for each child and liaising with a member of the managing or governing body with specific responsibility for children with special needs. The Report states that 'special classes and units wherever possible be attached to and function as part of ordinary schools rather than be organised separately or attached to another kind of establishment'. Recommendations were made about staffing levels, overall LEA plans for children with special needs, for the development of existing special schools as resource centres of specialist expertise, an so on; in all, about 250 recommendations were made in the Report. However, little by way of additional funding was made available for its implementation, and the Education Act (1981) proved in time to be a pale shadow of Warnock's vision.

The 1981 Act did embody parental involvement in assessment procedures and specified parental rights of appeal against LEA decisions. However, for many parents the procedures involved a bureaucratic rigmarole of such complexity that all but an articulate few were alienated from the outset. More to the point, nothing was said about resourcing the integration of children with special needs which had been recommended by Warnock. Neil Kinnock, then Labour education spokesman, declared that the Act was 'like Brighton Pier, good as far as it goes, but a poor way of getting to France'.

An inherent tension in the provision for special education needs of children presenting with problematic behaviour was thus created, and persists. On the one hand, many educationists are certain of the efficacy of integration in mainstream schools of pupils with behavioural difficulties; on the other hand, it is not possible to do this successfully without the provision of *appropriate*, *well-organised* resources, whether these are in addition to current resources or drawn from ones already existing in the school or LEA by changes in staff deployment policies. The 1981 Act had a number of 'get-outs for harassed administrators', among these the requirement that the placement of a child in a mainstream school must be compatible with 'the efficient use of resources'. In addition, the placement in the mainstream of pupils with special needs was ruled out where this could be construed to affect adversely the education of other children. This last point could be seized upon to justify a policy of excluding children presenting problematic behaviour at an early age. A headteacher's responsibility is to the efficient education of all the children in school. There is little evidence, however, that suspension of difficult pupils can be relied on to improve their subsequent behaviour (Gale and Topping, 1986). Indeed, there is sparse evidence that the removal of misbehaving pupils does improve the lot of those left behind.

Mortimore *et al.* (1983), in a survey of headteachers in the Inner London Education Authority (ILEA), reported that a number of headteachers of ordinary schools declined to use off-site units. Of those who did use the units, a small majority reported vague 'beneficial effects', but a third reported no positive effects or a deterioration. Likewise, schools reporting that the absence of a 'unit' child improved the behaviour of the pupils left behind were only slightly more numerous than those schools reporting no significant difference. By contrast, Coulby and Harper's (1985) evaluation of a team for peripatetic support of disruptive pupils in the mainstream reported that intervention with the disruptive pupil in the host school resulted in an improvement in the behaviour of the rest of the class in 44 per cent of cases, and 57 per cent of the involved teachers reported feeling more conflict about handling other similar cases in the future.

It has become clear that implementation of the 1981 Act has resulted in little increase in the integration of children with special needs. Sharron (1984) reported an alarming increase in the proportion of primary-aged children entering segregated special education prior to the implementation of the Act early in 1983. Enrolment in primary schools had fallen by over 13 per cent between 1978 and 1982, but the special school population had fallen by only 6 per cent. In schools for the maladjusted, rates of enrolment had increased by 12 per cent in the primary school range and over 9 per cent in the secondary school range.

In 1985 the Fish Committee reported on special education in the ILEA. The Report endorsed a pro-integration line, and recommended close association between remaining special schools and mainstream schools. There was evidence of 'widespread anxiety and confusion' about the 1981 Act assessment procedures. The Statementing process involved long delays and parents from ethnic minority groups were particularly dissatisfied. Ordinary schools often had problems identifying pupils' special needs, and links between the class teacher and specialist withdrawal teachers was often poor. There was a lack of nursery provision and other services for the under-fives. Liaison between professional agencies was poor and the allocation of responsibility for different types of provision could be 'confusing and arbitrary'. In so far as the Fish Report represented an evaluation of the effectiveness of the implementation of the 1981 Act in one LEA, it clearly implies that the Act could hardly be construed to have been cost-effective, particularly poignant in an authority which had in the preceding years spent many hundreds of thousands of pounds on off-site units for disruptive children.

Wedell *et al.* subsequently (1987) reported that Department of Education and Science (DES) figures showed that disadvantaged urban areas were 'Statementing' fewer children than the better-off shire counties. New 'labels' had come into being, and Statements tended not to reflect the interactive view of causation put forward by the 1981 Act. Only a minority of LEAs claimed to be sending fewer children to special schools (26–49 per cent depending on the type of school), and for children with emotional and behaviour problems there was a tendency for *more* children to be placed in special schools.

We now consider the variety of facilities and resources for meeting the needs of children who present behavioural difficulties in terms of their relative effectiveness and cost-effectiveness.

Provision

The publication of the Underwood Report in 1955 resulted in an increase in the numbers of Child Guidance Workers. Subsequently the Summerfield Report (1968), the Warnock Report (1978) and the Education Act (1981) considerably swelled the ranks of educational psychologists. As the numbers of these consultants were increasing, evidence was slowly accumulating that their effectiveness in one-to-one casework and generalized advisory work was low (Topping, 1986b).

In the 1950s and 1960s, boosted by the Underwood Report, the numbers of day and residential special schools for 'maladjusted' children increased substantially. After the mid-1960s evidence was already accumulating that the effectiveness of such establishments in terms of improving attainment and behaviour were, on the whole, extremely modest in relation to the high cost.

In the 1970s, off-site units proliferated with amazing speed, especially in southern England. But in the 1980s research evidence has indicated that such units have many disadvantages. Although cheaper to run than special schools, their effectiveness is low, save for a few exceptional cases.

Expensive systems have been implemented on the basis of 'seeming to be a good idea' and tended only to be evaluated at a later stage, when often there is so much financial, social and emotional investment in the existing institutions that changes become hard to implement. As we move towards the end of the century, an era of relative financial stringency has led at least some educational managers to take care to initiate all new projects on a pilot basis and to build in evaluation from the outset. Hopefully, this practice will result in the more efficient use of scarce resources, thereby benefiting more children with special needs to a greater extent than hitherto; further details of these developments will be found in Topping (1983). A comprehensive range of possible resources for helping children with problematic behaviour is given in Figure 1.

In the figure resources are presented in the form of a 'cascade', so that provisions lower down the cascade imply greater cost for the operation and involve greater interference or restriction with the life of the pupil affected by them. The underlying principle is that in resourcing the special needs of a child with problematic behaviour, one should start with the 'lightweight' interventions and only try facilities lower down in the cascade if the early interventions are unsuccessful. Likewise, in terms of re-integration, pupils should not be 'stuck' for ever at

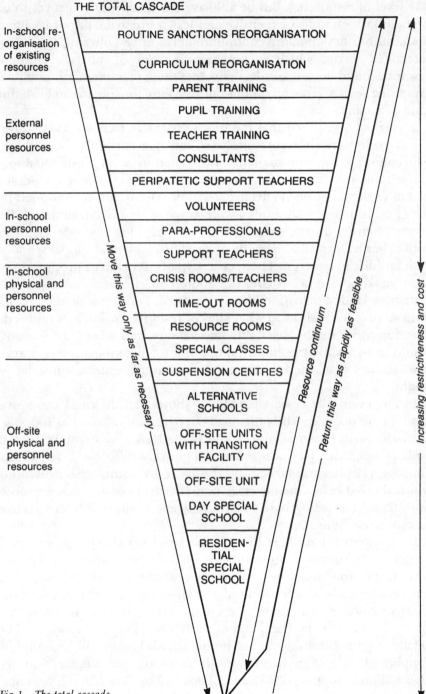

Fig 1   The total cascade

one level of resourcing, but be able as their behaviour improves to be phased back on to less expensive and less restrictive kinds of facilities. Some authorities operate a continuum of resources, offering a coherent integrated service which encompasses a range of different kinds of resource found in the cascade, delivering them in a systematic and pro-grammed way. A growing number of LEAs are looking to establish this kind of facility.

It might be assumed that the more expensive facilities lower down the cascade were the more effective; and that currently the children who end up at the bottom of the cascade in the day and residential spe-cial schools and off-site units must be by definition the 'worst' cases for whom nothing has been effective. Neither assumption is supported by the facts. In many authorities a wide range of resource facilities of dif-fering intensity do not exist, so children may, for example, be dealt with either by 'consultants' or by dispatch to residential special schools, with nothing in between. The special schools have thus a proportion of their intake whose needs could be more cost-effectively met by a less restrictive kind of provision, if only it existed. Furthermore, the predic-tions of professionals as to what kind of resource facility a pupil needs are of notoriously low reliability and validity, and where 'assessment' results in bypassing the empirical test of actually trying out less restric-tive facilities first, the effectiveness of many placements must be in doubt.

In any event, the research evidence shows that the most expensive facilities are not necessarily the most effective (summarised in Topping, 1983). Virtually identical conclusions in the USA have stemmed from a body of research which was at least 50 per cent different (Safer, 1982). Topping (1983) summarised his findings by listing the provisions which showed better than average cost-effectiveness, and placing those in order of increasing cost and restrictiveness within a 'cost-effective cascade' (see Figure 2).

It is suggested that where LEAs are seeking to establish a coordinated service or 'resource continuum' for children with special needs on account of problematic behaviour, they would do well to establish a service which could offer some if not all of the facilities in the 'cost-effective cascade'. For those interested in pursuing the research evi-dence on some of the cheaper and more cost-effective inputs, further details of parent training and of home–school liaison will be found in Topping (1986a); and further information on routine sanction re-organisation in Topping (1987), and Chapter 10 by Gersch in this volume.

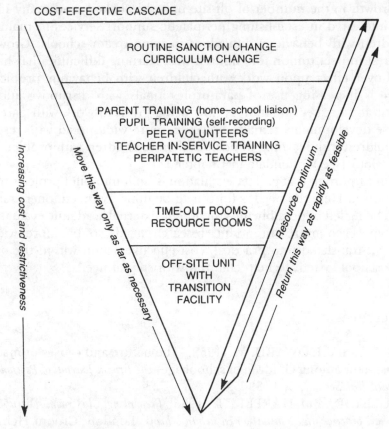

Fig 2 *Cost-effective cascade*

The future

Over the last few years some of the interventions in the cascade (Figure 2) have shown promising development. Some schools have become more adept at pupil training, and the quality of teacher in-service training (INSET) has improved in certain areas. High schools, in particular, are scrutinising more carefully their routine sanctions; developments in pastoral care have led to the introduction of social skills training as an integral part of the curriculum; and there is an increased interest in child self-management, often involving pupil self-recording (see Scherer in Chapter 5), a welcome change to the directive, punitive nature of some previous responses to children with problematic behaviour.

Growth in the number of off-site units has halted, and many LEAs are interested in establishing peripatetic support services to maintain children with behaviour difficulties in mainstream schools. Growing interest in peer tuition for children with learning difficulties has had a spill-over effect upon work with children with behaviour problems; there is increasing use of para-professionals with disruptive adolescents; and greater attention is now being given to work with parents. These developments remain, however, more widespread with respect to children with learning difficulties than to children with problematic behaviour (see Wolfendale in Chapter 15).

It is important that greater evaluation is built into pilot projects from the outset. Here the need is for this to be done by practitioners rather than being left to possibly unsympathetic external academic evaluators. Perhaps even more important, research needs to be more widely known, translated into practical, cost-effective action within the ordinary school system to help children with special needs.

References

BURT, C. and HOWARD, M. (1952) 'The nature and causes of maladjustment among children of school age' *The British Journal of Psychology, Statistical Section*, 5, 1, 39–59.

COULBY, D. and HARPER, T. (1985) *Preventing Classroom Disruption: policy, practice and evaluation in urban schools* (London: Croom Helm).

DAVIE, R., BUTLER, N. and GOLDSTEIN, H. (1972) *From Birth to Seven* (London: Longman).

GALE, I. and TOPPING, K.J. (1986) 'Suspension from high school: the practice and its effects' *Pastoral Care in Education* 4, 3, 215–24.

H.M.S.O. (1955) *Report of the Committee on Maladjusted Children* (the Underwood Report) (London: H.M.S.O.).

H.M.S.O. (1978) *Special Educational Needs* (the Warnock Report) (London: H.M.S.O.).

INNER LONDON EDUCATION AUTHORITY (1985) *Educational Opportunities for All?* (The Fish Report) (London: I.L.E.A.).

MORTIMORE, P. *et al.* (1983) *Behaviour Problems in Schools: an evaluation of support centres* (London: Croom Helm).

RUTTER, M., TIZARD, J. and WHITMORE, K. (1970) *Education, Health and Behaviour* (London: Longman).

SAFER, D.J. (1982) *School Programs for Disruptive Adolescents* (Baltimore, Maryland: University Park Press).

SULLY, J. (1894) *Teacher's Handbook of Psychology* (London: Longmans, Green & Co).

TOPPING, K.J. (1983) *Educational Systems for Disruptive Adolescents* (London: Croom Helm, New York: St. Martin's Press).

TOPPING, K.J. (1986a) *Parents as Educators: training parents to teach their children* (London: Croom Helm).

TOPPING, K.J. (1986b) 'Consultative enhancement of school-based action' in: Tattum, D. (ed.) *The Management of Disruptive Behaviour in Schools* (Chichester: Wiley).

TOPPING, K.J. (1987) 'School Sanction Systems: myth and reality' in: Hastings, N. and Schwieso, J. (eds.) *New Directions in Educational Psychology: Vol. 2, Behaviour and Motivation* (Lewes: Falmer Press).

WALL, W.D. (1973) 'The problem child in schools', *London Education Review*, 2, 2, 3–21.

WEDELL, K., WELTON, J., EVANS, J. and GOACHER, B. (1987) 'Policy and provision under the 1981 Act', *British Journal of Special Education*, 14, 2, 50–53.

WHITMORE, T.K. (1975) 'What do we mean by maladjustment? – then why don't we say so?' in: Laing, A.F. (ed.) *Trends in the Education of Children with Special Learning Needs* (Swansea: Faculty of Education, University College Swansea).

Chapter 3

Contemporary Behavioural Psychology and Problem Behaviour in School

Robert Cameron

Introduction

Despite the complexity of human behaviour, applied psychologists are developing strategies which can help parents and teachers to manage problem behaviour more successfully. In this chapter some of the problems of these approaches are discussed and a step-by-step procedure for tackling behaviour problems is offered, and the advantages of using a problem-centred approach are highlighted.

Human behaviour

Among the many phenomena offered for scientific analysis the behaviour of people must rate as among the most complex. Researchers in psychology have long been aware that even if they place human beings in the most artificial situations and attempt to reduce their options to the barest minimum, then the behaviour of their experimental subjects can vary from the predictable to the totally unexpected (more often than not, an ingenious mixture of both).

Despite the rich variations between and within individuals, common features do exist and social scientists can make important and accurate statements about people's behaviour if they are aware of sociological features, such as cultural and class norms, shared beliefs and social environment, or psychological variables like home background, attitudes, educational attainments, and so on. Indeed, the thrust of much social science research has moved away from individual or idiosyncratic aspects of human behaviour (taken as 'given') and concentrated on searching for some of those laws and relationships which govern the behaviour of individuals, as well as small and large groups of people.

One way in which it has been attempted to make sense of the complexity of human behaviour has been to set up abstract models of human behaviour. Psychological models have viewed people from a variety of different perspectives, including those of problem-solvers, machines, scientists, biological entities, social animals and information processors (see Chapman and Jones, 1980).

One obvious attraction of some models is the possibility of understanding and explaining human behaviour when the complex behavioural matrix has been stripped down. Another useful feature of models is their power to allow us to see what should be done when the human system is placed under strain or when certain aspects begin to fail or malfunction, as when personal or inter-personal problems arise. However, we shall see that approaches which can be used satisfactorily to explain human behaviour may also run into difficulty when the focus moves from explanation to *change*.

Problems within people

Historically some of the most powerful, enduring models employed to help teachers, parents and childcare staff to deal with the behaviour problems of children have been those which have viewed the child as the significant component of the problem. Some models have focused on the quality of early relationships ('She's had a difficult childhood . . .') or the processes of development and maturation ('They are very immature for their age . . .'); others have examined the nature of unconscious emotions and conflicts ('He's emotionally disturbed . . .') or have highlighted the importance of differences in personality ('Some aspects of her personality are abnormal . . .') or unusual features of intellectual functioning ('His ability profile is uneven . . .'). Such traditional psychodynamic, psycho-medical or psychometric views of a pupil's problem behaviour have helped parents and teachers to glimpse something of the complexities of behaviour and allowed researchers to begin to identify some of the differences which exist between and within individuals. Similarly, the close examination of within-child variables has sometimes enabled researchers to provide a more detailed explanation of why pupils exhibit problem behaviour. However, applied psychologists have recognised that within-child approaches have a number of built-in deficits both for children and teachers. Such models have led to the widespread labelling of children (e.g., 'maladjusted', 'lower ability', 'emotionally damaged', etc.), and although there is little evidence that exceptional children need to be treated differently from so-called 'normal children', the problems which arise from expectancy effects are well documented (see Scambler, 1984, for an overview of the problems of 'stigma' and 'spoiled identity'). The greatest drawback of models which concentrate on endogenous features of children is that the data collected do not readily generate strategies which the teacher can use for *changing* the problem behaviour.

Behaviour in context

Not surprisingly, over the past two or three decades there has been a steady trend in applied psychology away from an over-concern with the traditional endogenous variables towards a closer examination of the environmental factors which provoke, maintain or alleviate problem behaviour. Thus the focus of problem-solving has changed from discussing likely within-person aspects and searching for causes of the problem behaviour to seeking answers to the question: 'what can we do to change the situation for the better?' In reality, such elaborate descriptions of possible causes of problem behaviour have rarely been necessary, anyway, since most parents, teachers and other direct-contact adults have always tended to ask precise questions about the problems they face with their children.

One way of generating answers to such questions is to help people to examine the environmental aspects which surround a problem behaviour and to consider how such controlling conditions relate to the onset or maintenance of that behaviour. A simple method of examining the often daunting complexity of any problem behaviour has been suggested by Westmacott and Cameron (1981), consisting of examination of three important sets of events which surround the problem behaviour:

(a) *Antecedents* (events preceding the problem behaviour). It may be possible to identify and change some of the factors leading up to the unwanted behaviour. In a school setting particular considerations might include appropriate choice of activity, the establishing of clear classroom rules, the development of helpful classroom routines and careful curriculum planning, as well as teacher expectations, timetabling, etc.

(b) *Background events* (the setting or context in which the problem behaviour occurs). There may be certain features of the setting

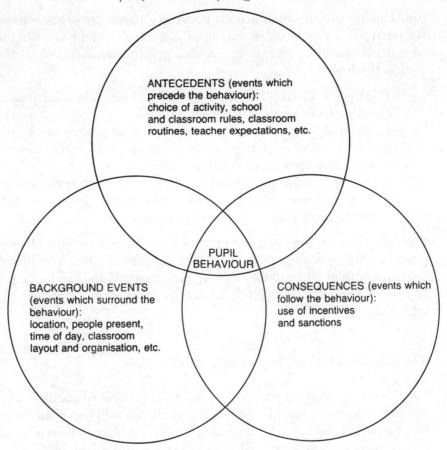

ANTECEDENTS (events which
precede the behaviour):
choice of activity, school
and classroom rules, classroom
routines, teacher expectations, etc.

PUPIL
BEHAVIOUR

BACKGROUND EVENTS
(events which surround the
behaviour):
location, people present,
time of day, classroom
layout and organisation, etc.

CONSEQUENCES (events which
follow the behaviour):
use of incentives
and sanctions

Fig 3   The ABC model of behaviour

which contribute to the problem behaviour. These are likely to
include the location, the people present and time of day, all of
which have implications for classroom management and layout.

(c) *Consequences* (events which follow the problem behaviour). It
may be possible to modify important aspects which occur as a
result of the behaviour. In particular, this can involve
improved problem management as a result of careful scrutiny
of incentives and sanctions available (Chapter 8), or just as
important, the possibility of teaching the pupil more appropriate skills (Chapters 10–12).

This simple behavioural model (see Figure 3) encourages a functional analysis of the relationships between a particular behaviour and the controlling events which surround it. Such a model has a number of general features which contrast with previously discussed within-person models:

·1. There is an emphasis on examining observable behaviour, as opposed to inner processes.
2. There is likely to be a clear statement of the desired behaviour.
3. The process of change involves helping the person with the problems to achieve the desired behaviour.
4. All the procedures leading to change are carefully monitored.
5. The outcomes of any agreed strategies for change are subjected to careful and systematic evaluation.

Such a systematic way of tackling problems has shown considerable promise, and a decade ago Berger (1979) concluded, 'there is sufficient evidence both in terms of the need of teachers and pupils and in terms of helpful application to justify the use of behavioural approaches in education'.

The rise and fall of 'behaviour mod'

Despite its reported effectiveness, many teachers and educationists are nevertheless suspicious of what they describe as 'behaviour modification', especially those in the normal school sector. Part of the reason for this is likely to have stemmed from a period in the late 1960s when over-enthusiastic 'behaviour modifiers' concentrated their attention on the consequences of learning and encouraged teachers to adopt what appeared to be 'universal' management strategies like the token economy. Many people in education were not convinced and many others must have winced at the brave new world suggested in one account of this new technology which appeared in *The Times* (11 July 1973): 'A new weapon in the psychologist's medicine bag – the Smartie!' The psychologists' obsession with consequences often meant that important antecedents like curriculum planning, and crucial background events like classroom management and resource allocation, were largely ignored. Thus not only were some of the most important controlling conditions in the management equation left out, but some of the most powerful sources of teacher expertise were left untapped, when strategies for change were being planned.

Such an overkill of 'behaviour mod' had the effect of ensuring that crude and simplistic interventions were often recommended by psychologists to deal with what teachers correctly saw as highly complex problems. It was a situation which disturbed many psychologists and led Berger (1979), in an article about behavioural approaches in education, to warn about 'the dangers of a mindless technology'.

An improved behavioural approach

The development of a more contemporary form of behavioural psychology became increasingly obvious in the late 1970s. Although building on some of the strengths of earlier models *contemporary behaviourism* had a number of additional features, which not only ensures a more thoroughgoing analysis of controlling conditions, but also promotes a more sensitive match between (a) strategies for changing problem behaviour and (b) the needs of particular individuals in particular settings. Cullen *et al.* (1977) have highlighted the main features:

1. The problem behaviour, together with its part in the person's total repertoire is examined (Chapter 5).
2. Data collected are interpreted in terms of the relationship between the problem behaviour and those environmental features which might provoke or maintain the problem (Chapter 9).
3. The agreed strategy for change is directly related to the implications of the data.
4. The outcome of the agreed strategy for change is evaluated and any modifications to the interactions (and also to the interpretation of the data) are themselves implemented and evaluated, thus evaluation is both ongoing and interactive.

Such a stance has led applied psychologists carefully to examine the controlling conditions in an individual's personal or social environment and offer clients the opportunity of viewing objectively problem situations.

Two of the chief advocates of this service stance (Howarth and Pearson, 1982) have suggested that it is appropriate to regard people as 'problem-solvers'; and supporting professionals as 'facilitators of solutions to problems'. While this is highly commendable, the practical task of turning people into 'problem-solvers' is not without difficulty. Indeed, a number of writers have even suggested that most people are not very good at problem-solving. In a classic book on this subject, Miller *et al.* (1960) made the important point that 'an ordinary person almost never approaches a problem systematically and exhaustively unless specifically educated to do so'. There are, however, as D'Zurilla and Goldfried (1971) have shown in their work with young children, hopeful signs that problem-solving skills can be taught successfully 'if . . . taught directly'.

The problem-centred approach

Over the past decade work has been undertaken at Southampton University to develop a procedure to enable both teachers and support professionals, including psychologists, to utilise a contemporary behavioural approach when helping teachers to tackle problem behaviour in school. The resulting 'problem-centred approach' has two major objectives: it provides an easy, self-correcting method of tackling a problem, and it is also designed to allow users to step back and view more objectively problem situations. The problem-centred approach provides an easy-to-follow, sequenced set of steps which enables users to move from problem to intervention to effectiveness evaluation. The original problem-centred procedure (Thomas and Walter, 1973) can be summarised as follows:

1. List each problem.
2. Select a priority problem from the problem list.
3. Specify operationally the priority problem.
4. Obtain a measure of how frequently the priority problem occurs.
5. Identify probable controlling conditions.
6. Specify a desired outcome.
7. Formulate and agree possible intervention designed to lead to the desired outcome.
8. Implement intervention.
9. Record and monitor intervention.
10. If successful, select next priority in (1) or agree no further intervention necessary; if unsuccessful, repeat (4)–(9).

The starting-point of this behavioural approach is the problem statement made by clients; assumptions concerning 'problems' include:

(a) The problems are such because people say they are (together with the implication that *they* therefore must be the ultimate judge of whether the problem has been resolved or reduced);

(b) Problems are relative and not absolute; they may be related to environmental circumstances and their level may be readily modified.

(c) Problem solutions are most likely to lie within the competence of the person who has originally stated the problem.

This approach is intended as a general guide for identifying problems and agreeing, planning and monitoring subsequent action with a wide range of individuals in a variety of settings. The problem-centred approach can therefore be used to clarify problems facing children, parents, individual teachers, the staff of an entire school or planners and policy-makers within an education system.

Steps to systematic problem-solving

Step 1: List assets

Interviews usually begin by asking clients to list some positive features of what, until now, may have been viewed totally as a 'problem situation'. (See also Chapter 6.)

Step 2: List problems, complaints, difficulties, etc.

This means writing down all the problem areas as stated by all interested parties. (See also Chapter 6.)

Step 3: Select a priority problem from problem list

The priority problem, in this case, may mean the 'most severe problem' or 'a problem to start working on', or it may mean 'the problem most likely to improve quickly'. Obtaining agreement is the major task involved in carrying out this step. (See also Chapters 3 and 4.)

Step 4: Specify priority problem operationally

Essentially, this means writing an adequate description of the priority problem. This procedure may be aided by asking questions like 'what exactly happens when . . .?' or 'what examples do we have of . . .?'. (See also Chapter 3..)

Step 5: Collect data relevant to problem

Here the objective is to collect information regarding the frequency or magnitude of the priority problem, thus obtaining a baseline measurement. (See also Chapters 3, 5 and 10.)

Step 6: Identify probable factors contributing to problem

This step concerns examination of the factors and conditions which may be associated with the problem behaviour. However, it is important to concentrate on factors/conditions that can be changed such as the antecedent, background and consequent events surrounding the problem behaviour.

Step 7: Specify desired outcome

In effect, this means agreeing on what is happening when the problem behaviour is either considerably reduced or alleviated. It is also necessary to agree the criteria by which successful change is to be judged; these are likely to relate to baseline data obtained in step 4.

Other considerations include:

(a) task analysis, where necessary, to plan appropriate steps towards the desired outcome;
(b) a re-check that the attainment of desired outcome would alleviate or overcome the priority problem, listed in step 2;
(c) a check that the desired outcome is not incompatible with the objectives of other people on the organisation as a whole.

Step 8: Plan possible strategies for change

Having discussed all possible intervention alternatives necessary to obtain the desired outcome, it should now be possible to select the best alternative and to clarify and agree details. (See also Chapter 13.)

Step 9: Implement intervention plan

Ensuring this step is successful may mean acquiring necessary resources and agreeing the personnel to be involved in planning, monitoring and follow-up. Again, it is important to ensure the intervention is not incompatible with the objectives of other people or the organisation as a whole.

Step 10: Record and monitor effects of agreed intervention

The main activities, at this stage, are the regular collection of data and an examination of progress, with changes in the intervention plan when necessary. (See also Chapter 3.) If the outcome is successful, then the next priority problem is selected from the problem list or it is agreed that no further intervention is necessary. If unsuccessful, steps 4–9 are repeated.

As can be seen, there is little room in the problem-centred procedure for a static or mechanistic approach which assesses problems out of context, uses explanations based solely on 'within-person' assumptions, ignores relevant environmental controlling conditions and does not generate observable outcomes and measurable change. Although it cannot be claimed that the problem-centred approach described here can be used to solve every problem, it does offer a number of advantages for supporting professionals:

1. It can be easily taught to direct contact personnel (e.g. teachers, care staff and parents).
2. It focuses on features of a problem situation that can be changed; 'problems', and not 'people', become the focus of change.
3. The involvement and agreement of everyone concerned is likely to improve the chances of a positive outcome to any problem situation.
4. It does not violate the principle of minimal intervention; when dealing with the problem, it generates simple strategies first, before moving on to more complex ones.
5. The assumption of positive change and the pursuit of constructive outcomes as opposed to 'solutions' are features of the approach; the starting-point is that people can change: things can improve.

The problem-centred procedure has been shown to be robust enough to deal not only with the problems of individuals (Stratford and Cameron, 1987), but also with organisational problems in a school setting (Stratford and Cameron, 1987; Stratford, 1987). A range of examples at different levels of service practice, including the client level, the staff level and the policy level, can be found in Cameron and Stratford (1987), where the importance of the problem-centred approach in the field of applied psychology training is discussed.

Overview

At the beginning of this chapter we noted that both the explicit and hidden rules which govern people's behaviour are highly complex and pose a daunting task for the social science researcher who attempts to untangle them. While research has tended to lend support to the well-worn adage, 'Now't queerer than folks!', some worthwile attempts to disentangle the general rules in human behaviour have also been made.

Originally, many of these efforts were directed towards within-person or endogenous aspects which explained some aspects of human behaviour but, in general, such models were limited in generating suggestions for change. While behaviour psychology in the form of 'behavioural modification' represented an environmentally focused approach to problem behaviour, early models were crude and often led to over-emphasis on a heavy-handed package solution to problems, a characteristic which failed to endear these approaches to teachers.

The radical contemporary behaviour movement, it is argued, represents a more promising approach to considering the functional relationships between the problem and the events that surround it and can provide a more subtle, as well as more positive, approach to behaviour management. Such an approach can help parents, teachers and others systematically to rearrange these controlling events to teach pupils new skills and successfully to manage disruptive behaviour.

Finally, it is recognised that there is no single all-embracing model of human beings. Rather there are a number of different formulations which may allow us to increase our knowledge of psychological process and widen our particular perspectives on behaviour. Contemporary behavioural psychology offers freedom to the analysis of human behaviour, which has the added advantage of being able to help direct contact people, such as parents and teacher, to change problem situations for the better.

References

BERGER, M. (1979) 'Behaviour modification in education and professional practice: the dangers of a mindless technology', *Bulletin of the British Psychology Society*, 32, 418–419.

CAMERON, R.J. and STRATFORD, R.J. (1987) 'Educational psychology: a problem centred approach to service delivery', *Educational Psychology in Practice*, 2, 4, 10–20.

CHAPMAN, A.J. and JONES, D.M. (1980) *Models of Man* (Leicester: British Psychology Society).

CULLEN, C., HATTERSLEY, J. and TENNANT, L. (1977) 'Behaviour modification: some implications of a radical behaviourist view', *Bulletin of the British Psychological Society*, 30, 65–69.

D'ZURILLA, T.J. and GOLDFRIED, M.R. (1971) 'Problem solving and behaviour modification', *Journal of Abnormal Psychology*, 77, 107–126.

HOWARTH, I. and PEARSON, L. (1982) 'Training professional psychologists', *Bulletin of the British Psychological Society*, 35, 373–377.

MARSH, R. (1973) 'A new weapon in the psychologist's medicine bag: the Smartie!', *The Times*, 11 July, p. 10.

MILLER, G.A., GALANTER, F. and PRIBRAM, K.H. (1960) *Plans and the Structure of Behaviour* (New York: Holt, Reinhart and Winston).

SCAMBLER, G. (1984) 'Perceiving and coping with stigmatizing illnesses' in: *The Experience of Illness* Eds Fitzpatrick, R. *et al.* (London: Tavistock).

STRATFORD, R.J. (1987) 'Helping schools to solve problems', *British Journal of Special Education*, 14, 3, 123–126.

STRATFORD, R.J. and CAMERON, R.J. (1987) 'Difficult behaviour in school: a problem centred approach', *Maladjustment and Therapeutic Education*, 4, 3, 25–32.

THOMAS, E. and WALTER, C.L. (1973) 'Guidelines for behavioural practice in the open community agency', *Behaviour Research and Therapy*, 11, 193–205.

WESTMACOTT, E.V.S. and CAMERON, R.J. (1981) *Behaviour Can Change* (London: Macmillan Education).

Recommended reading

CHEESMAN, P.L. and WATTS, P.E. (1985) *Positive Behaviour Management* (London: Croom Helm).

HERBERT, M. (1981) *Behavioural Treatment of Problem Children: A Practice Manual* (London: Academic Press).

SECTION B

Assessment of Disruptive Behaviour

Chapter 4

Monitoring and Analysing Disruptive Incidents

David Steed and Jean Lawrence, with Martin Scherer

Introduction

Collecting data, if it is to be acceptable to busy teachers, needs to be neither overly time-consuming nor bureaucraticised and to give some assurance that it will lead to better functioning of the system and a more effective harnessing of resources. Incident monitoring – using paper-and-pencil exercises – has now been used satisfactorily in a number of contexts. The simple request for a description seems to offer some reassurance that the perceptions and feelings of the key participants are not being ignored, nor the incident condoned. We know that some schools are more effective (Reynolds, 1975), while others seem to generate delinquency (Powers, 1967). Collecting data on the characteristics of schools – i.e. curriculum, timetable, structure of management, etc. – is thus important in understanding how schools may affect behaviour.

This chapter describes two uses of incident forms in different contexts; the first in primary and secondary schools (see Lawrence *et al.*, 1977, 1986), and the second in a regional centre for disruptive adolescents. Definitions of disruptive behaviour are important and need to be rigorous enough to develop suitable procedures for meeting such behaviour, yet not too tight so as to exclude information or deny individuals the freedom to report on what causes them most concern. In the school inquiries disruption was defined as anything which seriously interferes with the normal running of the classroom or school. In the disruptive centre it was anything which might result in an assault on a person or damage to property, or require restraint by a member of staff.

Incident monitoring in secondary schools

The two secondary schools which undertook incident monitoring were both multi-racial: the first was a boys' school of 800 pupils, in an outer city district, grouped into three broad ability bands with pastoral and disciplinary procedures organised on a year basis; the second a co-ed school of 1,200 pupils. Such contextual details are clearly important when designing a monitoring system to ensure careful mapping of the many factors to be taken into account in interpreting findings.

The procedure was as follows. Agreement was reached with the staffs in the two schools on a general definition of disruption, in preparatory visits by the three researchers. Incident forms were circulated to all staff, who were asked to record details of any incident which occurred in the periods chosen for monitoring – i.e., time, place, severity, pupils involved, age, sex, nature of the disruptive activity, etc. This was supplemented by a short written description of the incident and by interview data immediately after the incident; further information was collected from senior staff. When the data was collected, a report was circulated to teachers as a basis for discussion. This was seen as essential if a genuine dialogue was to develop between teachers and researchers. Some of the findings were new, others confirmed what was already known, but not necessarily by all staff. It was a measure of the success of the monitoring that with only one or two exceptions, all the teachers were involved. In general, those who reported incidents were younger and less experienced, but disruption was not restricted to this group. The findings in the two schools show similarities and differences; it is suggested that the extent to which teachers reported incidents is a measure of the frustration they experienced at not being able to engage children in worthwhile teaching experiences – an aspect of pupil disruption which has been underestimated.

The data suggests that teachers' perceptions were closely associated with the work ethos of the school – disruption was anything which prevented this from operating such as refusal to work, slowness in settling, aggressiveness and insolence. Incident forms sometimes highlighted a mismatch between the misbehaviour and the response of the system. A pupil sent from a classroom to the head of year, for example, could be led, because of similar incidents reported and acted on by other staff, into consequences which the teacher reporting the initial incident had not intended (in one extreme instance) to suspension. Knowledge of this led many teachers to contain problems in the classroom rather than to seek the available assistance. Such information is helpful in examining assumptions about how a school's discipline works and in matching the aims of the school with what it achieves with its pupils; it also serves as a useful corrective to the commonsense assumption by teachers that disruption largely occurs in large, low-ability groups and in corridors, whereas the data showed it occurred across the ability range, in groups of varying size and mainly in classrooms. It also revealed discrepancies in understanding between pupils and teachers, teachers and teachers and between junior and senior staff. There was more disruption than appeared in official records, but it was of a different order – less serious, but not less stressful to the teachers who reported it. Another insight was the clustering of incidents at certain times of day – in the early morning before break in one school, a finding which was new to the school, enabling timetabling to be reviewed.

The inclusion in one of the two schools of opportunities for pupil responses to incidents was helpful in providing fresh and challenging insights on organisational factors; pupils named by teachers in incidents were asked for their accounts. When one considers how often delicate negotiations are involved in incidents reported to senior staff, two accounts may well be more helpful in providing a wider view. Such data, too, is itself an occasion for staff development.

These two school projects were undertaken in response to requests from the respective LEAs and involved three researchers working intensively during the periods of monitoring. Other instances where schools have undertaken monitoring using similar procedures have been at the initiatives of individual teachers and managed wholly within existing schools resources; an example where incident forms were used to provide data from a large cross-section of schools without the presence of the researchers is the Primary School Inquiry (Lawrence and Steed, 1986).

Incident monitoring in primary schools

There has been a relative dearth of information about disruptive behaviour in primary schools, although aggression has been studied in the nursery school (Manning et al., 1978; Manning and Hermann, 1981). The Primary School Survey (Lawrence and Steed, 1986) collected data from over 500 teachers in 77 separate schools suggested by their local authorities as representative of the varying levels of difficulty by intake.

The quality and quantity of the data in these studies seems to confirm the incidents as a natural focus for research. Patterns may be seen to emerge which place them in the context of the whole way of life of the school (its timetable, administration, curriculum, staffing, pupil intake, etc.) and offer an opportunity to take a global perspective on the school and on disruptive behaviour.

Critical Incident reporting

While monitoring using Critical Incident reporting has seemed useful in schools, it raises a number of questions. A key issue is who initiates the project. The agent may be an interested staff member, the LEA, the headteacher or a researcher; the project will inevitably reflect this in its approach and in the time allocation and interpretation of data. Further questions arise concerning the competence of the agent to organise whole-school exercises, to collect and organise complex data in terms of simple statistics and to present clearly written, well-structured and easily read reports; competence extends to ability to free oneself from bias. Whatever the history of a monitoring project, it would seem important at an early stage for a group of staff to become involved in the organisation and interpretation of data to protect against extremes of subjectivism.

In some schools there may be good reasons for suggesting that monitoring is not undertaken until preliminary activities, such as small-group discussions or inputs from outside agencies, have been undertaken, for example, where morale is low and staff may feel that nothing will come out of such an exercise. Additionally, there may be situations where disruption is so severe and demoralising that monitoring is not feasible.

Where it is undertaken, staff motivation to report needs careful examination. For instance, there may be a 'warm up' effect, so that more weight should be given to reporting once teachers have got into the swing of it than to that of the first few days. Similarly, reporting may be influenced by the presence of the director of the project to the school and by daily reminders on the notice board.

Presenting data, too, involves hazards, for example, in concentrating too much attention on the names of individual pupils thrown up by monitoring. It is important to remember the shortness of the period sampled and the overall aim of the project to look at the school's patterning.

Disruptive behaviour in the primary school inquiry
incident report form
(Definition of disruptive behaviour: *Behaviour which seriously interferes with the teaching process and/or seriously disturbs the running of the school*).

Incident Sheet

1. a) Teacher status (e.g. assistant, supply, probationer)
....
   b) Number of years' teaching experience ....
2. a) Time of day (e.g. before school) ....
   b) Day of week ....
3.　Age of pupils ....
4.　Type of class or group ....
   (e.g. withdrawal, whole class, remedial)
5.　Vertical or horizontal group ....
6.　No. of pupils in class or group ....
7.　Subject/activity in progress ....
....
8.　Type of teaching in progress:
   a) whole class .... b) group work ....
   c) individual work .... d) other ....
....
9.　Place (e.g. classroom, hall) ....
10.　Was it serious or very serious? ....
11.a) How long did it last? ....
   b) Sex of pupil(s) ....
12.　No. of pupils involved: ....
   a) One .... b) two/three ....
   c) group .... d) most/all of class ....
13.a) Was this incident reported onwards by you? YES/NO ....
      If YES, to whom, and for what purpose? ....
....
   b) Was it reported to you? YES/NO (give details) ....
....
14.　Which of the following best describe the incident:
   a) fearfulness, severe anxiety ....　l)　stealing ....
   b) fussiness ....　m) bad manners ....
   c) tearfulness, unhappiness ....　n) dirtiness ....
   d) temper tantrums ....　o) erratic behaviour ....
   e) disobedience ....　p) withdrawal, solitariness ....
   f) vandalism ....　q) clowning ....
   g) destructiveness ....　r) restlessness ....
   h) truancy ....　s) irritableness ....
   i) poor concentration ....　t) aggression to pupils ....
   j) bullying, spitefulness ....　u) defiance ....
   k) lying ....　v) abusive/bad language ....
　　　　　　　　　　　　　　　　　　　　w) not listening ....
15.　Was the incident avoidable? If so, in what way? ....
....
....
16.　Initials of teacher completing form ....　17.　Sex of teacher (M/F) completing
　　　　　　　　　　　　　　　　　　　　　　　form ....

Practical uses of Critical Incident forms: an example

Here we show how information provided on a Critical Incident Form by those involved in or observing a disruptive incident can help towards understanding and meeting the special needs of pupils. The incident form was developed from use in two regional centres for disturbed delinquent boys, and a day special school unit. The account starts with the initial statements of those involved in an adapted incident.

Teacher's view: Jason came into class late, in a sullen mood. He initially refused to work, and soon got into disagreement with two other pupils. Jason threatened one of the pupils with a compass. When I went to remove the compass from Jason, he attempted to strike me and ran out of the classroom, shouting. I followed Jason, stopped him by the open fire-escape doors and retrieved the compass. The Deputy Head happened to be around, and I felt Jason was not in a fit state to return to class. This is the third time Jason has caused problems, attacking other pupils and running out of class. The pupil should be suspended for this action.

Pupil's view: Mr W. is always picking on me. He started as soon as I got into class. Then Paul started winding me up, and I told him to shut up. Mr W. started and I threw my pencil down. He grabbed me and I ran out of the class, where he twisted my arm up my back, and took me back.

Class pupils' view: The class consisted of eight pupils. Those sitting on the same table as Jason quickly offered their account, stating that Jason had started on them as soon as he came into the classroom and had thrown a compass at them like a dart. They complained that Jason was always causing trouble and that the teacher was 'too soft on him'.

Cleaner's view: The cleaner, a mother of five adolescents, usually completed her work by cleaning the staffroom, office and corridors during the first lesson. She reported, 'That kid is always running in and out of class, shouting, I don't know how young Mr W. puts up with it. He tries so hard. That kid needs a sharp clout around the ear'.

Deputy head's view: Teaching in the adjacent classroom, I heard strong words and then doors slam. Standing in the corridor, I observed Mr W. follow, restrain a very agitated Jason and remove a compass from him. I sat Jason to work quietly in my class for the remainder of the lesson.

Caretaker's view: The school's caretaker had witnessed the final part of the event and independently complained to the headteacher: 'I saw this teacher using his weight to force the boy against the wall and then through the door back into school.'

Immediate conclusions

We may note several immediate impressions on the initial reports of this incident.

1. This was a severely disruptive, threatening and stressful incident. Pupils in this and other classes are disrupted.
2. The various reports are ready in appropriating blame. The pupil himself, the pupils on Jason's table and teacher will be worried about the subsequent judgement of colleagues, senior staff and parents. Their reports will be influenced by how they feel they may be judged.
3. In their reports each participant shows little reflection of their own actions.
4. This incident has not occurred in isolation. It involves several participants, both before school and during the first lesson. However, little attention is paid to the antecedents of the event.
5. No action is taken. Without such action, there is a danger that the incident and the actions of all concerned are implicitly condoned. Punishment or criticism may increase the probability that, in future, such events may be kept quiet.
6. A school is a multi-professional context including cleaners and caretakers. If these professions are to work in partnership, their observations and concerns need to be taken into account.

Incident Report Forms

This establishment used an Incident Report Form, a development of which is shown here. First, it asks a number of factual questions: the place, time, participants and activity. Next a number of possible descriptors of the event are presented. In this case, the teacher may be expected to ring 'pupil–pupil' and connect this in sequence to 'adult intervention', 'non-compliance' and then 'physical attack' and 'restraint'. This provides an immediate picture of the incident. The form then asks for a description of the events that have led up to the incident (antecedents), what actually happened (behaviour) and what followed (consequences). Finally, there are two sections for action recommended by the report author and that taken by the senior staff (headteacher, year

Incident Report Form

School: _____

Date: _____ Time: _____Report author(s): _____

Place: _____ Activity: _____

Pupil(s) involved: _____

Pupils present : _____

Adults involved: _____

Adults present: _____

NATURE OF THE INCIDENT (please ring): if one aspect leads to another, please connect, '<———>'

Pupil–pupil	Pupil–adult	Several pupils
Non-compliance	Teasing/taunting	Verbal abuse
Physical taunt	Physical abuse	Physical attack
Adult intervention	Restraint	Property damage
Racism	Sexism	

What was the serious aspect of the incident and how serious do you judge it?

_____

_____

_____

_____

ANTECEDENTS OF THE INCIDENT:
How did the incident develop? What factors may have led or contributed to it?

_____

_____

_____

_____

_____

_____

_____*(please continue on reverse)*

INCIDENT: What actually happened and who was involved?

_____

_____

_____

_____

_____

_____*(please continue on reverse)*

CONSEQUENCES: What happened afterwards? What did the pupil(s) get out of this behaviour?

_____

_____

_____

_____

_____

_____

WHAT ACTION do you recommend should be taken to help prevent a re-occurrence of the event? (You may find it helpful to refer to the Teacher Information Pack (TIPS); Behaviour sections for Aggression (1); Attention-seeking (3); Bullying (6210); Calling out (11); Distructive (14); Disruptive (15); Hitting out (18); Racism (26); Social skills (34); Stealing (37); Teasing (40 and 41); Uncooperative (44); Techniques sections; Motivation (5); Rewards (9); Problem-solving (8); Trouble-shooting (13).

_____

_____

_____

_____

_____

_____

_____*(please continue on reverse)*

DISCIPLINARY ACTION and by whom?
Detention during break/after school.
By teacher supervising/class teacher/deputy/head.

Other: _____

_____

ACTION TAKEN BY HEADTEACHER
a) In relation to the pupil(s):

_____

_____

_____

_____

_____

_____

_____

b) In discussion with relevant staff:

_____

_____

_____

_____

_____

SPECIFIC ACTION TAKEN (please ring):
  Social skills training (1 and 5); Counselling (3); Detention, Daily report, Contract (2);
  pecial provision, Suspension, Exclusion.
LETTER TO: parent/guardian, EWO, PSW, SW, EP.
INTERVIEW WITH PARENTS: by head/deputy/class teacher/social worker/EP.
Please copy and file under a) Pupil's file; b) Incident file. Attach copies of any letters for the
pupil's file.
Thank you for your valuable time. I am sorry you have endured the incident. The informa-
tion will guide us in the development of policy for the school and/or procedures to meet
the needs of the pupil.

PUPIL'S VIEWS (this section may be completed with/by pupil or following interview with
the pupil):
A serious incident has been reported to me. Can you tell me what happened?

_____

_____

_____

_____

_____

_____ *(please continue on reverse)*

What may have caused you to do it? Did anything happen before?

_____

_____

_____

_____

_____

How can we help you and others to make sure this does not happen again?

_____

_____

_____

_____

_____

Thank you for your help

or house head), or special needs coordinator (cf. **Teacher Information Pack**, Dawson, 1986). The form contains a separate section for the pupil's view (cf. Chapters 7 and 16).

When should incident forms be completed?

Any stressful incident is likely to raise fears of allegation and counter-allegation. Clearly, there is a need for a period of calm reflection. However, the greater the delay between the incident and the report, the greater is the probability that the report will be influenced by extraneous factors. Since the aim is to obtain an accurate account, incident reports are best completed the same day, or there is a danger that the incident is forgotten and the task of completing the form appear unnecessary and tedious.

Who should request incident reports?

Here the centre concerned maintained incident reports as part of its standard procedures. Teachers collected a form from the staffroom and, when completed, handed it to the deputy head, who then decided whether any further action was needed. In the majority of incidents, this entailed only a discussion with the pupils concerned and feedback to the teacher.

Information to be gained from incident reports

Next the report is duplicated, one copy placed on the pupil's file. Jason had not struck the teacher, he had just walked out of the class when the teacher came up to him, but it may have appeared that he went to strike the teacher. He acknowledged that he had left the class with the compass and that he had felt like scratching himself with it.

Other pupils admitted that they found Jason irritating. It was fun to wind Jason up and this was a way of avoiding the work in class. They also largely confirmed Jason's account of their provocation.

The teacher reported that he consistently experienced problems with Jason. Maybe Jason had just wanted to leave the class. From the case file, Mr W. was aware of and concerned about Jason's history of unpredictable outbursts, running out of lessons and the difficulties he subsequently got into, including self-mutilation.

The caretaker acknowledged that he had only seen a part of the incident and was reassured to know that the deputy head had been present and the incident was being investigated. He said that he had previously found Jason crying in the school grounds during classtime.

Collecting the information starts to resolve the problem

1. Investigating the incident showed that it was not condoned.
2. Encouraging all to contribute prevented anyone supposing that their feelings and concerns were not being considered.
3. The information gathered immediately pointed to solutions and the need for further information. Among the information sought was examination of previous incident reports since Jason's admission. These showed a pattern of disruptive incidents during lessons that followed the start of school, breaks or lunchtimes. While there was no pattern of specific teachers or subjects, two pupils were usually involved: Jason and one other. Further inquiries revealed that Jason was unpopular and isolated in his peer group. The reports also showed that Mr W. endured a higher rate of incidents and a greater probability that pupils would run out of his class.

A pattern of events emerges

Jason got into trouble before lessons. In the presence of peers alone, their bullying caused him to withdraw. In the presence of peers and adults, he could draw attention to his plight and was protected from bullying by the intervention of the teacher. By disrupting the lesson, Jason gained attention from both peers and teacher. 'Winding up' Jason in the class enabled peers to avoid the set work. Allowing Jason to run out of the lesson 'solved' the problem. This incident was different as Jason had a dangerous implement and a history of self-mutilation. When this was explained to the caretaker, he felt the teacher had acted correctly. Nevertheless, the incident caused concern that physical restraint had been used and that Jason and the teacher deserved assistance and support. The pattern of events needed to be broken. In particular, the sequence of misbehaviour, attention and avoidance of work needed to be broken.

Provision resulting from incident report

Both Jason and his teacher suggested action that they may have taken to prevent the incident escalating; these suggestions were incorporated into the planned provision:

1. Jason should be allowed to work on a table on his own.
2. At the first sign of disruptive behaviour by Jason and any other pupil, Jason would be asked to work in the adjacent class with the deputy head.

3. A list of ten appropriate classroom behaviours was established, by the achievement of which pupils earned points. Pupils who earned above a number of points and had completed the set work were allowed 10 minutes' free time at the end of the lesson. Pupils who failed to earn a minimum number of points for each target were held in detention for up to 10 minutes at the end of the lesson.

4. Jason agreed to a contract, which afforded him special privileges for arriving 5 minutes early to class, settling at and concentrating on his work. With the teacher, he would briefly discuss his attitude and progress at the beginning of each lesson. The privilege was access to a computer during breaktimes (cf. Chapter 10).

5. Jason's breaktime problems were partly (and temporarily) resolved by using the computer during the first break. An observation procedure was established to gain further information on Jason during other breaktimes. From this observation the centre considered breaktime provision (cf. Chapter 12). A social skills programme was designed for Jason.

6. The teacher was asked to consider his classroom management and presentation of classwork (cf. Chapter 8). He requested and was supported in attendance at a course for the management of disruptive pupils.

7. While physical restraint was rare, the incident revealed the need for a policy towards pupils apparently in danger of harming themselves or others and a working party was established.

8. Jason's statement that he was the subject of racial abuse caused concern and surprise. Both Jason and his taunters were black, but Jason was of Nigerian descent while his taunters were of West Indian descent. Specialist advice was requested from the LEA and incorporated into the centre's INSET.

With the exception of action 6, these suggestions were recorded in the section 'Action taken by a senior teacher'. It may be noted that no blame was apportioned, nor any punishment given. Jason's key teacher discussed the possible unintended dangers of using an implement in a threatening manner; there may be incidents where punishment is considered necessary or a teacher is formally advised about his management.

In the complex organisation of a school we should expect troublesome incidents. An incident report form, contributed to by participants, may present valuable information that prompts possible solutions. The report needs to include both antecedents and consequences of the event, as well as the behaviour itself. Over time the reports may reveal a pattern of incidents that offer valuable assessment of a pupil's needs, suggest changes in a school's policy or organisation and monitors the progress of both.

Discussion and conclusions

Teachers and pupils quite clearly remember incidents even after long periods of time. At every level, teachers deal with incidents. They are crisis points in 'disruptive behaviour', often leading to reporting onwards and entry of the child into the official system of coping. They are often quoted in explaining official sanctions such as suspension and exclusion; they are notable and noted events.

Incident monitoring thus appears a feasible technique for the study of disruptive behaviour in assisting schools and LEAs. While the procedure does not pretend to provide objective and quantitatively measurable data of disruptive behaviour, the global approach offers an alternative to piecemeal strategies and overemphasis on the child's behaviour. For the LEA it may offer, for example, an alternative to the setting up of special units and provide a broad preventative strategy rather than a policy which focuses upon the disruptive child and on such measures as suspension and exclusion (Young *et al.*, 1979, 1980). Monitoring offers schools, by identifying stress points, the possibility of targeting their resources more effectively. It is, then, a useful behavioural approach to system change through selective intervention.

A broad approach through monitoring, which points to the relationships between structures and disruptive events, has led in some schools to self-monitoring by the school and to staff development alongside a school policy on behaviour. Staff support and development can probably best be accomplished in an atmosphere which acknowledges that disruption is normal and need not be considered an indication of professional ineptness or incompetence. The benefits of close and regular monitoring might include, then, improved staff morale by acknowledgement that problems are understood and recognised. Routinely collected information could give indications of the effectiveness of measures taken and of the need for further development in the classroom, curriculum and other aspects of school life and organisation. Involvement of staff in such research and development could contribute importantly to their cohesion and meet some of the criticisms that senior management do not understand the problems of teachers at the 'chalk face'. Equally, it might enable junior staff to understand the enormous task faced by senior staff with administrative and pastoral responsibilities in coping with the problems referred to them. Change and development under these circumstances might then be seen as less threatening, more easily related to the agreed educational aims within the constraints and opportunities of the school's particular circumstances.

In itself, monitoring could constitute a form of in-service training, allowing staff to take up a more analytical, diagnostic stance on those very problems which commonly generate considerable emotion. In addition, a comment frequently made by all the schools referred to its therapeutic qualities. It, too, offers pupil and teacher a degree of protection from later subjective recall that may be harmful to one or both. If pupil disruptiveness is seen as a chicken-and-egg problem (Steed, 1985), then monitoring incidents may well provide useful clues to resolving the riddle.

References

DAWSON, R. (1986) *Teacher Information Packs (TIPS)* (London: Macmillan).

LAWRENCE, J., STEED, D. and YOUNG, P. (1977) *Disruptive Behaviour in a Secondary School* (London: Croom Helm).

LAWRENCE, J., STEED, D. and YOUNG, P. (1981) *Dialogue on Disruptive Behaviour – a Study of a Secondary School* (London: PJD Press).

LAWRENCE, J., STEED, D. and YOUNG, P. (1984) *Disruptive Children: Disruptive Schools* (London: Croom Helm).

LAWRENCE, J., and STEED, D. (1986) *Incidents of Disruptive Behaviour in the Primary School and Other Papers* (London: D.J. Press).

MANNING, M., HERON, J. and MARSHALL, R. (1978) 'Styles of hostility and social interaction at nursery, at school and at home' in: *Aggression and Anti-Social Behaviour in Childhood and Adolescence* Eds. Hersov, L.A. and Berger, M. (Oxford: Pergamon).

MANNING, M. and HERMANN, J. (1981) 'The relationships of problem children in nursery schools' in: *Personal Relationships in Disorder* Eds. Duck, S. and Gilmour, R. (Brighton: Harvester Press).

POWERS, M.J. *et al.* (1967) 'Delinquent schools', *New Society*, 19 October.

REYNOLDS, D. (1975) 'When teachers refuse a truce' in: *Working Class Culture* Eds. Mungham, D. and Pearson, G. (London: Routledge and Kegan Paul).

REYNOLDS, D. (1976) 'The delinquent school' in: *The Process of Schooling* Eds. Hammersley, M. and Woods, P. (London: Routledge and Kegan Paul/Open University).

RUTTER, M. *et al.* (1979) *Fifteen Thousand Hours* (London: Open Books).

STEED, D. (1985) 'Disruptive pupils, disruptive schools: which is the chicken? Which is the egg?', *Educational Research*, 27, 1, 3–8.

YOUNG, P., LAWRENCE, J. and STEED, D. (1979) 'Disruptive behaviour: LEA policies. A research note', *Policy and Politics*, 7, 4, 387–93.

YOUNG, P., LAWRENCE, J. and STEED, D. (1980) 'LEAs and autonomous off-site units for disruptive pupils in secondary schools', *Cambridge Journal of Education*, 10, 2, 55–70.

Chapter 5

Checking Pupils' Behavioural Skills

Martin Scherer

Traditional assessment, usually conducted by professionals working outside the class, has relied on ability and personality tests that result in intelligence quotients, personality labels, reading, writing and number ages. Assessment of behavioural problems often takes place at the time of crisis. If there is to be a move from crisis intervention, labelling and segregation, towards integration and provision, then teachers require a method of assessment of pupil's needs that may be undertaken in the classroom and prompts provision to take place in the classroom. Teachers need to ask themselves: 'What are the social, study and academic skills the pupil needs in order to learn the subject I am about to teach in this classroom?' To answer the question, teachers require a method of assessment that results in a list of behavioural skills that the pupil does have (abilities/assets), does not have (disabilities/deficits) and perhaps those behaviours of the pupil that are disruptive, irritating or annoying (excesses).

This chapter discusses how such a list may be achieved and how the pupil's skills may then be checked. The deficits may form the goals of provision and contribute to educational advice in Statements produced under the provisions of the Education Act (1981). The design of checklists as an aid to assessment and their use within a single class (and across classes) is discussed. A behaviour checklist is offered as an appendix.

Why check pupils' behaviour?

It is often assumed that pupils know how to behave in class and teachers know what behaviours to expect. This may be an error. Primary schools commonly seat pupils around tables; secondary schools commonly seat children in rows. There is a complex set of skills associated with each of these seating positions. Further, every school and every teacher will have different expectations of how a pupil should behave. This may be obvious in the comparison of craft and academic subject lessons. However, it is equally true of the same subject taught by different teachers. School rules are one attempt to establish conformity and reduce confusion, but variation inevitably exists through the inter-pretation of rules. Simply punishing a pupil because he/she does not exhibit the appropriate behaviour may only aggravate the problem.

We may assume that pupils' 'know how to behave but won't do it'. It may be true that a pupil learnt the skills in earlier years, but for one reason or another has not exercised those skills lately. It may also be confusing to use a well-practised skill in a different context, or in the complex world of unstated rules and expectations in the classroom. It may be safer to assume that a new pupil does not have the required skills until he/she is observed confidently using them.

Throughout pupils' school careers their academic performance is checked on. Acquisition of appropriate classroom social and study skills are equally important precursors of learning. Also, if teachers are to manage the organisation of their classrooms, they need a clear outline of the behaviours they expect to manage.

Who should check behaviour?

Traditionally a pupil's behavioural skills are checked on when the pupil shows problems; at this point, assistance is sought. If the pupil is seen as misbehaving, the school's disciplinary system may be brought into force. If the problem persists, specialist assistance may be sought, typically from an educational psychologist. The pupil may be withdrawn from class and 'assessed'. However, all this is radically changing. The Warnock Report (1978) recommended that the first stages of assessment should be carried out by the classroom teacher, presumably in the classroom. The role of the educational psychologist is becoming one of supporting teachers rather than assessing problem pupils. Greater support is now given in assisting teachers increasingly to assess and meet behavioural problems. However, there is a need for methods that fall within the experience of the teacher and are compatible with the complex demands of teaching.

Exams and personality tests

Teachers are most familiar with checking academic skills, commonly by marking course work, tests and examinations. Traditional methods of checking behavioural skills are not substantially different and involve a number of personality and intelligence tests.

One of the most common personality adjustment tests known to teachers is the Bristol Social Adjustment Guide (BSAG, Stott and Marston, 1971). The BSAG is based on a number of descriptors of pupil behaviours; these are observed by the teacher, who is subsequently asked to complete the questionnaire, and the assessment of the pupil results on a number of scales. Intelligence, reading, spelling and numerical ability tests are equally used by teachers and others.

Personality, intelligence and ability tests are usually 'standardised', tested on a large number of 'normal' pupils across the country. Pupils who are subsequently tested are compared to this standard, resulting in a comparative reading, spelling, number age or intelligence quotient. In a similar manner to these norm-referenced tests, the performance of pupils in exams is compared to the performance of the other pupils in the class, school or, in public examinations, the pupils in the area of the examining body; hence the pupil's test mark is judged by reference to the average performance of the pupils undertaking the test. By giving a grade or percentage mark, tests and exams are also related to a perfect performance, with the top grade usually set at 100 per cent. Often such criterion referencing in exams is related to the norm or average performance of pupils undertaking the test. If the average performance of pupils is high, say, 70 per cent, the average pupil may be awarded only a 'C' grade, being the typically average grade. The opposite is also true, when the exam proves difficult for the majority of pupils.

Problems of academic and personality tests

1. The standard of normality is changing. The Education Act (1981) states that a pupil has a learning difficulty if he/she 'has a disability which prevents or hinders him from making use of the educational facilities of a kind generally provided in schools, within the area of the local authority concerned'. The Act offers a new definition of normality: first, it is defined in terms of the educational environment, as well as the pupil's abilities; and second, the comparison is restricted to the educational environment of the LEA concerned. While the Act compares the pupil to the 'majority of pupils of his

age', it makes no statement that the majority refers to the national majority. Therefore, nationally norm-referenced personality and ability tests may not be applicable to the assessment of special needs.

2. Exams and personality tests are taken under constrained circumstances that bear little resemblance to class or future work or social life. Exams predict only future performance in exams. Even here, as the subject and place of education changes, the prediction becomes weaker. The skills demonstrated in the examination room or assessed in the psychologist's office may not generalise or be appropriate to the classroom. Assessment needs to occur in the context in which the skills are used.

3. The grade or mark gained provides limited information; it gives only an average performance across the area of the test, failing to reveal areas of strength or weakness. Teachers are generally unfamiliar with diagnostic tests, and have little experience of personality tests. Consequently, it is easy to forget the purpose of measuring pupils' academic or behavioural performance. The test may become an end in itself, merely a statement of pupil performance; and while the results may provide professional credibility in school or assessment reports, they provide little information of the pupil's specific needs or how to meet them.

4. Tests are more objective than the subjective judgement of teachers. However, tests take a single measure of the pupil's performance, which may be affected by a number of factors of which the examiner has little if any knowledge. Little confidence, then, can be placed upon attributing performance to any one factor.

5. Tests may be a method of evaluation rather than assessment; and terms and definitions are changing rapidly. Broadly, assessment is a measurement of the pupil; evaluation is a measurement of the provision (cf. Child, 1986). However, both activities may be expected to have some purpose beyond measurement. The function of assessment may be the discovery of the pupils' disabilities and designing of provision to overcome them. The function of evaluation is rather to improve the course. Despite the fact that exams are predominantly used as a statement of the pupil's achievement at the end of the course, they are more correctly a form of course evaluation. As a consequence of testing, the pupil may be streamed, placed into similar-ability classes, including remedial or special education. Personality and adjustment tests are similarly used: the pupil may be subsequently streamed, placed in classes of similarly

behaving pupils including attendance at offsite units, or in day and residential schools. Personality tests may be used to evaluate the provision.

The above problems, together with the development of GCSE, may be currently leading education away from formal examination and personality testing towards a greater reliance on course work marking and more direct methods of assessing pupil behaviour.

Checking skills

From the course curriculum the teacher may list specific skills to be taught. The list may be short if global descriptions are used: 'Understands decimals . . . uses tools appropriately.' A more detailed list provides greater information: 'addition, subtraction, multiplication and division of whole numbers in units, tens and hundreds, and decimal fractions to one, two and three places . . . Use of cross cut, tenon saws to make a variety of [named] wood joints.' Such a curriculum list may be devised for all subjects; by observation, test or course work, the pupil demonstrates each skill and is checked off the curriculum list on that pupil's record sheet.

Assessment of disruptive behaviour

Crisis intervention

The traditional approach to disruptive or delinquent behaviour focuses on the presenting problem. There are, however, a number of limitations with this 'crisis-centred' or 'crisis intervention' approach. First, attention to the 'problem' may encourage provision that seeks to 'get rid of', punish or suppress the problem behaviour. This may simply aggravate the problem, driving the pupil to avoid the punishment by misbehaving elsewhere. Alternatively, the pupil may be taught appropriate behaviour to replace the problem behaviour. However, it is likely that a disruptive pupil lacks a number of skills, solving the presenting problem may 'lift the straw from the camel's back'. At some point in the future, another skill deficit may cause stress and lead to similar problems. Third, the crisis-centred approach is, perhaps, not unlike closing the door after the horse has bolted. While this may be the only recourse to external agencies, schools should be able to assess the pupil's needs before the crisis occurs.

Assessing the pupil's needs

A comprehensive assessment of pupils' needs is required that may be used by teachers in classrooms, providing detailed information of the pupil's social and study skills; three terms have emerged:

Assets. Those skills possessed by the pupil which may be used to build more complex skills.

Deficits. Those skills the teacher wishes the pupil to acquire.

Excesses. Those behaviours that occur in excess and may be irritating, disruptive or detrimental to the pupil's learning in class. (Westmacott and Cameron, 1981)

The resulting assessment will be more positive and indicate the provision that should be made. It results, first, in a list of the pupil's successes, which may be congratulated and positively reported; second, a list of behaviours the pupil needs to acquire, for which intervention programmes need to be designed; and finally, the behaviours that need to be reduced if they cannot be ignored or do not decrease as a result of increasing the pupil's skills.

It is possible to draw up such a list for an individual pupil; however, the resulting list is likely to be influenced by problems presented at the time the list is completed. What is needed therefore is a complete list of the behavioural requirements of the classroom against which the pupil's skill assets and deficits can be checked.

Writing a list of classroom social and behavioural skills

Such a list may be compiled by a single teacher. It is similar to the increasing practice of displaying a list of rules on a classroom wall. This practice is included as one of the procedures of Assertive Discipline (see Chapter 9). Many behaviours included are commonly expected by teachers; others are more specific to a particular classroom and teacher. The list will vary across different ages, classes, subjects, teachers and schools (see list of classroom rules, p. 77). However, such classroom rules are not seen as a method of assessment.

An alternative is to establish a list of skills by common agreement of school staff, and perhaps pupils, across the school. In constructing this list, teachers may consult any similar existing systems; for instance, the BSAG lists behaviours under sections, as follows:

ASKING TEACHER'S HELP

Constantly seeks help when he could manage for himself/
. . . seldom needs help/. . . too shy/not too shy but . . .
too lacking in energy to bother/tries to argue with teacher/n.n.

Readers may find some of these descriptors curious, or may point to what are felt to be glaring omissions: 'fails to put up his hand . . . interrupts the teacher.' The BSAG is clearly influenced by the authors' theoretical assumptions about the nature of the variables it seeks to assess: over-reactivity, hostile, inconsequential. To some extent, all lists will be influenced by the authors' implicit or explicit assumptions.

Achieving an agreed list of classroom behavioural and social skills is a valuable exercise in its own right. First, it brings unstated expectations into the open; behavioural expectations and social norms are a part of the school system. Second, it encourages teachers to examine what they expect of the class. Third, it may bring about a greater consistency across classrooms; with greater consistency, the expectations may be more realistic to pupils who may be less likely to accuse individual teachers of being different or unjust. The list of behaviours which follow were achieved by this means, originating in a regional resource centre for disturbed delinquent adolescent boys. It was influenced by a number of other published lists and has since been adapted through use in two other schools.

Until an agreed social and study skills curriculum is achieved there will be a number of examples of classroom social skills lists. Once the list has been achieved the behaviour the pupil shows may be 'checked off'; examples of checklists include: Disruptive behaviours: Coulby and Harper, 1985; Galvin and Singleton, 1984; Study skills; Jackson *et al.*, 1979; Croft, 1979; Social skills: Spence, 1980; Adolescent skills: McGinnis and Goldstein, 1984; Career problems: Crowley, 1983; Various: Cautela *et al.*, 1983. A brief scan of the major educational publishers will reveal many more. Once a curriculum is agreed, social and study skills may become an accepted part of the school curriculum.

What is a checklist?

Checklists have become very common in recent years. The simplest is the shopping-list, where as the items are purchased, they are checked off. Some items will be found to be unavailable, not suitable or beyond the resources of the user; every checklist has similar problems. Hence all contain the opportunity to answer: 'n.n. – nothing noticed; n.k. – not known; or n.a. – not applicable; they also provide the opportunity to add items e.g. the BSAG provides a section, 'Anything special about this child which is not covered in this form?'.

A skills·checklist, unsurprisingly, comprises a list of skills that may be checked. By presenting the list rather than presenting a final 'standardised, authoritative assessment', this assessment method lays itself open to examination and criticism. In any particular use, the list will always be inadequate or it may include irrelevant items. There is, however, a danger that checklists may be used in a cookbook fashion: the list becomes the ingredients. Rather the checklist should be used as an aid or prompt to assessment. Once identified, the skill deficits and excesses may be subject to more detailed investigation (see e.g. Chapter 6).

A checklist derives its value only by reference to a context, including curriculum demands or teachers' expectations. Lists of excess behaviours, which relate to the unique problems of individual pupils, will always appear curious or irrelevant in the case of most pupils.

Curriculum topics may be listed and checked off. All exams and some personality adjustment tests are based on observable skills. The movement towards use of the checklist constitutes a return to basics: it avoids reduction of the pupil's various skills to a single measure. If education is to move away from labelling and streaming or segregating pupils, then education needs a device for assessing the individual pupil's needs.

When to use checklists

1. *In the context at the time of teaching.* Completing the checklist in the class at the time of the lesson and in the presence of the pupil will enhance the teacher's recall of that pupil. Some skills may be checked off as the lesson progresses: at the start of the lesson (e.g. arriving on time); during the lesson (e.g. legible handwriting); and at the end of the lesson (e.g. clearing up). The 'Class Rules' list may be similarly used to indicate the skills of which the pupils as a whole are generally deficient.
2. *For the new pupil, after admission and/or after a period of settling.* Pupils may go through a 'honeymoon' or settling-in period when their behaviour is exceptionally good or very disruptive. Using the

Date: ___ / ___ / ___ .

Lesson: _____

Class: _____

Teacher: _____

Subject: _____

CLASS RULES

	Pupils who do	who don't
1. Arrive on time and line up quietly		
2. Enter classroom quietly and take your coat off		
3. Sit quietly		
4. Get out appropriate books and equipment		
5. Respond clearly and politely to register		
6. Look at and attend to teacher during work presentation		
7. Put your hand up if you don't understand		
8. Work quietly alone or with other as directed		
9. Encourage and thank other pupils who are working with you		
10. If you need to walk around the class to get equipment be quiet and do not disturb other pupils		
11. Politely ignore disruptive pupils		
12. Put up your hand when answering teachers' questions or asking for help		
13. Wait for the teacher to reply		
14. State when the set work is completed		
15. Use any spare time by checking the work or reading quietly		
16. Thank the teacher for marking your home or class work and any help given		
17. Apologise for any offence caused to teacher or pupils		
18. Ask if you can put your point of view		
19. Tidy your work, clear up and put things away before you leave		
20. Leave quietly when dismissed		
21.		
22.		
23.		
24.		
25.		

Notes:

The 'Rules', adapted to suit your own requirements, may be advertised on the classroom wall. With a new class or pupil, you may take one or two lessons to establish positively and practice the rules. The rules may be used as the targets of a classroom token or points system (see Chapter 9)

Pupils: Include the initials of pupils here.

Pupils who do: Praise and thank these pupils immediately after they have done it. Their behaviour may act as a model for other pupils and your praise may encourage others to learn.

Pupils who don't: In a positive and friendly manner stop the pupil. Explain the rule clearly and ask them to do it again. When they have, thank and praise them.

checklist immediately after entry to the class may reveal the skills that have been acquired, or which they may need to learn in the new class. Comparing the results of checklists before and after the settling-in period may show the success of the pupil and teacher.

3. *Before and after a programme to meet the pupil's needs.* As a result of using a checklist, a teacher may identify one or two skill deficits as the targets of a programme. Following the programme, the checklist may be used to evaluate its success and may reveal that other skills, of which the pupil showed a deficit, have increased and behavioural excesses decreased. Changes may be attributed to the success of the programme. Little change may encourage the redesign of the programme.

4. *Before and after admission to special placements.* A special school may find it an advantage to send a checklist to previous schools. The information gained may show what social skills need to be acquired.

How are skills checked?

There are a number of answer formats:

List item:	*Answer formats:*
'arrives on time'	1 Yes/no
	2 Always/sometimes/never
	3 More than/equal to/less than.
	pupils in the class/school

The most common answer formats are 1 and 2. Both are factual but the second permits more information; the pupil has acquired the skill but may not always demonstrate it. The third follows the definition of a special need given by the Education Act (1981). The teacher cannot be expected to have recent experience of the schools in the area of the local authority concerned, but he/she will have experience of the class or school concerned. A fourth format is based upon a behavioural model of learning (Haring *et al.*, 1978):

Acquired	Has the pupil acquired the skill? It may be weak, occur hesitantly or infrequently.
Fluent	is he/she able to produce the skill when required, frequently and confidently?
Generalised	Can he/she use the skill in a variety of contexts (e.g. arriving on time in all lessons and classrooms)?

Adapted   Can he/she use the skills as a component
of a more complex skill, such as arriving
on time for additional lessons or activities
outside normal lesson times?

This is the most demanding answer format. It affords the greatest information to meet the pupil's needs.

A checklist may use one or a variety of answer formats, depending on individual checklist items. The checklist may ask for additional information and leave space for additional items or comments. Finally, most checklists will provide the opportunity to answer, n.k. – not known or n.a. – not applicable.

What to do with the results

On completion, take the checklist and highlight pupils' assets and deficits in different colours. The skills may then be listed in an assessment report under the relevant titles, as shown overleaf (letters in parentheses indicate sections of checklist). List the deficits in order of priority. Here the teacher may add further information: Deficit 7 notes that the pupil cannot apologize to peers or teacher and adds that he is unable to do so in the presence of peers. Presumably the pupil can apologize in private. Positively phrased, as in the checklist, the deficits become the goals of provision. The targets of provision may be the subject of further measurement.

Detailed assessment prompts provision

By virtue of the frequent contact with the pupil, the teacher may be able to recommend provision. Here teachers comment on the major presenting problem but also attend to what may be the cause – e.g. avoidance of ridicule. The pupil may avoid ridicule by gaining handwriting and spelling skills rather than by disruption. The teacher is not a remedial specialist, so suggests further detailed assessment and provision. Neither does the teacher have any contact with the pupil outside class, but asks about this area of the pupil's skill. Suggestions are valuable, even when the teacher who completes the checklist is not the teacher who meets the pupil's specific needs.

Statements and reviews

The Assessment Report and checklist may be submitted as part of the

---

Assessment Report

Pupil's name:_____Age_____/_____

Date of admission to class: /   /   Dates of assessment   /   /

Class_____Subject_____Teacher_____

1) Briefly describe the pupil's skill assets:

Sean arrives on time, acceptably dressed and with the right books and equipment (A). He shows normal physical abilities (B). He gets down to work (C) which he normally dates, titles and completes (E). Sean is pleasant towards his teacher when he succeeds at his work. He speaks well and clearly (I) and is able to apologize and accept responsibility for his misbehaviour (H).

2) List the pupil's skill deficits:

(1) Handwriting skills (E)
(2) Spelling
(3) Repeatedly asks questions about the task (D)
(4) Cannot borrow or lend equipment without provoking peers (D)
(5) Avoids teacher being close when he is working (D)
(6) Avoids teacher marking his work during the lesson (D)
(7) Cannot apologize to peers or teacher in the presence of peers.
(8) Cannot avoid teasing by peers (L)

3) How do you feel the pupil's needs may be met?

Sean's major problem in class in his disruptive and aggressive behaviour. However it seems that an immediate need is to improve his handwriting and spelling which he tries to avoid the teacher attending to or marking during the lesson. Perhaps his disruptive behaviour is a cover for this disability, which he feels his peers are teasing him about. In his favour is that he clearly wants his peers' friendship and is able to discuss his behaviour with me at the end of the lesson. I would recommend:

(1) Detailed analysis of handwriting and spelling skills.
(2) Additional teaching in these areas.
(3) Counselling to encourage Sean to accept that his teacher wants to help, not criticise or punish.
(4) Assessment of his peer interaction outside class.

Since the assessment I have talked to Sean about his handwriting and spelling. We agreed that I would not mark his work during the lesson with a red pen and that I would silently correct his spelling. I have given him a spelling book for use at all times. He now sits at the front of the class with a spare desk beside him. Things seem to be improving.

educational advice. The checklist may be repeated a year later prior to the annual review. This may show that the pupil's handwriting and spelling are now within range of peers. Other behavioural deficits may remain and need to be overcome.

Increasing confidence

The teacher has shown that he/she is aware of the pupil's special education needs, is able to make provision and achieve success. The success may lead to confidence to make further provision for this and other pupils and attend assessment and review meetings.

Are checklists a reliable assessment method?

No method of assessment is utterly reliable. The Education Act (1981) requires educational advice to be given by the headteacher, preferably in consultation with a teacher who has frequent contact with the pupil. Hence a teacher's professional but subjective report is sufficient for the purposes of the Act. In the present climate of greater accountability subjective reports may not suffice.

By attending to a wider range of skills that are more specifically defined and checked while in the presence of the pupil, checklists may be a more reliable assessment method. The checklist provides a permanent and detailed record.

Repeated use of checklists

Greater confidence may be gained by the repeated use of the checklist in the same class, by the same teacher. As the checklist is based on the observation of a single teacher, the assessment should refrain from making generalizations about other subjects and teachers. Comparison of the repeated checklists may increase confidence and reveal useful information.

1. *Same lesson, same teachers*. Repeated use by the same teacher, in the same lesson, over several weeks may show:

    (a) that the single assessment is reliably repeated;
    (b) that the behaviour is improving or deteriorating over time.

2. *Same teacher, different subjects*. This is probably the position in primary rather than secondary schools. Differences may be attributed to the effect of the subject on the pupil's behaviour.

3. *Same subject, different teachers*. This situation is less likely to occur in many schools, especially secondary schools, but it would show if some aspect of the teacher had an effect on the pupil's behaviour.
4. *Different subjects, different teachers*. The conclusions that can be drawn are more tentative, but a pattern may be revealed. For instance, if the pupil generally behaved well with female but not male teachers, the special need of the pupil may be determined to lie in social skills with male adults. Differences in teaching style, age of the teacher or academic content of the subject may be revealed by asking all teachers to complete the checklist.
5. *Same subject, different teacher, different class group*. This situation may happen where streaming occurs and the pupil's class group changes. Comparison of checklists may indicate that a pupil regularly showed misbehaviour in certain class groups. The pupil's special needs, then, may lie in social skills with peers. Again, the conclusion needs to be tentative because more than one aspect – both teacher and class group – is changing.

Repeated use of checklists requires someone to sit down and compare results. This is a cut-and-paste job: cut the answer formats from the checklists and paste to a single master list. It may be useful to group the answer formats by academic/craft subjects; male/female teacher; and large class/small class. Any pattern that exists stands out, and may point to the required provision. Repeated use may enable a more reliable, general assessment. It may reveal, too, useful information about the circumstances in which disruptive behaviour occurs.

For example:

Background

Marisa was transferred to secondary school with a history of antagonism and verbal aggression towards teachers. Her academic achievements were above average. Within two months she had attacked a teacher and was the subject of concern in several other lessons. She was suspended with a view to full assessment on return. As part of the assessment the Head of Year requested that all Marisa's teachers complete a behaviour checklist.

All male teachers with one exception, maths, reported that Marisa was a socially skilled, charming pupil, whose work was excellent. All teachers agreed that she completed the set work in class, often faster than other pupils. She was very popular amongst peers. Rather than confirming the impression that Marisa was aggressive towards teachers in general, the assessment revealed that Marisa was aggressive towards female teachers, with one exception, her art teacher.

Since early childhood, when her mother died, Marisa had been raised by her father; social reports expressed concern about 'father's frequent changes of girlfriend'. It may be easy to speculate that Marisa resented these intrusions from girlfriends and projected her feelings on to female teachers. Such speculation is dangerous, for it does not help solve the school's immediate problem, Marisa's aggression. It fails to explain her positive behaviour towards her female art teacher. Instead, perhaps, Marisa was a bright pupil who was easily bored in class except art, and gained considerable peer attention by 'winding up' teachers. Most of her teachers in junior and the first year of secondary school were female. Perhaps her antisocial skill of winding up female teachers had yet to generalise to male teachers.

One of the major problems of the procedure leading to Statements in special education needs is the time it takes. What provision is made for the pupil in the intervening period? Until the Statement was completed, it was agreed to transfer Marisa from lessons taught by female teachers to male teachers, wherever possible. In two classes this was not possible. A contract was established, allowing Marisa to take her art project into those lessons and do it when she had satisfactorily completed the set work of the lesson. As the art teacher was a tutor of a class in the same year, she was transferred to this group.

Within six months, Marisa had settled down and was working well in most lessons. However, she had now become disruptive in her maths lesson with a male teacher. Again, in maths she showed she could complete the work, despite her disruptive behaviour. She would often lead other pupils 'astray'; the teacher would not permit Marisa to bring her artwork to the lesson; and she refused to undertake extra work in class. The problem was 'solved' by placing Marisa alongside a pupil who had difficulties in maths and praising her for assisting that pupil.

In a sense, the school had destroyed its case for special education for Marisa. Or, perhaps, it had discovered successful provision for her? Marisa was a bright pupil, who found most academic subjects boring and tedious. She would escape her boredom by disrupting the lesson, thereby becoming a popular deviant peer leader. The exception was art, a subject which she enjoyed and in which she excelled. Future provision may require Marisa to illustrate her work in all subjects with good diagrams and drawings.

Conclusions: stages of assessment

Behavioural checklists are merely what the title suggests and academic, social and study skills, and behavioural excesses, may be listed. When the skills are positively stated, the deficits become the goals of provision and need to be prioritised. Used repeatedly across subjects, classes and teachers the checklist may reveal more detailed assessment and increase users' confidence in the results. Repeated administration may be used to evaluate provision.

Checklists may be established for the stages of a complex task, as well as the skills required for the task. Here we may conclude with an assessment checklist for the classroom teacher:

Stages of behavioural intervention in class

1	List the skills you require of pupils in class
2	Observe the pupil during the lesson
3	List and prioritise the pupil's assets and deficits
4	Choose the priority deficit
5	Ask colleagues how they may meet the deficit
6	Achieve detailed assessment of the priority deficit
7	Design a programme to meet the priority deficit
8	Evaluate the programme
9	Repeat the checklist
10	Check again the pupil's skills and move to the second priority deficit

References

CAUTELA, J.R., CAUTELA, and ESONIS, S. (1983) *Forms for Behaviour Analysis with Children* (Champaign, Ill.: Research Press).

CHEESEMAN, P.L. and WATTS, P.E. (1985) *Positive Behaviour Management* (London: Croom Helm).

CHILD, D. (1986) *Applications of Psychology for the Teacher* (Eastbourne: Holt, Reinhart and Winston).

COULBY, D. and HARPER, T. (1985) *Preventing Classroom Disruption* (London: Croom Helm).

CROWLEY, A.D. (1983) *The Career Problem Checklist* (Windsor: NFER-Nelson).

GALVIN, P., and SINGLETON,R., (1984) *Behaviour Problems: A System of Management* (Windsor: NFER-Nelson).

HARING, N.G., LOVITT, T.C., EATON, M.D., and HANSEN, C.L. (1978) *The Fourth R: Research in the Classroom* (Columbus, Ohio: Merrill).

JACKSON, P.F., REID, N.A., and CROFT, A.C. (1979) *Study Habits Evaluation and Instruction Kit*, New Zealand Council for Educational Research, Wellington (distributed in UK: NFER).

JESSNESS, C.F. (1970) *Behaviour Checklist* (Palo Alto, Calif.: Consulting Psychologists Press).

McGINNIS, E. and GOLDSTEIN, A.P. (1984) *Skill Streaming the Elementary School Child* (Champaign, Ill.: Research Press).

SPENCE, S. (1980) *Social Skills Training with Children and Adolescents: A Counsellor's Manual* (Windsor: NFER).

STOTT, D.H. and MARSTON, N.C. (1971) *Bristol Social Adjustment Guides* (London: Hodder and Stoughton).

ULLMAN, L.P. and KRASNER, L. (1969) *A Psychological Approach to Abnormal Behaviour* (Englewood Cliffs, NJ: Prentice-Hall).

WESTMACOTT, E.V.S., and CAMERON, R.J. (1981) *Behaviour Can Change* (Basingstoke: Globe Education (Macmillan)).

Appendix: Schools Skills Checklist
(Scherer, 1988)

Pupil's name _____

D.O.B.   /   /   Age   /   D.O.A.   /   /

School _____ Class group _____

Teacher completing the checklist _____

Tutor/subject taught to pupil _____

Checklist completed following:
observation/questions to pupil/self recall of teacher?

Use of checklist with this pupil: 1st/2nd/3rd DATE: /   /

Please circle or tick as appropriate
First use mark with /
Second use form a x
When the skill is acquired fill the box
Please return to _____
by   /   /   / Thank you

Answer Format
LT: Less than a normal pupil
AS: As a normal pupil
MT: More than a normal pupil
NA: Not applicable
NK: Not known

	LT	AS	MT	NA	NK
A) ARRIVING AT SCHOOL/LESSON					
Arrives on time _____					
Knows the journey to school_____					
The route to all lessons_____					
His/her personal timetable_____					
Arrives appropriately dressed _____					
Please list clothing required but not worn_____					
Pupil does not have the clothing/declines to wear it? ____					
Personal hygiene: clean/dirty_____					
Personal smell: normal/objectionable_____					
B) PHYSICAL ABILITIES					
Hearing: normal/needs testing/impaired					
Uses hearing aid _____					
Sight: normal/needs testing/impaired					
Uses glasses _____					
Use of hearing aid/glasses:					
competent/forgets/loses _____					
Gross loco-motor skills: normal/disabled:					
Please describe any disability _____					
Able to negotiate classroom: _____					
Physical deficit/skills deficit? (Please ring)					
Able to manipulate equipment: _____					
Physical deficit/skills deficit? (Please ring)					
C) STARTING THE LESSON					
Lines up appropriately _____					

	LT	AS	MT	NA	NK
Enters the classroom quietly and as required					
Makes appropriate greeting to the teacher					
Goes to/sits in appropriate place					
Seated in an upright but relaxed position					
Brings equipment:					
Equipment the pupil needs:					
Waits quietly for teacher to commence					
Responds clearly to register					
Volunteers to give out books/equipment					
Gets work books, materials and equipment out					
Attends to teacher's presentation					
Looks at teacher during presentation/instructions					
Responds to teacher's questions					
Makes enquiries about task if unsure					
Commences the task immediately					
Follows simple instructions					
Follows complex instructions					
Follows instructions given to himself					
Follows instructions given to a group					
Follows written instructions					
Can follow workcards					

D) GETTING ON WITH THE LESSON

	LT	AS	MT	NA	NK
Stays in appropriate place					
Puts hand up or asks quietly for teacher to assist					
Waits patiently for teacher's assistance					
Accepts teacher working in close proximity					
Shows s/he understands by nods, yes, I see, etc.					
Uses equipment safely and sensibly					
Fetches equipment without disturbing others					
Talks quietly to peers as appropriate					
Works appropriately with peers in pairs					
Works appropriately with peers in small groups					
Duration of attention to task					
Identifies components of a task					
Organises components of a task					
Will persevere in solving a problem					
Completes set work					
Commences next task, without instruction					
Requests next task					
Requests extra work					

E) PRESENTATION OF WORK

	LT	AS	MT	NA	NK
Work dated and titled					
Handwriting legible and neat					
Uses ruler					
Numbers answers					
Uses subheadings					
Diagrams, drawings neatly presented and labelled					

	LT	AS	MT	NA	NK
Does not waste paper in exercise books					
Books are covered and looked after					
Work books present a neat record of progress					
Work books are lost or mislaid					
Practical work neatly stored away					
Understands teacher's marking system					
Welcomes teacher's use of red marking pen					
Accepts teacher's mark and comments					
Accepts disappointment appropriately					
Accepts criticism of work					
Learns from criticism of work					
Will self-mark honestly					
F) PEER INTERACTION SKILLS IN CLASS					
Ignores disruption					
Apologizes to peers for any offence					
Encourages peers involved in group tasks					
Accepts contribution of peers in group tasks					
Assists peers as appropriate					
Quietly asks for loan of equipment from peers					
Able to share equipment/books with peer					
Advises peer against inappropriate behaviour					
G) RECEIVING AND GIVING PRAISE					
Seeks praise publicly					
Seeks praise privately					
Looks and smiles at teacher					
Uses expressions of gratitude					
Compliments efforts of others					
H) APOLOGISING SKILLS					
Listens to the complaint					
Looks down when receiving complaint					
Stands still, with hands held behind or in front					
Apologizes					
Accepts responsibility for his part					
Asks for opportunity to explain					
Will wait for the end of the lesson to discuss					
Re-assures that the event will not repeat					
I) CONVERSATION SKILLS					
Speech is at appropriate volume					
Speech is at appropriate pitch					
Accent is easily comprehended					
Facial expressions reflect speech content					
Introduces himself to known group					
Introduces himself to new group					
Introduces others					
Aware of appropriate moment to contribute					
Waits for appropriate moment to interrupt					
Apologizes if interruption is necessary					

	LT	AS	MT	NA	NK
Acknowledges contribution of others					
Keeps to the topic of conversation					
Allows others to enter conversation					
Listens to others' contribution					
Looks at contributors					
KNOWLEDGE OF SCHOOL RULES					
Able to recall school rules					
Abides by school rules					
HOMEWORK					
Willing to accept homework					
Attempts homework					
Completes homework					
Plans a quiet place to do homework					
Hands homework in on time					
J) AT THE END OF LESSONS					
Completes task or section					
Clears up and puts books, equipment away					
Helps peers to clear up					
Helps teacher to clear up					
Asks/waits to be dismissed					
Leaves quietly					
WHAT THE PUPIL ENJOYS RECEIVING IN CLASS					
Giving out and collecting books/equipment					
Being a classroom monitor					
Assisting teacher					
Assisting peers					
Conversation with the teacher					
Free time at the end of the lesson					
Free time to engage in a quiet activity					
Free time to listen to a tape recorder					
Curriculum games at the end of the lesson					
Extra time in a given lesson					
please name:					
Extra time helping a given teacher					
please name:					
Marks in exercise books					
Stars in exercise books					
Charts showing personal progress					
Maintaining own chart					
Display of chart on the wall					
Earning points/tokens					
Certificates for good effort/work/behaviour					
After school leisure activities					
please name:					
Praise					
Public praise					
Letters home praising the pupil					
Parents visiting school to hear of progress					

	LT	AS	MT	NA	NK
K) SOCIAL INTERACTION IN AND OUT OF CLASS					
Positively greets peers					
Positively greets staff					
Opens doors for people					
Walks in corridors					
Shares sweets with peers					
Shares possessions with peers					
Makes realistic loans					
Makes fair swaps					
Returns peer's possessions without damage					
Accepts denial without aggression/sulking					
L) TEASING AND BULLYING					
Copes with teasing/taunting					
Jokes about taunts about himself					
Avoids/ignores provocation					
Asserts himself					
Escapes from bullying without use of aggression					
Defends himself with minimum force					
Defends others from teasing/bullying					
Able to recognize own needs					
Perceives others' needs for help					
Able to ask for help					
Offers to help others					
M) SHOWING FEELINGS					
Shows when hurt or offended					
Recognises others' feeling of being hurt					
Verbally or non-verbally shows being happy/sad/angry/frustrated/anxious					
Recognizes another when happy/sad/angry/frustrated/anxious					
Can verbally describe and explain when another is happy/sad/angry/frustrated/anxious					
N) PLAY AND LEISURE ACTIVITIES					
Shows leisure skills for use in breaks					
Able to organize own play activities					
Initiates play with others					
Accepted in play with others					
Joins in one to one play					
Joins in group play					
Able to perceive the rules of the game					
Abides by the rules of the game					
Leads peers in appropriate play					
Appropriately follows group leader					
Able to identify deviant leaders					
Plays as a member of the team					
Accepts losing					
Shows compassion for the loser/s					

Chapter 6

Assessment by Baselines

Martin Scherer

Introduction

At the beginning of the year, a teacher was faced by a class, 'known to be a handful'. With some concern, the teacher first established a list of class rules. Gradually all the pupils settled down, except for three. The teacher felt that these pupils had special needs. Initial discussion with colleagues centred on carefully describing the behaviour. Without a clear description, colleagues had difficulty in making suggestions. What evidence could the teacher present to give confidence that any had special needs?

The teacher had some problems in describing the behaviour exactly. It seemed that every description could be countered by some example of the pupils' behaviour that contradicted and required a wider description. Some colleagues felt that the term 'disruptive' was sufficient in itself. In the end, the teacher settled on *any behaviour that diverted the teacher from teaching unless the pupil was seeking help*. The teacher then decided to count the number of such incidents, separately for each of the three pupils and collectively for the remainder of the class:

pupil:	J.R.	K.B.	I.G.	Ave. (other pupils)
no. of disruptions:	2	16	7	0.7

These results were surprising. First, while the average number of disruptions by other pupils was low, it led, in practice, to a high rate of disruptive behaviour, of 43 incidents per lesson (approx. one a minute). Second, although JR showed a low rate of disruptive behaviour, the teacher was not convinced. The next, and each subsequent, day seemed to fail to confirm his early expectations of the results of the previous day. The number of disruptive behaviours of each pupil seemed to vary from day to day. Faced by a mass of confusing figures, a colleague suggested that he graph the results. On the horizontal axis he put lessons, on the vertical axis the number of disruptive behaviours per lesson (see Figure 4). Even then the graphs did not seem to 'say' anything, so he added the average number of disruptive behaviours of the other pupils (broken line). Immediately the graph told him that all three pupils were more disruptive than the class average. After several days' results, he felt more confident.

However, the graphs also seemed to present other conclusions. While there were one or two days on which K.B.'s disruptive behaviour increased, on the whole it was decreasing; I.G.'s disruptive behaviour was gradually increasing; and J.R.'s disruptive behaviour varied widely from lesson to lesson, but taken as a whole neither to be increasing nor decreasing. It was stable at around 9 disruptions per lesson.

Having made a closer observation of the disruptive behaviour of all three pupils for 5 lessons, the teacher found it easier to describe the behaviour of each. The behaviour of I.G. was particularly disrupting to the lesson. He would flick other pupils with rulers, propel bits of chewed paper from a ruler, stab with pencils, prod under the table and pass books around the class. Not only did this behaviour involve a large number of other pupils, but the evidence showed it to be getting worse. The teacher decided to intervene. While he had previously allowed pupils to sit where they wanted, he now moved IG to sit at the front at a

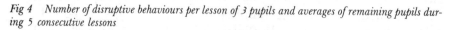

Fig 4   Number of disruptive behaviours per lesson of 3 pupils and averages of remaining pupils during 5 consecutive lessons

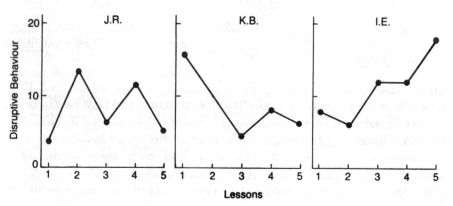

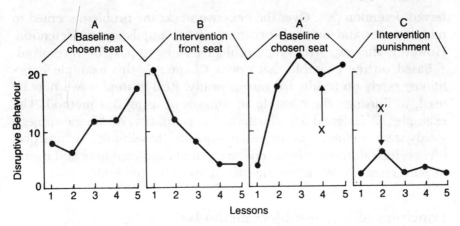

Fig 5   Number of disruptive behaviours per lesson of a pupil during baseline (A, A'), and two differ-ent interventions (B, C) (X = lesson when pupil sent to deputy head; X' = lesson after which pupils served detention)

single desk. He carried on monitoring the behaviour (condition B, Fig-ure 5). While it was worse on the first day, the strategy clearly worked. I.G.'s behaviour decreased to near the level of the average pupil. Per-haps I.G. had learnt his lesson? The teacher and I.G. agreed that I.G. could return to his chosen seat and that he would 'behave'. The teacher carried on monitoring (condition A', Figure 5).

The same disruptive behaviour returned. I.G. protested that he had been trying and that the teacher had not reminded him. The teacher denied this; on one day the behaviour was so bad that he had sent him to the deputy head (X). The teacher glanced at his graph, which confirmed his suspicions. Although I.G.'s disruptive behaviour was increasing no longer, it had stabilized at a higher rate. On discussing the problem with colleagues, one asked: 'What did you expect? You have taken the pupil away from his mates to stop the behaviour then put him back.' With hindsight, this seemed obvious but, perhaps, not so obvious at the time. The teacher recalled that when I.G. was sitting at the front, pupils behind and around I.G. did not tolerate his disruptive be-haviour.

At the beginning of the next lesson, the teacher spoke to the pupils I.G. chose to sit with, stating that if they did not help him to behave appropriately, they would all serve detention. The teacher carried on monitoring (condition C, Figure 5). The strategy worked for the first lesson, but in the second lesson the problem returned: all five pupils served detention (X'). Over the next two weeks the problem seemed to return twice, and on each occasion, all six pupils served detention. However, after two weeks the problem seemed to have been resolved.

Based on the example that opens Chapter 7, this example is fictitious; rarely do results fall out so neatly. Real examples will now be used, to illustrate the possible advantages of using this method. The example is designed to illustrate the simplicity of 'single-subject,' steady-state methods' or more colloquially 'baselining'. In practice, there is little difference between the method described here and its use in pure research. What are the principles of the method?

Principles of single-subject methods

Clear description of behaviour

In common with most psychological research, the description is chosen by the investigator. The only requirement is to state clearly the description in a manner that enables others to repeat the method.

Repeated measures increase confidence

A single measure may not be convincing. Hence the method seeks to repeat measures consecutively, under similar circumstances, with as far as possible, the same lesson, teacher and subject each day. The number of repeated measurements selected is up to the investigator – with ideally 5 or 10 repeats, or until the behaviour has stabilized.

Comparison of the effects of different procedures

There are three different procedures or conditions in the above report (Figure 5):

A *Baseline*   Before the teacher intervened, he objectively observed and recorded the behaviour. This is the baseline, or control condition, from which the effects of all subsequent procedures can be judged.

B *Intervention 1*   Here the teacher moved the pupil to sit in a different position.

A' *Second baseline*   The teacher next returned the pupil to the same place (return to baseline).

C *Intervention 2*   The teacher used a new procedure; in the above case, punishing all pupils encouraging or showing the disruption.

For short, this is labelled an **ABAC** design. The classic design is **ABA** but there are many variations (see later).

Examination of results

The example was deliberately constructed to show the three most commonly useful baseline results (Figure 4):

A *Stable baseline* J.R.'s results were described as erratic but stable. Both are relative terms. What is 'stable' is a matter of opinion, and of experience. In the end, the investigator must make his/her own judgement and stand by it.

   In the above study the teacher also recorded the behaviour of all other pupils and arrived at an average. The results showed that J.R.'s disruptive behaviour was clearly far above the average. The comparison reflects the 1981 Education Act's definition of 'special needs'. The result may give the teacher another measure to increase his confidence in the decision to intervene.

B *Decreasing baseline* K.B.'s disruptive behaviour is clearly decreasing. Should the teacher intervene? Perhaps not, for the disruptive behaviour may go of its own accord. If the graph represented an appropriate behaviour, the teacher would be concerned and may intervene to reverse the trend (see Figure 6).

C *Increasing baseline* I.G.'s disruptive behaviour is rapidly increasing. This caused considerable concern. The result gave the teacher the confidence to intervene. Again, if the graph represented a desired

Fig 6 Unstable baselines

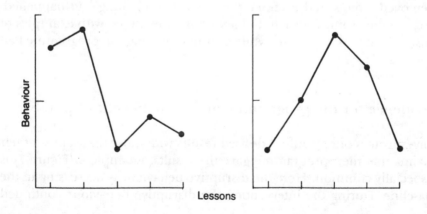

behaviour, the result may give the teacher confidence to wait and see if it increases to appropriate levels before intervening.

D   *Combinations*   Figure 5 shows an increasing baseline that stabilizes in the last two days of condition A', and the opposite in the subsequent condition (C). Generally an investigator would not have confidence until a specific trend emerged. Sometimes the fluctuations in the rate of the behaviour are considerable (Figure 6). This is frustrating, it tells the investigator nothing – except to start again. Perhaps a different or more specific definition of the behaviour, or different method of recording, will help to gain a clearer picture?

Results examined by eye

This is a common procedure with all applications of this method whether in pure or applied research, or applications in the classroom. Commonly known as 'eyeballing', the investigator looks for clear differences between conditions. This is shown in all the conditions of I.G.'s programme (Figure 5); the following examples (Figure 7) show no discernible effect.

Example 1:   The intervention (B) is more stable than the baseline (A) but there is no discernible difference between the two.

Example 2:   The opposite of (1).

Example 3:   The baseline (A) is increasing; the intervention is also increasing. There is no evidence here that the intervention has any effect.

Example 4:   The opposite of (3).

In all four examples, if the separating line between A and B was removed, you would be none the wiser that anything had happened. Regrettably, some journals and textbooks are littered with examples of results that look like these, while claiming still that the programme had the desired effect.

Evidence for the programme or for the benefit of pupils

Investigators often confuse desired results with those that support their claims that their programme gave the results. Example 4 (Figure 7) is especially common. Here the disruptive behaviour is decreasing in the baseline. During the intervention the disruptive behaviour continued

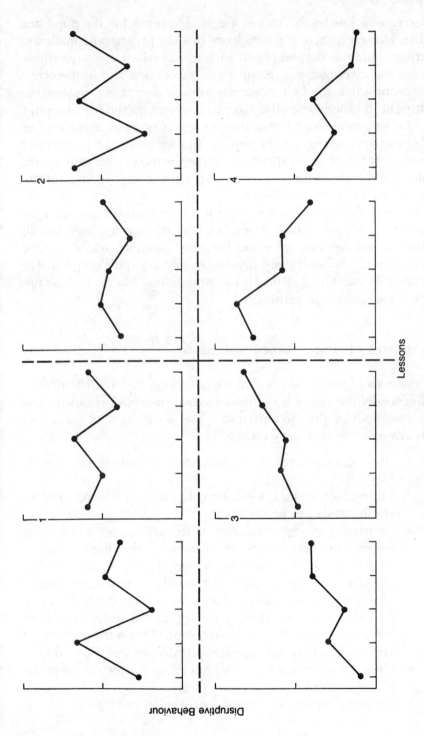

Fig 7   Comparison of conditions showing no discernible effect of the provision (B) in comparison to baseline (A)

Lessons

Disruptive Behaviour

to decrease to low levels. This is a desirable result for the pupil and teacher. However, there is no evidence that the programme made any contribution to this desired result. Such results raise serious questions: why did the investigator go to such effort to design and implement a programme when the behaviour was already decreasing, as desired? What right did the investigator have to intervene in the life of a pupil when he was improving? Sometimes there is reason to intervene when the behaviour is a danger to the pupil(s). In such a case, the programme should show the result of speeding up the decrease. Alternatively, the results should show the effects of a programme speeding up the increase of a desirable behaviour.

Ultimately the benefit to the pupil must have precedence over the desire to show neat results. A teacher may attempt to speed up the decrease of a dangerous behaviour but show no effect. While no effect may be shown, neither is there any damage to the pupil's progress. The advantage of baselining is that if the programme has an undesirable effect, it can quickly be terminated.

Advantages of single-subject methods

The methods of science do not 'prove' anything, they merely increase confidence by the use of a rigorous method; objective measures and clear statement of the circumstances. The advantages of the above approach to assessment may include:

1. *The method is exploratory.* It makes few assumptions, but seeks to find out.
2. *The results are graphed.* A picture tells a thousand words. From a graph trends can be seen easily.
3. *The results make comparisons between the pupil's present and past performance,* not between the pupil and any other pupil or group of pupils. In the example above (Figure 4) the teacher included the average performance of the remaining pupils. This may be informative but may not be valid. The performance of any individual pupil within that average may have been worse than the pupil in question. That is the problem of averaging, it may hide the real picture and true variation.
4. *The results pertain to a real person,* not an average or any other statistical concept.
5. *The method requires few resources or specialised training.*

6. *The method is not the 'property' of any particular approach.* The single-subject method was described in the work of the Freudians in 1895. However, they made exaggerated claims for both the importance of their results and their methods (Hersen and Barlow, 1976). Consequently, the single-subject method was 'thrown out with the bath water'. It was not until recently, after considerable struggle by contemporary behaviourists, that the method was accepted as one of the most rigorous methods in the social sciences and, perhaps, the most rigorous in the applied field.
7. *The method cannot be used to investigate all questions,* for instance, it cannot be used where measurement cannot be repeated.

Why not use statistics?

Many may ask if statistics are not better than examination by eye. While statistics have been adapted for use with single-subject designs, their use breaks one of the basic assumptions of statistics and has caused controversy (Kazdin, 1981). Second, in single-subject designs, statistics are generally used when differences are not discernible by eye. Hence 'eyeballing' is probably a more rigorous test than statistical analysis. This may be especially true for the new investigator, who may reject 'close results' that others may accept. Third, statistics do not prove anything, they merely state that a result has a greater or lesser probability of being the result of chance. Results above or below the standard of probability may be accepted or rejected, even though they are respectively false or true.

In general, eyeballing may be a more demanding test than statistical inference. When intervening in the lives of pupils, we may prefer the more rigorous test.

The basic method

Describing behaviour

In conversation people are usually imprecise in their descriptions of behaviour. Often teachers are obliged to use short-hand terms in the brief space allowed in school reports. Westmacott and Cameron (1981) give numerous examples of imprecise statements, for which they use

the term 'fuzzy: unclear, imprecise and frequently ambiguous statements used to describe problems'. Even here the definition is that of a
concept. Real examples illustrate:

Fuzzy:	*Performance:*
'He's disruptive'	Shouts out loudly when the teacher is talking to another pupil
'He lacks motor coordination'	Runs, jumps, climbs and balances as well as the rest of his class but cannot catch a tennis ball with one hand.
'Numerically backward for his age'	Can add, subtract, multiply and divide whole numbers but not fractions

Westmacott and Cameron present the 'come and see . . .' test. If you
know what to expect from the description without seeing the behaviour, then it may be a precise description. If you cannot, it is a fuzzy
description. 'Come and see I.G. being a disruptive influence' is not as
helpful as 'Come and see I.G. passing books, flicking rulers . . .' The
major problem with fuzzy descriptions is that the only action they
prompt is to ask someone to define or diagnose the behaviour.

There are basically four classes of behaviour description:

1. *Structural.* Describes the appearance or structure of the behaviour: 'Runs around the classroom.'

2. *Functional.* Describes the behaviour by its effects. The example that opens this chapter uses a functional definition: *Disruptive behaviour is any behaviour that diverts the teacher's attention from teaching, excluding the pupil's requests for help.*

3. *Performance.* Describes both the structure of the behaviour and the events that may prompt it: 'Runs around the classroom when peers call him a blockhead.'

4. *Operational.* Describes both the appearance of the behaviour and its effect: 'Runs around the classroom until the teacher stops him.'

The most complete definition describes the structure of the behaviour,
the events wherein it occurs and that may prompt it, and the events that
follow and may maintain it. The problem is that an assessment seeks to
discover the events that may be prompting and maintaining the behaviour. The pedantic critic will always find fault with a description.

The best definition is one that suits the circumstances and enables the particular investigation.

Definition drift

Definitions are likely to change over time. An exploratory approach may be less likely to drift, but is still vulnerable as people adapt to events. Teachers 'get used to', become 'more tolerant of' disruptive behaviour. The more imprecise the definition, the more likely it is to drift.

The researcher's solution to definition drift is to use a second observer as an occasional check. The level of agreement between the two observers is then presented as a percentage. The facility of a second observer is rarely available to teachers who are usually the only adult in the classroom. Second observers have to be trained, both in general and in particular, in the use of the description of the behaviour and the method of recording decided on by the teacher. The classroom is a private place. The occasional presence of an additional adult is likely to have a dramatic effect on pupil behaviour.

Measuring the behaviour

Some behaviours may occur frequently, such as calling out in class. Others occur infrequently but for a long time, such as attention to the task. Others occur both infrequently and for a short duration but are very intense, such as shouting. Each needs to be measured differently:

Frequency:	Perhaps the most common measurement and the easiest, unless the behaviour occurs very frequently.
Duration:	Less common because of the difficulty of recording. Requires a stop-watch; may be replaced by analysis using interval-sampling methods.
Intensity:	Even less common because of the measurement problems; requires equipment or a judgement on a scale 1 (hardly noticeable) to 10 (unbearable). The judgement is likely to drift as the teacher adapts or as the activity in class changes.

The best measure to use is one that gives a fairly high count but makes minimum demands on the teacher, who is simultaneously teaching. Hence frequency counts are most common. However, it depends on which aspect of the behaviour you wish to increase or decrease.

Recording the behaviour

Basically there are two methods of recording (Kazdin, 1981):

1. *Constant.*	The teacher records every time the behaviour occurs, the simplest and most common method in the classroom.
2. *Interval sampling.*	At the end of an interval, say, 5 min, the teacher observes the class and records. The behaviour observed might be specific and discrete (was he, or was he not, doing it), or involve counting responses over a period of time. The problem with this method is that it requires extra equipment: such as a classroom clock, stop-watch or watch with bleeper.

The easiest method is by pen and paper. Draw up a recording sheet with the date, time, class, subject and teacher. Write the pupils' names in the left-hand column and the behaviour in the right-hand column; if recording frequency, simply put '1' alongside the pupil's name, bunch in fives to aid counting at the end of recording; and if time-sampling, put '1' if he was so behaving and '0' if he was not. Carry the pen and recording sheet at all times. Rushing back and forth to the teacher's desk disrupts the teaching and is likely to be noticed and have an effect on pupils' behaviour. Alternatives – especially for use outside the class-room – include the cricket umpire's method, marbles in the pocket, collected in the hand and transferred to the other pocket. Digital coun-ters designed like a stop-watch or wristwatch are available and useful, and the back of the hand is still a very common place to record small records! It is unlikely that a teacher is able to record simultaneously more than a single behaviour of three pupils or three behaviours of one pupil.

If the method of recording is obvious to pupils, then it will probably have an effect on their behaviour. If they are aware that you are record-ing 'on-task' behaviour, and you use a bleep to tell you when to record, then they will learn to get their heads down when the bleep goes. Simi-larly, pupils are likely to pick up the signal if you are looking straight at them when recording behaviour. You are also likely to show approval or disapproval when looking albeit unintentionally. Such 'side-effects' are beneficial. At times there are distinct benefits in informing pupils that you are recording and sharing the result with them. Pupils may be encouraged to record their own behaviour.

Self-training

Training is essential. The more experience you have, the more accurate you will be. Often the first few lessons of recording will produce erratic baselines. This initial trial period is very useful; it tests out whether the description of the behaviour and method of recording are workable. After an initial testing out of the procedures, both the description and recording method may be refined.

Presenting the results

Usually behaviour is recorded on the vertical axis and days or lessons on the horizontal axis. The behaviour is often presented as the number of times, or rate, per lesson. However, rates per lesson is valid only if the lessons are of equal duration. In the case of lessons – or observations – of varying durations, the rate per hour may be presented. If time-sampling is used, the proportion may be expressed as a percentage.

Don't be deceived

The task of the investigator is to present the results clearly. The reader needs to make sure he/she is not hoodwinked. Figure 8 (overleaf) shows how the axes can be stretched and shrunk to increase the appearance of the rapid effects of a provision to reduce disruptive behaviour.

The data is exactly the same, but gives a very different impression. Be cautious about presentation of any data that has been 'translated' by statistics. Even the most simple of statistical methods may be used to hide imperfections; only astute readers will prevent this.

Design of the investigation

Reversal designs are commonly labelled by the sequence of their conditions:

A: This is the baseline alone and will produce results on which decisions are based, including decisions not to proceed any further, as in the case of K.B. (Figure 4).

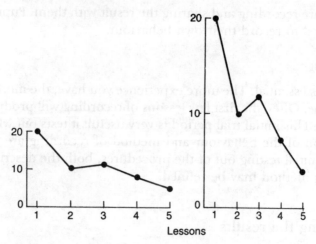

Fig 8   Effects of shrinkage and compressing axes to alter appearances of results

AB: Here a baseline A is followed by an intervention B. The
         AB design is the most common, in practice; if the bene-
         ficial effect is achieved for both pupil and teacher, then
         the method has served its purpose. However, there is no
         real evidence here that the intervention has had any effect
         at all (section A3, Figure 7). The change may be due to
         something beyond the investigator's control or know-
         ledge; the solution is to reverse the procedure: return to
         the baseline.

ABA':   If the rate of behaviour in A and A' is similar, and both
         are different to B, then there is evidence that the inter-
         vention (B) has had effect. This can be seen from Figure
         4, above, although the example is not perfect. Now the
         investigator can go on adding conditions C. After each
         intervention condition, the design is reversed to check
         the effects of the intervention.

Probes: Repeated reversals, each involving many lessons or days,
         are time-consuming. Hence many investigators will only
         reverse for one or two days (a 'probe'). It is less time-con-
         suming, but the evidence is less convincing.

Exploratory approach. It may seem that the investigator planned the
design from the start, but invariably the plan is changed by events. The

most realistic approach is exploratory. Start with a baseline (A), and look at the results. The results will prompt action. Design the next step, a change in definition, measurement of recording (A') or an intervention (B), and look at the results. The cycle is repeated.

Ethical problems. There are serious ethical problems with reversal designs – e.g. is it ethical to return the pupil to the condition that previously maintained his disruptive/aggressive/dangerous behaviour? For this reason, many investigators use a BAB design, where they start and finish with the intervention. The alternative procedure that does not face the same ethical problems is *multiple baselines*.

Multiple baselines are more complex and demanding, but they do not involve reversals. They involve taking at least three pupils with similar behavioural problems or one individual pupil with different behavioural problems. Each behaviour or pupil is observed simultaneously in the same context, and a baseline is presented for each. Each pupil or behaviour, in turn, is then the subject of the same intervention. If the behaviour of the target pupil or the target behaviour of the single pupil changes, but the others remain constant then the change in behaviour may be attributed to the intervention. A multiple baseline is shown in Figure 10.

Why use single-subject methods?

We may now examine the use of single-subject methods in assessment and evaluation, both of pupil performance and provision. All the examples presented here have emerged from the classroom. They are therefore not ideal and show various adaptations of the basic method. It is up to readers to examine the methods and their results; many have been published, so the reader may refer to the publications for further information. Whatever the limitations of the data, they are more reliable than subjective assessment and evaluation. The reports are chosen to illustrate the advantages of using a rigorous, single-subject method.

More objective and detailed assessment

Aggressive behaviour happens relatively infrequently but is the cause of considerable concern. Often it is not clear what provokes the aggression. In the following example the teacher discovered that over 30 per cent of aggressive behaviours of a new pupil were in response to teasing by peers. The school operated a points system and 40 per cent of the incidents were as a result of losing points for misbehaving (Parkin and Scherer, 1987). Having gained a clear assessment of what was provoking the incidents, the teacher decided to take a step-by-step approach, or multiple baseline approach. The first programme rewarded the pupil for showing an appropriate acceptance of the points award (Figure 9).

The aggressive incidents were infrequent, so were calculated for a week, and shown as the rate before the programme was instituted (baseline). The rate of aggressive incidents was recorded again after the programme had been established (intervention). The results show that the number of aggressive responses to points award had substantially decreased. Aggressive response to peers, not the target of the programme, had remained at the same level. The two types of aggression were different, prompted by different events. Had the teacher not differentiated between them in the initial assessment, any provision may have had confused results. A programme for aggressive responses to peers would be the next stage of provision. Confidence in these results may be increased by the clearly separate effect of the programme on a multiple baseline. However, confidence may be reduced by the lack of a repeated measure. That is one of the problems of aggressive behaviour; it occurs only infrequently while, nevertheless, causing considerable concern.

Fig 9   Rate of a pupil's aggressive response to teasing or correction by teacher, before and after provision to reduce aggressive response

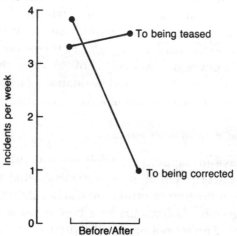

Avoiding ethical problems

A school's staff meeting agreed that a particular pupil seemed to look somewhat glum and despondent whenever praised. Such a response may deter the praiser, or be labelled 'maladjusted'. Before intervening, a baseline was taken. First, the pupil was observed at the end-of-day 'feedback session', where the whole school (staff and pupils) met. Praise was verbally given to pupils who had achieved or made effort in class. The observer recorded whether or not the pupil looked at the praiser, or another significant adult, and whether or not he/she smiled or looked pleased. Second, a form was passed among the teachers, who were asked to record if the pupil's response was normal when praised in class or house. The results showed that all adults felt that the particular pupil's response was normal, and that when observed being given praise in the feedback session, he/she smiled at the praiser (Watts and Scherer, 1987).

A staff meeting registered concern about the level of swearing among pupils in the playground of a residential school. One suggestion was that at assembly all pupils be cautioned about swearing; however, others felt that so doing would provide to pupils a means of provoking adults and gaining attention. During the baseline all incidents of swearing overheard during one playtime per day were recorded.

The results showed that usually no more than five incidents of swearing were heard per playtime in a school of 50 boys (Figure 10). Exceptionally, one day was different. It may have been just such a day that gave rise to the concern expressed originally: should, then, the school have chastised pupils on that evidence? Perhaps the evidence did not justify such action, the school may have continued monitoring to see if swearing was always high on Fridays.

In both the above cases, unwarranted interventions into pupils' lives was avoided, and time and effort saved. The potential effects of demand bias in assessment and labelling behaviour are that problems may be created that do not exist (Lindsey and Aronson, 1968; Ullman and Krasner, (1975).

Resolve disagreements and conclude debates

In a special education context three procedures were used to maintain the appropriate behaviour of disruptive and delinquent boys: an immediate points system, daily report and a contract. Staff discussion of the relative merits of each did not resolve the question of which to use. All boys were on a contract (A, A', A''), two were observed (Figure

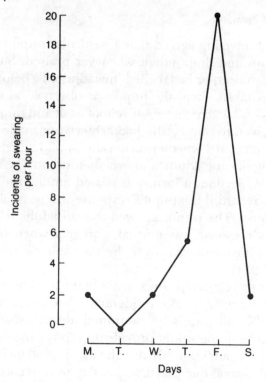

Fig 10   Incidence of swearing each day of week, excluding Sunday (per hour) in residential school playground

11) (Scherer and Redmayne, 1985). Adding a daily report to the contract increased the proportion of on-task behaviour in class. Adding
contingent points (immediate delivery) showed the highest rate of on-
task behaviour in class.

The use of a single-subject evaluation resolved the debate. Contracts
are closer to the procedures of 'normal society and school'. Hence it
was decided to start with immediate points, and gradually support the
pupil through a daily report to a contract. Confidence in these results
may be gained by use of a reversal design.

Enhancing professional autonomy

Traditionally teachers have applied the advice of inspectors, consultants and managers. However, it is the teacher who is in closest contact with the classroom.

Within a Secure Unit a particular system was felt, by some teachers,
to create some of the problems it aimed to prevent, namely violent and

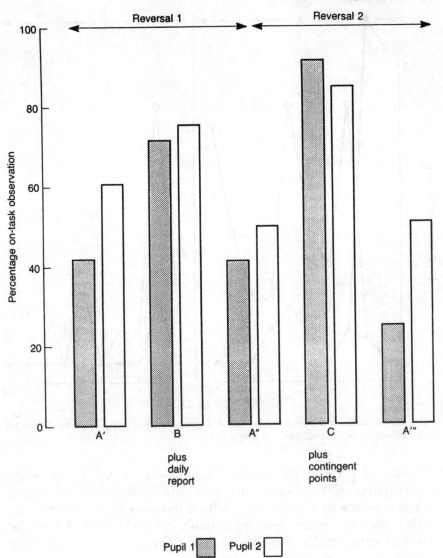

Fig 11   Percentages of observation when 2 pupils (clear and shaded histograms) were observed to be on-task; results showing 3 baselines (A', A'', A''') where contract alone in force (during condition B a daily report was also in operation and during condition C a contingent points system was in operation); the study shows 2 reversals (A' – B – A''' A'' – C – A''')

aggressive behaviour. Initial surveys gave some support to this belief. Nevertheless, the consultants found the arguments unconvincing, and managers felt the proposed alteration would be unmanageable. It was decided to change the system for a trial period (Scherer and Brown, 1984).

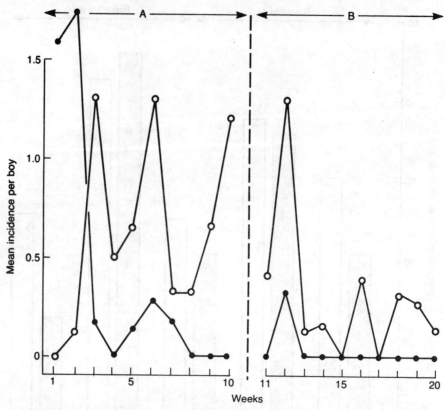

Fig 12   Mean incidence of violent (solid circles) and aggressive (open circles) behaviour per boy per week during baseline (A) and change in system (B)

Figure 12 presents the results before and after the change in the points system; violent behaviours are shown by closed circles, aggressive behaviours by open circles. After a few days in the baseline (A), both behaviours settle down to a stable rate. The rate of both behaviours substantially decreases after the first few days of the intervention (B). Other data showed that the concerns of managers were not justified. The data came from the daily recording systems of the unit. Many schools regularly record information of pupil behaviour, e.g. attendance and lateness records.

Critical examination of the above data may cast serious doubt on the validity of any conclusion that the change in the system resulted in a drop in aggressive and violent behaviours. Teachers were the only group in this multi-occupational context to produce any hard data, hence their arguments had greater force. Reversing the design may have resulted in a return to the previous rates of aggressive and violent behaviour. This would have been unethical and may be contrary to the Health and Safety at Work Acts.

Objective teacher appraisal

The performance of teachers is likely to be the subject of regular appraisal, perhaps including the headteacher's visits to the classroom. The following examples may illustrate a more objective approach to appraisal.

Despite general advice and support through a points system, a probationary teacher faced continuing management problems in a junior special school class. The headteacher established an individual INSET programme for the teacher. Before and after the INSET, two independent observers recorded teachers' attention to pupils' disruptive behaviour and appropriate behaviour in getting on with set work:

	Pre-training:		Post-training:	
	pupil behaviour (%)	teacher attention (%)	pupil behaviour (%)	teacher attention (%)
on-task	30	12	66	76
off-task	70	57	34	19
disruptive	30	31	20	5

The results show that following the in-service training (INSET), teachers' attention shifted from inappropriate behaviour to appropriate behaviour, and that as this happened, the pupils' behaviour shifted from disruptive to on-task.

The second example again involves an INSET programme, designed and presented by the headteacher. A school for emotionally and behaviourally disturbed pupils had extensive experience in using a points system; however, during the INSET discussion revealed that teachers did not appreciate a fundamental principle of such systems, namely that to have any effect on behaviour, the points must be delivered immediately after the behaviour. The INSET was based on working meetings where the teachers examined and redesigned their systems to meet the individual needs of their classes and pupils. One teacher set a number of classroom behaviour targets, then according to the type of lesson, gave immediate points, or delayed delivery of points until the end of the lesson. The teacher then asked the headteacher to act as an observer. By chance three lessons followed each other on different days when the teacher first used delayed points (A), then immediate points (B) and, again, delayed points (A'). The results for six pupils who attended all three lessons are shown in Figure 13 (Scherer 1987); it was shown that when the teacher used immediate points, the rate of rule breaking was substantially less (B). Confidence may be increased by two aspects of the design: first, there is a reversal ABA'; second, the result of one pupil is replicated across 5 others.

Two conclusions may be drawn. First, that the teacher showed considerable expertise in the immediate delivery of points to a large class of disturbed pupils. Second, that the immediate system was more effective. The teacher had previously lacked confidence in her own performance and the validity of the principle of immediate delivery. Following the evaluation, the teacher adapted the system of immediate delivery for use in all lessons to support pupils in learning to abide by the class rules. The teacher also permitted the presentation of her results to the staff group, gaining considerable respect for her efforts.

Objective evaluation of INSET

Teaching is a partnership between the teacher and managers providing support and training. If INSET has a value, it is in improving teacher performance in the classroom. Appraisal of the teacher is as much an evaluation of INSET and managerial support as it is the individual performance of the teacher. An objective picture is required. Both of the above examples illustrate that case.

Objective self-appraisal

The report in Chapter 10 of this book showed that the teacher used single-subject designs to evaluate his provision for three disruptive pupils in a comprehensive school maths class (Scherer, 1984). The same teacher then gained promotion to a Regional Centre for severely disruptive and delinquent boys and used the same method to evaluate an amended provision (*ibid.*). Self-appraisal gives greater personal confidence than appraisal by others. If teachers are to be autonomous professionals, they need an objective method of self-appraisal.

Is the school doing its job?

All schools will offer a general therapeutic and educational milieu. Too often, this provision may be accepted without question or recognition.

On admission, a ten-year-old boy seemed unable to converse, even to answer questions. The general approach of the school was to expect

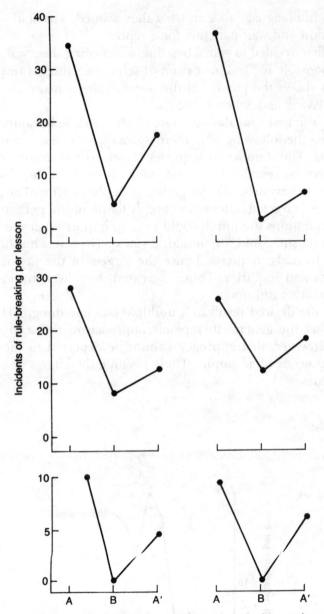

Fig 13   Number of rule-breaking incidents for each of 6 pupils during lessons where points delivered immediately (B) or delayed until the end of lesson (A, A')

pupils to use language to gain what they wanted. The staff would put the question and wait patiently for a reply.

It was first decided to gain a baseline: a recording sheet was sent to all staff responsible for lessons or out-of-school activities with the pupil. Figure 14 shows the picture of the pupil's statements, enquiries, and requests (Watts and Scherer, 1987).

During the first four days the rate of all verbal behaviours was low; and during the following days there was a rapid increase in the rate of statements. The number of inquiries increased less dramatically. The level of request remained low and stable throughout the observation. With three behaviours, this design is a multiple baseline. The approach of the school targeted statements in reply to questions; perhaps in reply to some questions the pupil would have to inquire what was available and what he/she could, or should, do next. However, he/she was not required to make requests, hence the targets of the provision were statements and inquiries. Those increased, but the behaviour which was not a target did not.

This is the desired result in a multiple baseline design. The results suggest that the general therapeutic approach of the school was effective. However, that approach cannot be expected to meet all the individual needs of all pupils. These become the targets of individual programmes.

Fig 14   Pupil's average statements, inquiries and requests during provision to increase verbal statements (per hour)

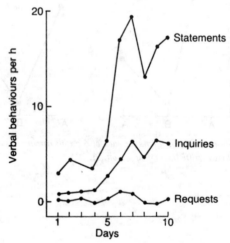

Pupil self-appraisal

A baseline showed that four disruptive pupils attended to the task set for less than half the lesson. The teacher negotiated contracts with each pupil, whereby they could gain access to certain privileges at lunchtime in return for attending to the set work. The rate of attending to the work increased to almost 100 per cent. The teacher then asked the pupils to monitor their own performance, making occasional checks himself. The checks showed that while attention to work decreased, it remained high at 80 per cent, or more (Shirodkar and Scherer, 1984). There seems no reason why pupils should not act as observers, especially of their own performance.

Conclusions

Investigation using single-subject methods is an adventure, an objective exploration, into the work we undertake as teachers and behavioural practitioners. The methods are relatively simple, require minimum resources, can be adapted for use in the classroom whilst allowing the teacher to teach simultaneously and are recognised as objective and rigorous. The results may assist us in evaluating any area of teaching and pupil performance, provide powerful support for our professional assessments and protect both ourselves and our pupils from continuing ineffective or even damaging provision. It may enhance professional autonomy and respect among colleagues and fellow professionals.

References

HERSEN, M. and BARLOW, D.H. (1976) *Single Case Experimental Designs Strategies for Studying Behaviour Change* (New York: Pergamon).

KAZDIN, A.E. (1981) 'Behavioural observation', in: *Behavioural Assessment* Eds. Hersen, M. and Bellack, A.S. (New York: Pergamon).

LINDSEY, G. and ARONSON, E. (1968) *The Handbook of Social Psychology* (Reading, Mass.: Addison-Wesley).

PARKIN, T. and SCHERER, M. (1987) 'Reduction of aggressive behaviour towards the teacher', *NCSE Research Exchange*,7, 9, 10.

SCHERER, M. (1984) 'Reducing disruptive behaviour in a secondary school classroom', *Orchard Lodge Studies in Deviancy*, 5, 29–36.

SCHERER, M. (1987) 'Teacher research of disruptive behaviour' *Educational and Clinical Psychology* (Leicester: BPS).

SCHERER, M. and BROWN, B. (1984) 'Eliminating exclusion time-out', *NCSE Research Exchange*, 3,4; see also *'Time out: an alternative to rooms' Behavioural Approaches to Children*, 8, 127–33.

SCHERER, M. and REDMAYNE, T. (1984) *NCSE Research Exchange 1985*.

SCHERER, M., SHIRODKAR, H. and HUGHES, R. (1984) 'Reducing disruptive behaviours: a brief report of three successful procedures', *Behavioural Approaches with Children*, 8, 52–7.

SHIRODKAR, H. and SCHERER, M. (1984) 'Development of appropriate classroom behaviour and maintenance by pupil self-evaluation in a special school classroom, *Orchard Lodge Studies in Deviancy*, 4, 25–36; See also *NCSE Research Exchange*, 3, 3.

ULLMAN, L.P. and KRASNER, L. (1975) *A Psychological Approach to Abnormal Behaviour* (Englewood Cliffs, NJ: Prentice-Hall).

WATTS, M. and SCHERER, M. (1987) 'Increasing verbal behaviour in a withdrawn ten year old', *NCSE Research Exchange*, 7, 10.

WESTMACOTT, E.J.S. and CAMERON, R.J. (1981) *Behaviour Can Change* (London:Macmillan).

Chapter 7

The Pupil's View

Irvine Gersch

Introduction

In this chapter, I would like to develop an argument in favour of increasing the direct, active and honest involvement of children in their assessment. Clearly, the assessment of children seems to be a growing area, particularly with maladjustment, and there are good pragmatic, moral and legally supported reasons for increasing the participation of children in the plans and programmes being drawn up for them.

I shall offer a brief critique of the current role of pupils in assessment and behavioural change, and describe four practical projects carried out by myself with staff in schools. It will then be possible to highlight particular areas of behavioural programmes which require careful consideration of the pupil's views. Finally, having addressed some questions for those professionals seeking to alter pupil behaviour, as a checklist, some general conclusions are drawn.

Background

Current role of children in assessment

Children are frequently assessed by a host of adult professionals. We assess pupil ability, schoolwork and attainment, learning skills, attitudes, behaviour and adjustment. Typically, children are assigned a relatively passive role in most of the assessments carried out, assessment usually being seen as something which is 'done to the child' rather than something in which they play an active part. To be fair, many psychologists and behavioural practitioners go a long way towards involving the child and family in decisions about treatment goals, rewards, targets and outcomes and exploring children's views and attitudes in some depth. None the less, it would appear fair to comment that more could be done generally to elicit pupils' views of their school life, work and behavioural programmes.

Why involve children more actively in their assessments?

There are several reasons why it might be helpful to engage children more actively in their assessments. These reasons fall under three main headings: pragmatic, moral and legally supported.

From a *pragmatic* point of view, children have valuable information to contribute to their school plans; their attitudes and views are likely to affect the success or failure of any plans or programmes drawn up for them; and the more direct the involvement of the child in the plan, the higher the chance of success. In school, it would seem sensible to ask pupils what they think are their strengths and weaknesses, which subjects they find hard to learn and what help they think they need. When devising behavioural programmes, it would also seem sensible to negotiate with children what counts as 'desirable behaviour', what steps should be taken to bring about change, appropriate reinforcement and methods of recording.

Morally it can also be argued that children have the right to be listened to when changes in their schooling, or indeed their behaviour, are suggested. Indeed one could raise ethical objections to another person attempting to modify one's behaviour without informed consent. It is my view therefore that not only should parental agreement be obtained when behavioural programmes are suggested for children, but that pupil consent needs to be obtained as well.

Legally, in certain circumstances, there is a duty to ascertain the views of children. This duty seems to be developed more in social work than in educational practice. For example, the Children Act (1975) (chapter 72, s. 59) requires that 'in reaching any decision relating to a child in care, a local authority shall . . . so far as is practicable, ascertain the wishes and feelings of the child regarding the decision and give due consideration to them, having regard to his age and understanding'. Educationally the Department of Education and Science (DES) Circular 1/83, in respect of the 1981 Education Act, states that in assessment, 'the feelings and perceptions of the child concerned should be taken into account, and the concept of partnership should, wherever possible, be extended to older children and young persons' (p.2). While it is fair to comment that a DES Circular is not legally binding, the spirit of the law would seem to be in favour of the inclusion of children's views.

Interactional view of behaviour

Recently there has been an increasing recognition of the fact that pupil behaviour does not occur in a vacuum, and that it can only be fully understood in the context within which it arises, and that behavioural adjustment depends upon the situation. Clearly, definitions of acceptable behaviour, disruptive behaviour or difficult behaviour will depend on the person who is responsible for those definitions.

Teachers, who it should be remembered have feelings too, may vary in their toleration of behaviour from day to day, lesson to lesson or indeed child to child. In short, it is important to bear in mind that definitions of behavioural difficulty are relative to the context in which they arise, and that a proper assessment of complaints or problems must take into account a number of different perspectives, including that of the child, the family, the teacher and perhaps other relevant people.

Pupil involvement: four practical projects

In this section it is intended to describe four projects on pupil involvement which relate directly to pupils whose behaviour has tended to cause concern.

The projects to be described are as follows:

- the development of a *child's report* in a social service setting;
- the development of *child's advice* under the Education Act (1981);
- a *pupil self-grading behavioural programme*;
- a programme based on *pupil–teacher working parties*.

The child's report

The report emerged from an Assessment Centre which catered for boys and girls, aged between 10 and 17 years, who were referred for an extended residential assessment. The aim of the assessment was to plan the best course of action, typically following a breakdown in the home situation. The assessment team included residential social work staff, education staff, a consultant psychiatrist, an educational psychologist and a social worker, all of whom prepared written reports on the child and family during the child's stay at the Centre. Towards the end of the child's stay, as in most Observation and Assessment Centres, all of the reports are collated into a booklet and discussed in detail at a case conference which aims to conclude with an agreed action plan about the child's future educational and residential arrangements.

The Child's Report is in fact a three-page form, on which pupils are asked to express their views under five main categories:

1. School.
2. Home.
3. Time at the Observation and Assessment Centre.
4. Hobbies and pastimes.
5. The future.

An evaluation carried out some two years after its inception revealed that the Child's Report was viewed by staff and children as worthwhile and valuable; that most of the children opted to complete the report (which was voluntary); that it had acted as a trigger for counselling on many occasions; and that it generally supported the philosophy of the Centre which stressed the importance of listening to children. A full account of the Child's Report and its evaluation is described elsewhere (Gersch and Cutting, 1985).

Child's advice (under the 1981 Education Act)

Following the positive evaluation of the Child's Report in a social services setting consideration was given to increasing the active involvement of children being formally assessed under the provision of the Education Act (1981). The 1981 Act requires, among other things, that local authorities re-assess all pupils who are thirteen years of age, in order to provide a new Statement of their special education needs.

In order to compile the Statement, local education authorities must seek the written advice of the child's headteacher, the school medical officer, the educational psychologist and other professional workers who are involved (e.g. social worker), and parental evidence is also invited. One glaring omission in the statutory requirements appears to be the fact that the child's views are not specifically requested, although as stated earlier, it is the spirit of the DES Circular 1/83 that children's views should be included and taken seriously.

It was decided to extend the Child's Report, previously outlined, and to produce a format which could be used by adolescent pupils with special educational needs. Pupils were given a report form which they were able to complete in order to state their views about their schooling and special educational needs, and which would become part of their legal Statement, added to the other reports drawn up by professional adults.

The report which was piloted (included in the Appendix) invited children to answer questions under the following headings:

1. School background.
2. Present school.
3. Special needs.
4. Friends.
5. Hobbies, interests and out of school activities.
6. The future.
7. Additional comments.

Thus far, experience has shown that children enjoy and value being consulted, they say sensible and interesting things and many pupils are very perceptive about their education. Some parents have requested that their own children complete a report when placements have been difficult. Some children have commented positively about being treated in a mature, responsible way. It does seem that guidelines and training are probably required for adult helpers and that care is needed not to bias children's views. Pupils may be unfamiliar with the exercise of expressing their views openly, without hurting the feelings of others, and may need support and guidance. With regard to the actual form piloted, there is some evidence from an initial evaluation that the particular form will require some amendment in order to make the format more attractive and the language more accessible to children with learning difficulties.

A pupil's self-grading behavioural programme

The third project to be described involves a behaviour modification programme in a mainstream fourth-year junior class, involving pupils tracking and grading their own work efforts. The project was undertaken with all the pupils in a single class and was devised by myself together with the classteacher (Gersch and Brown, 1986).

A behavioural programme emerged which involved every child in the class being given a work record sheet (see below), which has space for 15 tasks to be completed. The tasks are set by the teacher, each day, in clear, precise terms. The child ticks the column when the task has been completed successfully and then gives him/herself a grade for work effort:

PUPIL SELF-GRADED WORK RECORD SHEET
(Gersch and Brown 1986)

WORK RECORD SHEET   SHEET NO.

Name ....   Work beginning ....

Class ....

Teacher ....   Date ....

	TASKS TO BE DONE	COMPLETED (✔)	PUPIL'S GRADE	TEACHER'S GRADE	POINTS (BASED ON TEACHER'S GRADE)
1.					
2.					
3.					
4.					
5.					
6.					
7.					
8.					
9.					
10.					
11.					
12.					
13.					
14.					
15.					

A = EXCELLENT EFFORT (4 points)
B = VERY GOOD EFFORT (3 points)
C = GOOD EFFORT   (2 points)
D = SATISFACTORY   (1 point)
E = NOT VERY GOOD   (0 points)

Total Points _____

Comment: ....

signed: .... (Pupil)

Comment: ....

signed: .... (Teacher)

Comment: ....

signed: .... (Headteacher)

Comment: ....

signed: .... (Parent)

Please return to class teacher

REWARD MENU
Reward
1 Point = 1 minute of free time
Maximum 60 minutes
Suitable free time activities: indoor games, art, reading, hobbies, etc.

Points awarded:

A = excellent effort   4
B = very good effort   3
C = good effort   2
D = satisfactory effort   1
E = not very good effort   0

The teacher writes in his/her grade, along the same scale, in discussion with the child. Finally, points are allocated in the final column according to the teacher's grading. The points are added up at the end of the week, each point earning 1 min of free time. Free time could include indoor games, free-choice activity or going to help in another class. Most important, the charts or record sheets are signed by the classteacher and headteacher and taken home every week. Parental involvement in such programmes can provide valuable motivation for children and is often underrated when behavioural programmes are suggested for children.

Several features of the behavioural programme which clearly involve the active participation of pupils in assessing their own performance are noteworthy:

1. The system encourages children to develop organisational skills and to think about their progress self-critically.
2. The programme encourages pupils to assess their own efforts, to compare their perceptions with those of the teacher who, in turn, is able to make explicit to children the criteria for success.
3. Children receive more frequent and more immediate feedback about their work than is common.
4. The system encourages children to take on a more responsible role in respect of their work.
5. Work tasks are broken down into small, manageable chunks, as is usually required for behavioural programmes.
6. Over time, children should be able to predict teacher reaction more accurately than hitherto. The whole process should encourage two-way negotiation and understanding between teacher and pupil.

In order to evaluate the system, all the pupils in the class were given a questionnaire to complete, classroom discussions took place, questionnaires were sent to parents and the teacher concerned was interviewed by the psychologist. The following findings emerged:

1. 94 per cent of the pupils said that they enjoyed the system.

2. 56 per cent of the pupils said that they were working harder than before.
3. 44 per cent of pupils said that they agreed with the teacher's grades; the rest felt that her grades were sometimes too low, and just occasionally, some pupils thought that the teacher's grades were too high.
4. All the children enjoyed earning free time and listed their preferred or most rewarding activities as playing, watching TV or video, drawing, chatting, chalking on the board and, interestingly, going to another class and helping younger pupils.
5. There was a limited parental response to the evaluation questionnaire and letter, although those who responded did so favourably, saying that they supported the idea of the reward system.
6. The teacher herself felt that the children were learning to become more self-disciplined and that pupil effort had improved for most children.
7. The grades given by teacher and pupil were becoming closer as time went on, and the teacher felt that the system had encouraged her to think carefully about the criteria for grading, so that such criteria were made explicit to pupils.
8. The teacher felt that the system was viable in the classroom, but it did require careful consideration, planning and organisation.
9. The fact that the report was sent home to parents seemed to be particularly important, adding to the influence of the system.
10. Finally, the teacher regarded the system as worthwhile and wished to continue using it, noting that other teachers in the school had shown an interest in utilising a similar procedure in their classrooms.

Pupil–teacher working parties

The final project to be mentioned in this section relates to the prospect of a school's system change involving staff and pupils working very closely together to identify problem areas and recommend solutions and improvements to the school as a whole. The project began in a secondary school where there was staff concern about the number of pupils in the fifth year not attending school, and a number of pupils in the same year who seemed disenchanted with school.

Following discussions with the headteacher, school staff, the School

Psychological Service and a local Youth, Education and Social Services Joint (YESS) Project, it was suggested that five working groups should be set up, each with the same brief and questions to answer, as follows:

- What is causing the misbehaviour and truancy in year 5?
- What could the school do to put this right?
- Produce up to three recommendations for action within the school.

The five working groups each consisted of a senior member of staff, two other teachers, three pupils and a consultant either from the School Psychological Service or the YESS Project. Each working party was invited to organise itself in what it felt to be the most appropriate way, collect any evidence it felt to be required, in any manner thought relevant, and report back their recommendations to the whole school staff at a specified date. It was also agreed that the pupils would receive a written report of the outcome of the project.

At the time of writing, the project has commenced and it is clear that a significant number of pupils have shown much interest in the idea. A large number of changes have been suggested to the school environment, lesson choices, after-school activities and, most important, a permanent pupil council was set up as a direct result of one of the proposals.

It is the contention of the author that the *process* of teachers talking openly to pupils about problems and possible solutions within the school as a whole – i.e. problems which are shared by school staff and pupils alike – is an important step forward in influencing the ethos of the school. This process could certainly be employed to deal with other problems and issues which arise in school.

Focus on behaviour change

In this section I shall focus on behavioural programmes specifically from the point of view of pupil involvement in assessment and decision-making.

Assessment of the 'problem'

Perhaps the first and most important point worth highlighting is that the assessment of the 'problems' can assume that the problem is located within the child. Clearly, this is a matter of some debate since when some difficulties arise in school, the pupils themselves may not feel that the problem belongs to them, but rather that 'it is the teacher's problem'. There seems a lot to be said for taking an interactional point of view, regarding problems as arising between two or more parties, and taking seriously each person's perspective. The implication from such a perspective is that one cannot complete a proper assessment of a behavioural difficulty simply by observing a child alone, or by listening to one party (e.g. the teacher). Behaviour is complex and has a social meaning and significance; it therefore needs to be assessed as such.

Negotiating change

It follows from the previous point that any recommendations for change need to be negotiated with all concerned. Specifically, if it is felt that a child needs to set about altering his/her behaviour, then clearly the reasons for change need to be agreed by the child, as well as the person aiming to modify the child. While one would always hope that full parental permission has been sought before a teacher embarks on any behavioural change programme, one would similarly argue for the child's agreement to a significant behaviour programme seeking to alter his/her behaviour. Apart from any ethical issues involved, it would seem vital pragmatically to ensure that children are motivated to reach goals which have been agreed.

Recording

The method of recording behaviour should also be negotiated between the pupil and adult seeking to alter the child's behaviour since ultimately very useful records may be kept by the child him/herself. Although very young children may have to rely on adult recording, and indeed this may be needed to monitor pupil records, it seems sensible to aim for circumstances which encourage children to monitor their own performance at a detailed level.

Setting and agreeing upon targets

When setting up behavioural programmes, clear behavioural objectives and targets need to be negotiated and agreed with pupils. It is all very well for adults to decide that child X should aspire to such and such behavioural target, but if a child has a different attitude to such an objective, the programme is unlikely to succeed.

Reinforcement

Many behavioural programmes rely heavily on a structured system of positive rewards or reinforcement and sanctions such that when children achieve certain behavioural targets, they obtain specific rewards. It is all too easy for adults to assume they know best what is likely to be the most effective reinforcement. Any behavioural practitioner should first carry out a 'reward survey' in which pupils are invited to list what they think are the most potent rewards for them.

Contracts

Many behavioural practitioners set out their programmes in the form of a written 'contract', signed by all of those concerned, including the pupil. Such contracts would appear to have much to commend them, not least because they assume a negotiation, in respect of the processes described above, between the adult attempting to modify the child's behaviour and the child him/herself. A formal written contract is a way of encouraging an honestly negotiated programme.

Evaluation

All behavioural programmes should be evaluated after a set period of time to see whether any positive outcomes can be shown. One needs to focus on objective evidence, and indeed there is no doubt that it is necessary to *count* behavioural responses rather than rely on impressions. None the less, impressions are not unimportant. The pupil's view of success or failure, progress or lack of it, should be taken seriously as an important piece of evidence, and thus elicited specifically.

This section has argued for maximising pupil involvement in the design, execution and evaluation of behavioural programmes. The child's view should be actively explored at every stage of the behavioural change process; defining the difficulty, deciding about whether a programme is needed, establishing choice of target behaviours, recording system and appropriate reinforcement, and finally at the point of evaluation.

Some questions for adults seeking to alter pupil behaviour

In this section I intend to raise some questions for assessors, teachers and behavioural practitioners. The following types of questions might well be posed, as a starting-point:

1. How is the child's view to be discovered?
2. What does the child think the assessment is for?
3. What does the child think constitutes appropriate/inappropriate, desirable/undesirable behaviour?
4. How do other adults view the child's role in the assessment process?
5. How is the child to be prepared for the assessment and introduced to the activity?
6. How is any information gained to be fed back to the child?
7. To what degree is the child currently involved in the assessment process?
8. Could the child be more actively involved?
9. Is the child's ability to respond, comprehend, negotiate or express a point of view being underestimated?
10. What would the child like to learn, what behaviour would the child like to change and what would he/she like to come out of the assessment?
11. Questions could also be asked about the child's view of appropriate behavioural targets, recording systems, positive and negative reinforcement (rewards and punishment) and methods of evaluation.
12. What does the child think of the whole idea of the behavioural programme?

Conclusions

I have discussed several projects in this chapter, each being a modest example of what can be done to increase the active involvement of pupils in their assessment and school life. There does appear to be considerable scope for increasing the active involvement of pupils in their schooling, in relation to dealing with disruptive behaviour, evaluating behavioural programmes, pupil recording, involving pupils in decision-making and generally in teaching children how to make decisions.

Whenever behavioural difficulties occur between pupils and teachers, one may expect that at least two points of view, or explanations, will arise. The work of Lawrence, Steed and Young (1984) emphasises the importance of analysing problems in as wide a context as possible, and reminds us that, all too often, adults do not listen sufficiently to what children have to say about disruptive events, triggers to such events and the meaning of such behaviour to them. There would appear to be much merit in a policy which invited pupils to discuss their perception of disruptive behaviour more openly, and to air their point of view.

It is noteworthy that we do not routinely ask pupils for feedback in respect of lessons, materials presented by teachers and styles of presentation, and teachers rarely invite children to provide constructive criticism of lessons and learning tasks. While pupils might need to learn ways of communicating feedback, free from emotional, personal or hurtful comments, it is felt that when behavioural difficulties arise, a relevant step to be taken might include the examination of the pupils' views of their curriculum, timetable and lessons.

Many schools now have pupil councils which encourage children to take part in decision-making in their schools, using a democratic process. Such councils offer pupils the opportunity to learn about decision-making and to take responsibility for their school. There may be merit in having class councils at a primary school level, but certainly in involving pupils when problems arise in the school as a whole.

Pupil profiling (MacNaughton, 1986) aims to encourage pupils to keep track of their own progress, through written records and lists of their own achievements, and to end up with a log of such progress for which they are primarily responsible. Although such projects are still in their early stages, there is evidence that pupils themselves are motivated to keep their own achievement profiles; they seem to be proud of them and the whole process serves to be positively motivating to pupils at school.

For the future, to take on a more active role in their assessment, children will be required to learn about the task of decision-making, and need more direct advice and guidance on study skills, managing their own learning, tracking their own progress and modifying their own behaviour. It would seem important to construe children as 'active learners' who need to know about psychology, learning theory, learning processes, memory and behaviour change, so that at the end of the day pupils can take increasing responsibility for their own conduct and plans.

The 1981 Education Act offers interesting opportunities for including pupils' views about their special needs and can be used as a possible vehicle for increasing pupil participation in the assessment process. However, whatever vehicle one uses, particularly in respect of disruptive behaviour and in the area of maladjustment, pupils' views needs to be taken seriously if any meaningful change is to result.

Acknowledgements

I would like to acknowledge the help and support of the children, teachers, headteachers, education officers and social service staff who collaborated with the projects described in this chapter. The views expressed in this chapter, however, remain my own responsibility and do not necessarily reflect the policy of the LEA in which I am employed.

Parts of the above chapter appeared originally in the following journals:

'DECP Newsletter' 1986 No. 23
'Community Care' 1985 No. 547
'Educational Psychology in Practice 1985' Vol. 2
'Quarterly Journal of the Association for Behavioural Approaches with
    Children' 1987 Vol. 8
and Chapter 10 of *Special Educational Needs and Human Resource Management* edited by T. Bowers 1987 Croom Helm Ltd.

We are grateful for the kind permission of the above-mentioned publishers to reproduce the relevant parts here.

References

THE CHILDREN ACT (1975) (London: HMSO), chapter 72.

DHSS (1981) *Observation and Assessment*. Report of a Working Party (London: HMSO).

DES and DHSS (1983) Joint Circular 1/83 and HC(83)3 (London: DES).

DES (1978) *Special Educational Needs* (The Warnock Report) (London: HMSO).

GERSCH, I.S. (1984) 'Behaviour modification and systems analysis in a secondary school: combining two approaches', *Behavioural Approaches with Children*, 8, 3, 83–91.

GERSCH, I.S. and CUTTING, M.C. (1985) 'The Child's Report', *Educational Psychology in Practice*, 1, 2, 63–9.

LAWRENCE, J., STEED, D. and YOUNG, P. (1984) *Disruptive Children – Disruptive Schools?* (London: Croom Helm).

McNAUGHTON, J. (1986) *Records of Achievement Project* (Pamphlets, Project Bulletin and Personal Recording Tutor's Handbook), Essex County Council Records of Achievement.

Appendix: Child's report. Guidelines for adult helpers

The aim of the Child's Report is to obtain as true a picture of the child's view as possible.

It may be that an adult helper will be required:

(a) to explain the form to the child;
(b) to elaborate specific points of the form;
(c) to answer specific questions;
(d) to help the child complete the form;
(e) to encourage the child to express his/her views freely;
(f) to support the child with the activity.

It would be best if the child completed the form in his/her own handwriting, if possible, but help can be given with spelling (if wanted), although spelling and grammar don't really matter.

It would be important to encourage the child to express his/her views in his/her own language, in the knowledge that there is no *favoured* answer, and that there are no 'right' or 'wrong' answers. We really want his/her views and opinions.

It would also be helpful to encourage the child to complete as much of the form as possible and to stress the importance of the child having a say in his/her educational plans.

It is quite acceptable to explain any 'hard' words or questions which warrant clarification, in terms the child can better understand.

For children who are unable to write, it would be appropriate to let them dictate their views to an adult and write down what they say verbatim.

It may be found appropriate to allow the child to complete the form, with the helper, in a quiet room away from other children, in order to ensure privacy.

Finally, it is worth underlining that the aim of the exercise is to encourage the child's active involvement in the assessment process, and for the child to express his/her own view as clearly as possible. Quite clearly, the helper will need to know the child well, to remain impartial, yet to know when to prompt and encourage without implanting their own ideas.

LONDON BOROUGH OF WALTHAM FOREST
EDUCATION DEPARTMENT
EDUCATION ACT 1981 – SECTION 5 ASSESSMENT
FORM SEN/CE
© Irvine Gersch

CONFIDENTIAL

CHILD'S REPORT

NAME:	
D.O.B.:	AGE:
ADDRESS:	
SCHOOL:	
DATE COMPLETED:	

This is a chance for you to say what *you* feel about your schooling, future plans and skills or topics which you would like to learn as well as any help you think you need.

The aim of this report, which you can complete if you like, is to tell your teachers, parents and other people who are concerned with your education, about *your* views and ideas.

Please fill in as much as you can, leave out any parts you like and remember that there are no right or wrong answers.

A. *SCHOOL BACKGROUND*

1. Which schools have you attended before your present school?

     _____

     _____

     _____

2. In which of these do you think you got on well?

     _____

     _____

3. In which, if any, of your past schools did you have any difficulties?

     _____

     _____

4. If you had any difficulties (in your past schools) what were they?

_____

_____

_____

_____

_____

B. *PRESENT SCHOOL* | Name of School: |

1. How do you think you are getting on in your present school?

_____

_____

2. What do you like doing best at school?
   What subjects do you most enjoy?

_____

_____

3. What do you enjoy least doing at school?
   Are there any subjects or activities you do not like doing?

_____

_____

4. What do you think you are good at doing at school?
   Which subjects?

_____

_____

5. What do you think are the hardest subjects for you at school?

_____

_____

6. Are there any particular teachers with whom you get on very well?
   If so, who?

_____

_____

_____

7. If you had a problem at school, with whom would you usually discuss it?

_____

_____

C. *SPECIAL NEEDS*

1. Do you have any problems at school? If so, what are they?

    _____

    _____

    _____

    _____

2. (a) Do you think you need any special help at school? YES/NO
       What sort of help?

    _____

    _____

    (b) Are you getting this help?   YES/NO

3. Are there any subjects which you find particularly hard to learn?
    If so, which?

    _____

    _____

    _____

    _____

4. (a) How would you describe your behaviour in class?

    _____

    _____

    (b) How would you describe your behaviour in school generally?

    _____

    _____

5. Are there any topics, subjects or skills which you would particularly like to learn at
    school, and which you think would be helpful to you?
    If so, what?

    _____

    _____

    _____

    _____

D. *FRIENDS*

1. (a) Do you have any friends at school?   YES/NO

    (b) Who are your special or best school friends?

    _____

    _____

    _____

2. Do you have friends who attend other schools? If so, what are their names?

    _____

    _____

    _____

3. What do you generally do when you meet your friends out of school?

    _____

    _____

4. What do you generally do when you are with your school friends at lunch times or break times?

    _____

    _____

5. Do you think you have any problems with any of the children at school? If yes, what sort of problems?

    _____

    _____

    _____

    _____

6. (a) Do you wish you had more friends?   YES/NO
    (b) If yes, do you need any help to make friends?   YES/NO

E. *HOBBIES, INTERESTS AND OUT OF SCHOOL ACTIVITIES*

1. Who is in your family?

    _____

    _____

    _____

    _____

    _____

    _____

2. (a) Are there any particular hobbies, special interests or sports which you enjoy.
If so, what are they?

_____

_____

_____

   (b) Can you swim?   YES/NO

3. Are there any hobbies or sports or activities you *would like to do*, which you do not do
at present? If so, which?

_____

_____

_____

4. (a) What do you like doing at home?

_____

_____

_____

   (b) What are you good at doing at home?

_____

_____

_____

5. Is there anything at home which you would like to learn to do, e.g. cooking, repairs,
electrical work, gardening, painting, shopping, etc.

_____

_____

_____

6. (a) Can you travel around the area by bus and train, on your own?
                                      YES/NO
   (b) Have you ever done so?   YES/NO

7. What is the longest journey you have made on your own, or with a friend or friends?

_____

_____

_____

_____

F. *THE FUTURE*

1. What sort of work would you like to do when you leave school?

_____

_____

_____

2. Would you like to know more about any particular sort of job?
   If so, what?

_____

_____

_____

3. Do you know anybody who is doing the sort of work you would like to do?
   Who?

_____

4. Have you discussed your future job with your parents?　　　YES/NO

5. Are there any subjects or topics or skills you would like to learn to help you prepare for when you leave school? If so, which?

_____

_____

_____

_____

G. *ADDITIONAL COMMENTS*

Any other ideas or comments you would like to make to your teachers? Please list anything else you want to add, which has not been covered already.

_____

_____

_____

_____

_____

_____

_____

Thank you for completing this report

SECTION C

Influencing Behaviour Change

Chapter 8

Analysing Classroom Organisation

Colin J. Smith

Introduction

Despite the horror stories which surface now and then, when it comes to classroom management, most teachers get most of it right, most of the time. In general, teachers and pupils enjoy each other's company and share an interest in maintaining a pleasant but purposeful working atmosphere. Therefore anyone who treats classroom management as a topic of academic study has to steer a course between theoretical abstraction and mundane repetition of traditional tips for teachers.

On the one hand, teachers may complain that terminology and concepts drawn from the fields of psychology and sociology elevate discussion to an unnecessarily rarefied level, distanced too far from the every-day life of the classroom. On the other hand, teachers may dismiss conclusions based on research findings as being little more than statements of the obvious, commonsense, 'tricks of the trade', normally acquired through personal experience.

In avoiding these dangers, it is important to remember that teaching, like any profession, involves a combination of 'craft' practice and 'technical' theory. This means using research and observation to identify the skills and techniques used by successful practitioners. Sometimes this will confirm the value of such self-evident virtues as good time-keeping and appropriately prepared materials (Rutter *et al.*, 1979). At other times, appraisal and analysis will question time-honoured assumptions about the nature of teaching.

For example, good discipline is often seen as a matter of making decisions about punishment and dealing with trouble-makers. A different perception emerges from the review of research by Calderhead (1984), which supports the view expressed by Kounin (1970), that 'what distinguished the effective classroom managers was not their ability to cope with classroom disruptions, when they arose, but their ability to prevent disruption occurring in the first place'.

In this context, the crucial decisions are those which relate to the establishment of orderly work procedures. For these to be properly informed decisions, it is important that teachers should be able to analyse the elements which together constitute their system of classroom organisation. This will be particularly useful for experienced teachers charged with the duty of acting as 'mentor' to new entrants to the profession.

Such teachers rarely have the time to examine and articulate their own techniques, which they have internalised through the years. The suggested framework for an analysis of classroom organisation offered here is not intended to be a revelatory insight so much as a reminder of those aspects of lesson planning and management which contribute to a smooth-running partnership in learning, between teacher and pupil. What follows is neither a checklist nor a prescription. It is a framework for analysis drawn from research, observation and years of talking to teachers about their craft and the theory behind it.

Denscombe (1985) categorises strategies developed to maintain classroom control as belonging to three broad types: domination, co-optation and classwork management.

Domination strategies are those used by teachers to impose control. Co-optation strategies attempt to engage the willing participation of pupils. Classwork management strategies seek to structure activities which promote order and discipline. Thus, according to Denscombe, teachers can be seen as gaining and retaining control through a combination of bullying, jollying and busying their charges along the road to learning. Without denying the importance of studying the nature of conflict and confrontation in the classroom, the focus of the present exercise is on the third approach.

Indeed, if one explores the 'goals of misbehaviour' (Dreikurs, Grunwald and Petter, 1971) which motivate misbehaviour in the classroom, problems arise more often from pupils trying to ward off inadequacy or to gain attention than they do from pupils seeking power or revenge. Effective 'classwork management' strategies should therefore reduce the potential for conflict and confrontation and avoid the need to struggle for control. This does not mean keeping children busy for the sake of the thing. It means engaging learners in useful and interesting activities appropriate to their levels of competence and ability. However, the most apparently attractive and well-planned lessons may fail to engross and absorb all pupils in active and productive work.

When this happens, teachers need to look not only at the learning package, but also at its delivery.

What follows is a distillation of research on the 'delivery systems' of classroom organisation. It identifies areas where teachers might reflect on their own experience and suggests further reading for more detailed investigation. It does not offer instant solutions or infallible remedies, but aims to promote more informed decision-making.

Relationships, rules and routines

There is a social climate and atmosphere in every classroom. Sometimes pupils bring in anxieties and antagonisms from home, playground or other lessons, but in the main, it is the teacher whose approach determines the prevailing mood within each lesson. Successful innovations with methods or material may depend critically on the state of the environment or milieu into which they are introduced. Such a milieu will have been established by the building of relationships and the development of rules and routines.

Wragg and Wood (1984) asked pupils to comment on over 30 statements about 'the best teacher in the world'. The five statements with which the pupils agreed most strongly were that this teacher would explain things clearly; call you by your first name; help the slower ones catch up in a nice way; help you learn a lot in every lesson; and be a good listener. These opinions are consistent with those expressed in other studies of pupil appraisal of teachers, reviewed by Wragg and Wood. Though also looking to teachers for care, compassion, security and indeed entertainment, pupils' main expectations are that teachers will instruct them competently and take an interest in them personally.

Good relationships within the classroom are likely therefore to develop from well-managed lessons. Studies of successful teaching, measured by academic attainment and acceptable behaviour, rather than student appreciation, accord well with pupils' opinions. Techniques identified with effective teaching have been summarized in 'four rules' of classroom management: get them in; get them out; get on with it; and get on with them (Laslett and Smith, 1984).

Effective teachers smoothly manage the transitions at the beginning and the end of lessons. They 'get on with it', in the sense that they maintain the momentum of a lesson by ensuring that there is a variety in the selection of content and in the pace of its delivery. They 'get on with them' by making the effort to know and treat each pupil as an individual.

Maintaining a pleasant but purposeful atmosphere conducive to developing good relationships, depends to a great extent on a teacher's ability to prevent the pressure of minor misbehaviours building up into deeper depressions or disturbances. Petty irritations are not allowed to interrupt the flow of lessons. Intervention, when necessary, is direct but undramatic, with attention focused on the task in hand rather than the transgression. Deviance is 'insulated' before it spreads to other pupils, and conflict is defused before it escalates towards a detonation of anger. Laslett and Smith (*ibid.*) describe a variety of ways in which such techniques are deployed and how they become part of a teacher's style. Attitudes and personal qualities, such as warmth, humour, imperturbability and resilience, contribute to an individual's teaching style, but it also derives from the rules and routines embodied in classroom organisation.

Rules indicate the boundaries for behaviour within a classroom, whereas routines regulate the flow of activities. Together they establish expectations for teachers and pupils about what will happen within a lesson. Bennett *et al.* (1984) demonstrate the considerable potential for misinterpretation and limited communication within classrooms. Rules and routines help reduce the potential complexities of learning to a simpler predictability. Pupils, who know how the lesson will flow, can plan their own work and anticipate events, so that the teacher needs to employ less active direction (Egan, 1981).

A predictable pattern to a lesson maintains stability, sets a measured pace and eases transition from one activity to another. One example of this approach to organisation has been described by the acronym SIMPLE (Laslett and Smith, 1984). In this plan, lessons

- Start with seatwork, recapping work previously taught.
- Introduce new work through teacher talk or demonstration.
- Make sure pupils grasp new ideas by question and answer sessions.
- Practice examples by working with the teacher then individually.
- Look back by reviewing new learning and linking it to previous work.
- Enjoy a game, story or some other form of relaxation.

The acronym SIMPLE is an appropriate reminder that routines, or for that matter rules, should not become over-elaborate. Too easily, the latter particularly, can become part of a tedious system of rituals and regimentation (Denscombe, 1985).

Rules should be kept under review, to ensure that they do not become merely oppressive; but provided that they are rational and sensible, they are the most direct way to establish a teacher's expectations. Medland and Vitale (1984) offer detailed advice on identifying and reinforcing 'social behaviours' necessary for specific activities. Though some teachers may find this approach and its language unduly 'technological', its consideration ought to entail some reflection on the conventions which develop even within more flexible approaches. How do pupils know what is expected of them? Would the more explicit statement of rules and routines help avoid confusion about what pupils are expected to do?

Assignments and rewards

Expectations are also conveyed by the type of work which is given to pupils. Organisation which is sufficiently considerate of·differences in ability, aptitude and motivation shows personal concern for the pupil, just as much as offering a friendly smile or a sympathetic ear.

Laslett and Smith (1984) discuss ways in which the teacher can demonstrate considerate organisation in the selection of subject-matter, the presentation of material and the setting of tasks within the pupil's competence. Particularly where failure has been encountered in the past, fresh impetus for learning can be given by introducing new material, new methods or different activities. If material cannot be matched to the pupil's ability in reading and comprehension, then help can be provided with oral summaries, preparatory explanations of key words and essential concepts and by simplifying assignments or substituting alternative activities. Lunzer and Gardner (1984) describe what they term DARTS (directed activities related to texts), which involve pupils in working together on tasks such as labelling segments of text, tabulating information and diagrammatic representation. In these ways, pupils are not only helped to cope with material which is difficult to comprehend in its original form, but they are also offered variety in methods of response.

The marking system is another aspect of considerate organisation. While marking must give realistic feedback on performance, it should also provide encouragement. A dual marking system can help to achieve this objective. It is easier for teachers to find something to praise if separate grades are given for content and presentation or for accuracy and effort. This also gives more opportunity for written comments, which show that industry and endeavour are appreciated even where, as yet, skill and talent are lacking.

Persistent failure leads so easily to attitudes of disaffected defeatism, that marking schemes should aim to maintain interest and enthusiasm for a subject, by being geared to involving rather than excluding pupils from whatever reward system operates in a classroom. Whether reinforcement is through social approval, praise, formal commendation, stars or points, all pupils should feel that they can gain a share of that acknowledgement not for being outstanding, but for consistently doing their best. Too often recognition appears to be reserved for the exclusively bright or the exquisitely neat, leaving most pupils feeling left out. For some tasks, at least, individual targets can be set, which invite pupils to compete to improve on a 'personal best' instead of always trying to beat the rest.

If assignments and rewards are to be successfully matched to different levels of attainment, then this involves some analysis of how teachers can focus on individual needs. Working with groups is the first stage towards a more individualised approach.

Working in groups

The traditional presentation of information and ideas is most readily accomplished through the equally traditional disposition of rows of desks with pupils all facing the teacher. This is also the arrangement most conducive to sustained attention on set tasks (Wheldall and Merrett, 1984). There is, however, a possibility that through ease and familiarity, some teachers remain attached to the whole-class, 'lecturing' style, even when it is not suited to their intentions. Within the context of mixed-ability teaching and an avowed concern for more pupil-centred learning, groupwork is an option which merits detailed consideration.

Even within schools notionally committed to mixed-ability teaching, often what happens in practice, might be described more accurately as 'mid-ability' teaching (Kerry and Sands, 1984). Anxious to retain cohesion, teachers pitch lessons at a level at which most pupils perform adequately, frequently leaving the more able unstretched and the less able untouched by what is going on. Sometimes, though seated in groups, children still were working on undifferentiated tasks. Group-work is not an easy organizational option: it requires – as Kerry and Sands stress – a high level of teaching skill to control, motivate and supervise pupils in this situation.

Assigning separate tasks to different sections within a class is often associated with ability grouping. There is always the danger that this approach will lead to stigmatisation and the lowering of both teacher expectation and pupil aspiration. Much will depend on the nature of the subject being taught, and the aims and purposes of the curriculum in that area, but consideration of the advantages and disadvantages of setting or streaming raises issues of school policy and educational philosophy, beyond the more pragmatic concerns of the present discussion.

There are other reasons why groupwork should be considered as an option for classroom organisation. Whether selected according to intellectual capacity or designed to contain a range of abilities, small groups offer opportunities for increasing pupil visibility, encouraging communication, promoting cooperative learning and arranging competition without undermining individual self-competence (Waterhouse, 1983).

One criticism of the serried ranks of traditional classroom design is that it can lead to a teacher's attention being focused on an 'action zone' around the front and middle of the class (Good and Brophy, 1984). Dividing a class into small groups will present the teacher with not one but a series of 'action zones', where it will be easier to 'see' children as individuals.

Although the bright, the backward and the baleful always make their presence felt, it is all too easy for the more modest pupil to fade into anonymity in a large class. The strengths and weaknesses of such children are more clearly evident when they are seen as part of a group of 6–8 than when they are seen as part of a class of 30 or more. Communication is encouraged not only because it is easier to get a turn at speaking, but also because it is simpler to form a circle, where participants talk directly face to face. Cooperative learning, with pupils working together towards a common goal, enhances understanding and motivation in problem-solving activities.

Competition can be an enjoyable way of enlivening learning essential facts. It can also be a source of embarrassment with heightened revelation of individual ignorance. However, when success for a mixed-ability group depends on overall performance, then the least able pupil is as important as the most able member of the team. Astute tailoring of tasks or questions can further ensure that competition between groups does not result in limelight-hogging on the one hand, or ego-bruising on the other.

Working in groups also helps a teacher spread limited resources. Smaller numbers can tackle projects, in turn, so that teachers do not have to find or make enough books or equipment for the whole class to work on the same topic at the same time.

Classroom design

Egan (1981) suggests that where arrangements permit a number of pupil behaviours to happen at the same time, there is undoubtedly 'a greater potential for meeting a broad variety of learning and behaviour needs'. However, Egan then goes on to warn that care needs to be taken with any system which increases movement around the room since the 'mall' approach to classroom design can often be overstimulating to students.

If teachers do wish to work with smaller groups, then they need to think about which arrangement of classroom furniture, which design or layout, is best suited to their purpose.

Groupwork is often organised with pupils sitting around tables, or with desks placed together to form a similar base. Waterhouse (1983) likens this arrangement to a 'dining-room'. Certainly, it is similar with the teacher and resources at the front of the room acting as a sort of academic serving-hatch. However, while lunchtime should encourage socialisation, the round-the-table seating arrangement while excellent for intended discussion activities, can be a source of non-productive distraction during other sessions.

Inevitably this arrangement means that for a large part of each lesson, many pupils sit with their backs to the teacher. When their attention is required, there is an unavoidably distracting, shifting of chairs and jostling of bodies. Often this is accompanied by a loss of concentration and a break in the momentum of work on the task in hand. Negotiating the way to and from the teacher's desk, whether in search of guidance or supplies, offers an additional source of diversion, when the route is less clearly evident than the straight line of traditional arrangements. Though readily surmountable through the establishment of rules and routines, these difficulties do add a little to the teaching burden.

Some of the problems of the 'dining-room' arrangement can be overcome by what Waterhouse describes as a 'peripheral' system. Here the pupils sit at desks or tables around the edges of the room with the teacher in the centre, together with 'resource islands' containing stores of stationery, writing and drawing equipment, reference books and workcards. This should make traffic management and the focusing of attention easier for the teacher.

Lemlech (1979) has advocated the use of 'learning centres' with resources grouped by theme rather than function. Centres are arrangements of tables, alcoves or desks and bookshelves, where books, paper, writing materials and other equipment are gathered to provide 'an environment arranged to accomplish a particular instructional purpose'. Thus one area of the room might contain everything needed to tackle a project in art, while elsewhere a science experiment was set up. Lemlech is insistent that each centre should have a specific instructional objective, so that children know exactly what they have to do and have all the materials with which to do it.

Centres can also provide practice in particular aspects of work in one area of the curriculum, so that in language development, for example, groups or individuals would work at different times at centres for reading with comprehension, creative writing and listening with understanding.

Providing support

The success of any grouping arrangement depends on establishing a system for getting access to support and guidance when it is needed. It is all too easy for attempts at working with small groups or with individuals to be frustrated by constant 'low-order' requests for help and assistance. Teachers intending to give time to some individual diagnosis and counselling can, for example, find their time consumed and their attention distracted as they are harassed for spellings (Bennett *et al.*, 1984). Responses to this problem involve making decisions about the allocation of tasks and material and also about the deployment of human resources.

Work can be allocated to groups, so that different groups take turns at those tasks, where most teacher attention and direction is engaged, while other groups are provided with activities, which do not require close supervision and guidance. Work can be allocated in several ways (Laslett and Smith, 1984).

A rota system, as its name implies, is rather like a rotation of crops, with groups spending a set period of time at different learning centres or on different activities. A quota system requires each group or individual to complete a set programme of work involving a number of activities according to the teacher's judgement of whether more practice is needed in particular areas. A branching system has the whole class starting together on a common activity, but once this has been completed, groups branch off to different assignments.

Whichever system is selected, material preparation should include the provision of clear topic outlines or study guides, which can be consulted before asking for further explanation from the teacher. Supplementary material is also needed to occupy 'waiting time' when activities have been completed and a group is waiting to move on to another area (Waterhouse, 1983). It is also essential to determine some form of traffic control for when groups circulate, otherwise the 'mall' system can rapidly become a maul or mêlée.

Support from other adults can ease many of the potential problems of working with groups. However, here too careful thought needs to be given to planning exactly how teachers will work together. Ferguson and Adams (1982) point out some of the issues, which arose from their observations of remedial teachers working alongside mainstream colleagues. Ostensibly there to provide specialist help, the remedial experts were perceived by other teachers and their students as 'teacher's aides', 'helpful visitors', 'faithful retainers' and even 'extra pupils'. Similar problems are likely to arise as non-professional help from parents or other volunteers becomes more commonplace. Peer tutoring, where more able pupils help their classmates, is another potential source of assistance, which also requires careful planning and management.

Whoever they are, helpers need to be given precise tasks and clear responsibilities. Whether in charge of an area of the room, running a particular activity, looking after equipment or providing information, it is important that helpers should know exactly what is expected of them. It is equally important that pupils know to whom they should turn for what sort of help, otherwise extra assistance can become an additional confusion. The object of the exercise is to 'buy time' for the teacher to provide more attention to the needs of individual pupils, and that is the criterion against which to judge this or indeed any of the other aspects of classroom organisation which have been discussed.

Defining teaching skills

In examining how they organise their classroom, teachers are applying behavioural analysis to themselves. They are considering antecedents, behaviour and consequences with regard to their own actions. Objective self-evaluation is never easy, but here it can be rewarding in two ways. It may suggest changes to the milieu, method or materials with which teachers work or it may identify elements of successful practice, which can be passed on as a management technique rather than a piece of personal magic. Either way, analysing classroom organisation is an opportunity to look afresh at both craft experience and technical knowledge. It is an opportunity for teachers to define and to hone the skills of their profession.

References

BENNETT, N., DESFORGES, C., COCKBURN, A. and WILKINSON, B. (1984) *The Quality of Pupil Learning Experiences* (London: Erlbaum).

CALDERHEAD, J. (1984) *Teachers' Classroom Decision Making* (Eastbourne: Holt, Rinehart and Winston).

DENSCOMBE, M. (1985) *Classroom Control: A Sociological Perspective* (London: Allen & Unwin).

DREIKURS, R., GRUNWALD, B.B. and PETTER, F.C. (1971) *Maintaining Sanity in the Classroom* (New York: Holt, Rinehart and Winston).

EGAN, M.W. (1981) 'Strategies for behavioural programming', in *What Will We Do in the Morning?* Eds Hardman, M.L. *et al.* (Dubuque, Iowa: W.C. Brown).

FERGUSON, N. and ADAMS, M. (1982) 'Assessing the advantages of team teaching in remedial education', in *New Directions in Remedial Education* Ed Smith, C.J. (Lewes: Falmer Press).

GOOD, T.L. and BROPHY, J. (1984) *Looking in Classrooms* (3rd edn) (New York: Harper and Row).

KERRY, T. and SANDS, M.K. (1984) 'Classroom organization and learning', in Wragg, E.C. (1984) *Classroom Teaching Skills* Ed: Wragg, E.C. (London: Croom Helm).

KOUNIN, J.S. (1970) *Discipline and Group Management in Classrooms* (New York: Holt, Rinehart and Winston).

LASLETT, R.B. and SMITH, C.J. (1984) *Effective Classroom Management: A Teacher's Guide* (London: Croom Helm).

LEMLECH, J.K. (1979) *Classroom Management* (New York: Harper and Row).

LUNZER, E. and GARDNER, K. (1984) *Learning from the Written Word* (Edinburgh: Oliver and Boyd).

MEDLAND, M. and VITALE, M. (1984) *Management of Classrooms* (New York: Holt, Rinehart and Winston).

RUTTER, M., MAUGHAN, B., MORTIMER, E. and OUSTON, J. (1979) *Fifteen Thousand Hours* (London: Open Books).

WATERHOUSE, P. (1983) *Managing the Learning Process* (London: McGraw-Hill).

WHELDALL, K. and MERRETT, F. (1984) *Positive Teaching: The Behavioural Approach* (London: Allen and Unwin).

WRAGG, E.C. and WOOD, E.K. (1984) 'Pupil appraisals of teaching', in *Classroom Teaching Skills* Ed Wragg, E.C. (London: Croom-Helm).

Chapter 9

Assertive Discipline

Lee Canter

Introduction

Lack of discipline in schools is a growing problem across Western society and may have first emerged to worrying proportions in the USA. Some British politicians seem to feel that the UK may look to the USA for ideas and solutions. If this is possible, the only reason may be that teachers in the USA have faced problems longer and have therefore been obliged to find workable solutions. Assertion training is a major field in the USA, one that is growing in all English-speaking countries. Assertive Discipline, developed in the USA during the mid-1970s, is now growing in Australia and interest is developing in the UK.

This chapter briefly describes the Assertive Discipline programme; a competency-based approach to discipline in the USA has been field-tested by over 600,000 teachers and principals nationwide. These educators report that the programme has reduced behaviour problems by 80 per cent in their classrooms or schools (Webb, 1983).

Assertive Discipline is designed to give an educator the skills and confidence necessary to 'take charge' in the classroom. It advocates a systematic approach to discipline that enables teachers to set firm, consistent limits for pupils – at the same time, keeping in mind each pupil's need for warmth and positive support. Consistent limit-setting requires the teachers to establish specific classroom rules. The pupils are taught the rules, the consequences they will choose to receive if the rules are not followed and the rewards they can expect for complying with the rules.

Why is this kind of competency-based training necessary? To be frank, educators simply were not trained to deal with the behaviour problems today's pupils present. As a result, teachers devote more time and attention to discipline and managing behaviour than appears to be the case in other countries of the world (Bloom, 1978).

Assertive Discipline is the result of seven years of research and evaluation into effective classroom discipline skills. The basic question in our research was, how can teachers encourage pupils to behave appropriately in the classroom? To find the answer, we studied effective teachers who given all the problems faced by today's teachers, successfully maintain appropriate behaviour. We found these effective teachers responded to their pupils in an assertive manner, by which we mean that they clearly and firmly express their expectations and needs and are prepared to back up their words with appropriate actions. In other words, they say what they mean and mean what they say.

Assertive, non-assertive and hostile teachers

Assertive teachers take the following stand in their classrooms: 'I will tolerate no pupil stopping me from teaching. I will tolerate no pupil preventing another pupil from learning. I will tolerate no pupil engaging in any behaviour that is not in his/her own best interest and in the best interest of others. And most important, whenever a pupil chooses to behave appropriately, I will immediately recognise and reinforce that behaviour.' Finally, assertive teachers effectively manage pupils in their classrooms. They have the skills and confidence necessary to take charge.

In our research we also focused on what types of teachers do not respond effectively to pupil behaviour. We labelled such teachers either 'non-assertive' or 'hostile'. Non-assertive teachers do not clearly or firmly communicate their wishes and needs to the pupils, or if they do, they are not prepared to back up their words with actions. They are passive or imprecise in directions they give to their pupils and lack the skills and confidence necessary to deal effectively with disruptive behaviour. Hostile teachers, on the other hand, get the pupils to do what they want, but in so doing they violate the best interests of the pupils. These teachers often verbally or physically abuse their pupils.

The following example shows how each of these three types of teacher would typically deal with a pupil's disruptive behaviour. Suppose the teacher wants the pupils to do their work without talking or disrupting one another. During the work period one pupil puts his work aside and begins to talk loudly to the pupils around him.

In such a situation, the non-assertive teacher would characteristically walk up to the pupil and ask him to get to work. When he doesn't, the teacher shrugs and says, 'I just don't know what to do with you'. The hostile teacher would storm up to the pupil and yell; 'You have the biggest mouth I have ever seen. Shut it or you'll be sorry!' But the assertive teacher would walk up to the boy, look him in the eye, and tell him firmly, 'Stop talking and get to work now. If you don't, you will have to finish your work during free time.'

Now here is an example to illustrate how the three types of teacher respond when a pupil behaves appropriately. Suppose one pupil in the class tends to become disruptive during the transition periods between activities. She gets very excited, fails to follow directions and often runs around the room yelling. Finally, the teacher sets firm limits by telling the pupil that that type of behaviour is inappropriate and will not be tolerated. Then one afternoon the pupil cleans up her activity appropriately and comes directly to the reading corner when she is asked to.

In a situation like this, the non-assertive teacher characteristically would not recognise or support the pupil's appropriate behaviour, either verbally or non-verbally. The hostile teacher would say to the pupil, 'It's about time I didn't have to chase you around the room to get you to clean up and sit down.' But the assertive teacher would typically say to the pupil, 'I like the nice job you did cleaning up and following directions. You did so well that you can pick a story for me to read to the class.'

Encouraging teachers to be more assertive

In order for teachers to become more assertive and thus more effective in dealing with behaviour problems, they need both confidence and skills. Many teachers do not expect to have or may not possess the assurance necessary to establish rules in their classrooms because they have little confidence in their ability to deal with problem pupils. Teachers, and many members of the public, may believe that certain types of pupils 'cannot' behave appropriately at school. Among the most common misconceptions are these: if the pupil has emotional problems, the teacher says, 'He is just too disturbed for me to handle in my class'. If the pupil has neglectful parents, the teacher says, 'Coming from those parents, how can you expect her to behave normally?' If the pupil is from a low socioeconomic background, it is: 'What can you expect from that kind of neighbourhood?' If the child is educationally handicapped, it is: 'She's eh – you can't expect her to behave.'

These are misconceptions. All pupils can behave appropriately at school (Chapter 16). It does not matter whether children are neglected, neurotic or deprived; they still can behave – they simply do not want to behave. When problem pupils are with teachers who expect them to behave and who assertively communicate their expectations to the pupils through both words and actions, the pupils will choose to behave appropriately. The first step in dealing with pupils assertively, then, is for teachers to develop higher expectations of their own ability to deal with all pupils. When expectations are raised, confidence levels will be raised as well (Canter and Canter, 1976).

Along with increasing their confidence, teachers need to increase their skills in dealing with pupils who have behaviour problems. The following are the competency skills guidelines teachers may follow in order to deal assertively with pupil behaviour.

The process of limit-setting

The key to the effectiveness of the Assertive Discipline programme is a process of limit-setting which encourages pupils to *choose* to act responsibly. Limits consist of classroom rules by which the teacher communicates to pupils what is expected of them and why. Research supports the idea that the effective teacher is one who establishes reasonable, definable and clearly understood rules (Hair, 1980). Research has also shown that effective teachers clearly state expectations on the first day of school and explicitly teach their rules to pupils early in the school year (Emmer and Everton, 1980).

In addition to knowing the rules, Assertive Discipline requires that pupils know precisely what will happen, should they choose to behave or misbehave. Limit-setting consequences need to be known by the pupils, so that they can make the choice as to whether or not the consequences will occur (Canter and Canter, 1976). It is through choice that we teach pupils about responsibility (Dreikurs, 1957).

Assertive Discipline and its limit-setting system of rules and consequences has been proven to reduce classroom disruptions and through the process help pupils (Ersavas, 1980) learn to act responsibly (Ward, 1983).

*The teacher must know at all times what he/she wants the pupils
to do*

Typical behaviours teachers want from pupils include: following directions; staying in their seats; raising their hands when they want to speak; getting to class on time; keeping hands, feet and objects to themselves; and bringing pencils, books and paper to class. The teacher must communicate these wants to pupils both verbally and visually.

*The teachers must know how to set limits systematically when the
pupils do not behave properly*

Consistency is the key to limit-setting. A teacher must provide a negative consequence every time a pupil choses to behave inappropriately. The consequence must be included in a systematic plan.

The teacher must know how to set up an effective Discipline Plan

To establish an Assertive Discipline Plan, the teacher must do the following.

1. Set down some basic general rules of behaviour, such as: follow directions the first time given; raise hand to be called upon before speaking; stay in seat; keep hands, feet and objects to yourself; no swearing or teasing. (Chapter 5)
2. Allow a maximum of five negative consequences for disruptive behaviour. The consequences must increase in severity and must be cumulative; for instance, the first time a pupil breaks a rule, he/she is given a warning. The teacher then records the pupil's name in a record book. The second time the pupil breaks a rule, a check mark is put next to the name and the pupil must stay after school for 15 minutes. The third time, a second check is made, which means 30 minutes after school. The fourth time, a third check is made, the pupil stays 30 minutes after school and the parents are called. The fifth time the pupil is sent to the senior teacher, the parents are called and the pupil stays 30 minutes after school (see Chapter 8).
3. Provide for the consistent use of praise, recognition and other reinforcers for appropriate behaviour.
    The teacher must know how to reinforce systematically the appropriate behaviour of pupils. Effective positive reinforcement of appropriate behaviour is the key to dealing assertively with discipline problems. For verbal reinforcement, teachers first give

directions to pupils, then immediately praise one or more pupils who comply with them. It is important to praise every pupil at least once per day. The most effective way of backing up verbal reinforcement is with action such as sending positive notes home. Sending two notes home per day per class is recommended.

In addition to individual praise, classwide reinforcement enables all pupils to earn a positive consequence for appropriate behaviour (Canter and Canter, 1976). One form of classwide reinforcement – the 'marbles-in-a-jar' incentive system – can be used even with difficult classes. Whenever one or more pupils behave appropriately, they earn a marble for the entire class. Each marble equals one point. When the class has earned a predetermined number of points, the pupils get a reward such as extra free time. The younger the pupils, the more frequent the rewards must be. The same goes for problem pupils, who should have a chance to earn three to five marbles a day, as compared with one a day for regular pupils. At the end of each day or period, the teacher counts up the marbles earned and keeps a running total. When the class has earned one reward, set a new goal. (Remember that the reward must be something the pupils really want.)

4. At the end of the day, all the names and check marks should be erased. Never erase a name or check mark as a reward for good behaviour, however.

5. In the case of severe disruption, the pupil may be sent immediately to the senior teacher responsible for discipline.

6. Sending a pupil to the senior teacher responsible for discipline is always the last consequence in the plan. The senior teacher must approve the plan before it is put into operation and must be notified if any changes are made. In addition, the senior teacher and the class teacher should decide in advance what will be done with pupils who are sent to the senior teacher's office.

7. The plan applies to all pupils in the classroom. If after three days or so the plan does not appear to be working with one or more pupils, it must be made more strict for those pupils. For instance, if a certain pupil continually disrupts, the teacher might say to that pupil: 'I will not tolerate your continued misbehaviour. Until your behaviour improves, the first time you misbehave you will not be warned. You will immediately receive two checks and spend 30 minutes after school.'

8. For pupils who present more severe behaviour problems, the

teacher should consider other consequences such as one of the following.

Send the pupils to an in-school time-out room (see later). The pupil is suspended from class and sent to a time-out room where he/she does academic work in silence, monitored by another teacher or an administrator. Disruptive behaviour in the suspension room earns the pupil extra hours of isolation.

The teacher must know how to elicit the cooperation of the headteacher and the parents in discipline efforts with problem pupils. A teacher's discipline plan, to be effective, must be shared with the headteacher and the parents, and it must systematically spell out when and how they may cooperate with the teacher in implementing the plan.

What Assertive Discipline can do for your school

The following research is offered to illustrate the positive effects Assertive Discipline can have, both on pupils and teachers.

In 1983, Linda Mandlebaum and colleagues at Bowling Green University examined the results of implementing the Assertive Discipline approach. They found a classwide reduction of two problematic pupil behaviours: out-of-seat and inappropriate talking. The research was conducted in a third-grade classroom in a metropolitan school district. The classroom teacher, with 20 years' experience, evidenced poor influence over pupil behaviour prior to the institution of Assertive Discipline and, as a result, was in jeopardy of losing her position. The researchers found that the teacher was able to reduce inappropriate behaviour as a direct result of using the Assertive Discipline programme. Mandlebaum concluded that the Assertive Discipline programme, is an effective and practical behaviour management strategy' (Mandlebaum, 1983).

Mandlebaum's conclusions are supported by teachers and administrators who attended Assertive Discipline training workshops across the USA and report significant reductions of discipline problems and improvements in pupil behaviour after the Assertive Discipline programme was implemented (Becker, 1980; Moffett, 1982; Ward, 1983; Webb, 1983). Follow-up surveys indicate that observable pupil behaviour continued to improve after two to five years (Crawley, 1982, and Bauer, 1982).

Other research projects based on surveys of pupils and teachers show a positive relationship between Assertive Discipline and (a) reduction of time devoted to discipline referrals, and (b) improvement of classroom discipline and improvement in pupil behaviour. These findings are supported by observation reports of school district teachers and administrators. School authorities in California, Arizona and Minnesota reported that administrative time devoted to discipline referrals dropped significantly after implementing the Assertive Discipline programme (Loss, 1981, and Ludlow, 1979).

Assertive Discipline has also been shown to increase the amount of time pupils spend on academic work (being 'on-task'). Sammie McCormack conducted a study in 1985 in 36 Oregon third-grade classrooms. The intention of the study was to analyse data about pupils' off-task behaviour. The 36 classrooms were divided into equal groups, half using Assertive Discipline and half not using the programme. McCormack found that pupils' on-task behaviour was repeatedly higher in classrooms using Assertive Discipline. She further concluded that,

> Assertive Discipline works to reduce off-task behaviour of pupils of varying reading levels, socioeconomic status, ethnicity, sex, parental influence, and parents present at home. Further, Assertive Discipline works for teachers who have varying qualifications, experience, and knowledge of the subject (McCormack, 1985).

Another area of research is concerning the effect Assertive Discipline has on the improvement of teachers' and pupils' self-concepts. This was studied by Ersavas, the first researcher to use pre-test and post-test surveys in the study of Assertive Discipline. She began by surveying four elementary schools where Assertive Discipline was not used. She then introduced the programme to the staff of those schools, and teachers implemented it. Not only did she find improved self-concept of teachers and pupils at each of the four schools, but also validated Assertive Discipline's effectiveness in improving classroom behaviour (Ersavas, 1980). A similar improvement in teacher and pupils' self-concept was also reported in two other studies (Henderson, 1982). Other positive self-concept findings were reported in 1984, when the Compton Unified School District in California (approx. 1,340 teachers) examined the results of implementing the Assertive Discipline programmes in an entire district (Swanson, 1984).

While research studies validating the effectiveness are important, as important is the testing Assertive Discipline undergoes in tens of thousands of classrooms every day in the USA. As enlightening as the research reports are the comments from teachers and administrators currently using the programme. Kenneth Moffett, superintendent in a school district in a low socioeconomic community with street gangs and drug problems, credited Assertive Discipline with 'virtually eliminating classroom disruptions' (Moffett, 1982). Phyllis Schuman, a junior high school teacher in the same district with 30 years' experience, summarised the feelings of teachers and administrators about the Assertive Discipline approach:

> I have seen dozens of approaches to discipline come and go. This system has done more to provide good discipline to our school than anything I have seen. We have more time to do what we are supposed to do, so – teach (Moffett, 1982).

Whether Assertive Discipline will enjoy the same success in the UK as in the USA only time, experience and research will tell. I suspect, however, that the majority of teachers in both the UK and USA share the same commendable goal: to spend less time on discipline and more time teaching.

References

BAUER, R. (1982) 'A quasi-experimental study of the effects of assertive discipline', *Dissertation Abstracts International*, 43. 25A (University Microfilms No. 82-14316).

BECKER, R. (ed.) (1980) *The Troy Reporter* (Troy, Ohio: Troy Schools, March).

BLOOM, B. (1978) 'New views of the learner: implications for instruction and curriculum', *Educational Leadership*, April, 563–76.

CANTER, L., and CANTER, M. (1976) *Assertive Discipline – Take Charge Approach for Today's Educator* (Santa Monica, Calif.: Canter).

CRAWLEY, K. (1982) 'Teacher and student perceptions with regard to classroom conditions, procedures and student behaviour in classes of teachers trained in assertive discipline methods', in *Dissertations Abstracts International*, 43. 2840A (University Microfilms No. 82-01140).

DREIKURS, R. (1957) *Psychology in the Classroom* (Evanston, Ill.: Harper and Row).

EMMER, E., and EVERTON, C.(1980) 'Effective management: at the beginning of the school year in junior high classes', Research and

Development Center for Teacher Education, University of Texas, Report No. 6107.

ERSAVAS, C.M. (1980) 'A study of the effect of Assertive Discipline at four elementary schools', unpublished doctoral dissertation, United State International University.

HAIR, H., *et al.* (1980) 'Development of internal structure in elementary students: a system of classroom management and class control', ERIC Document Reproduction Service No. ED 1829 067.

HENDERSON, C. (1982) 'An analysis of assertive discipline training and implementation on inservice elementary teachers' self-concept, locus of control, pupil control ideology and assertive personality characteristics', *Dissertation Abstracts International*, 42. 4797A (University Microfilms No. 82-09893).

LOSS, J. (1981) 'Assertive Discipline: a new tool but not a plug in module', *Minnesota Elementary School Principal*, Fall, 17.

LUDLOW, A. (1979) 'How to get tough', *Newsweek*, 10 July, p. 69.

McCORMACK, S. (1985) 'Students' off-task behavior and assertive discipline', unpublished doctoral dissertation, University of Oregon, p. 79.

MANDLEBAUM, L.H., *et al.* (1983) 'Assertive discipline: an effective behavior management program', *Behavioural Disorders Journal*, 8, 4, 258-64.

MOFFETT, K., *et al.* (1982) 'Assertive discipline', *California School Board*, June-August, 24-7.

SWANSON, M. (1984) *Assessment of the Assertive Discipline Program* (Compton, Calif.: Compton Unified School District).

WARD, L. (1983) 'The effectiveness of assertive discipline as a means to reduce classroom disruptions', in *Dissertation Abstracts*, 44,2140-2141A (Doctoral dissertation, Texas Technical University).

WEBB, M. (1983) 'An evaluation of assertive discipline and its degree of ef-fectiveness as perceived by the professional staff in selected school corporations', in *Dissertation Abstracts*, 43,25A (Doctoral dissertation, Indiana University).

Chapter 10

Using Consequences in Class

Martin Scherer

Introduction

A probationary teacher was experiencing difficulties with a particularly disruptive third-stream maths class. He raised the problem with his head of department. She responded that perhaps after the first year, or rather after the first term of the second year, these pupils may accept his presence and settle down. At first, the comment was reassuring, it suggested that his own teaching wasn't the problem. He was experiencing the normal 'testing out' period of the new teacher in a difficult school. Later he was dismayed, alone he would have to suffer the disruptive behaviour and its associated stress for a further 12 months. The pupils would gain an inferior education and suffer the stress.

In this chapter we look at an alternative approach, illustrate its use in classrooms, evaluated by action research. It may suggest some surprisingly simple and effective methods of changing disruptive behaviour. Before using consequences to change behaviour, it is necessary to describe that behaviour in precise terms, and the behaviours required of the pupil.

Traditionally, we view people as responding to events in their social environment. An alternative view is that people behave to produce or avoid certain consequences in their social environment. Having done so, those consequences have the effect of maintaining the behaviour:

$$\text{Behaviour} \rightleftharpoons \text{Consequences}$$

This may seem like common sense, but it is a relatively recent view of human behaviour. It may not always seem so obvious. Becker (1971) reported a study in which a teacher had asked for help with a number of pupils who were repeatedly getting out of their seats. He noted that the teacher firmly told them to sit down. The teacher felt this was a successful strategy, so Becker asked her to increase the number of times she told them to sit down. Instead of decreasing their behaviour, this procedure increased the number of times they got out of their seats. Becker then suggested trying the opposite, not telling them to sit down, the result of which was that fewer got out of their seats, on fewer occasions.

Is this surprising? These pupils wanted the teacher's attention, even if it came in the form of a rebuke. They found they could always get attention by getting out of their seats.

What we can learn from Becker's study is that:

1. People behave to produce or avoid consequences, and those consequences act to maintain or suppress their behaviour.
2. We can only discover what is the effect of a consequence by its effect on behaviour. While a rebuke may seem something to be avoided, some pupils will work hard to get it. A teacher's attention is often a very powerful consequence, and we should not underestimate it.

Using consequences: immediate delivery

The probationary teacher, above, used consequences. The traditional consequences available in class are verbal rebuke, lines, detentions, letters home, sending to the deputy or head of department. The latter have consequences for the teacher and may suggest incompetence, something the teacher would wish to avoid. All the other consequences came some hours after the pupil's misbehaviour. They seemed to have little effect, if they were complied with at all. The teacher's first step was to hold detentions immediately after the lesson, in breaktime – again, to little effect. The detention at the end of the lesson came anything up to an hour after the misbehaviour; further, although the teacher did not 'intend' it, the detention was not only a consequence of misbehaviour, but also followed appropriate behaviour.

The teacher's next step was to make a more tenuous link between behaviour and consequence. The first time a pupil misbehaved the teacher wrote his name on the blackboard. Subsequent actions of misbehaviour resulted in a 'I' alongside the name. The teacher concluded the lesson a few minutes ahead of the bell; he allowed the best behaved pupils to leave first. By the time the bell went the misbehaving pupils were still seated. The teacher sat down and commenced marking. At the end of each minute he wiped one 'I' off each pupil's name on the blackboard. When all the 'I's had been removed, he allowed that pupil to leave.

That strategy was gradually effective. As the teacher had collected the number of disruptive incidents both before and during the procedure, he was able to make an objective comparison (Scherer, Shirodkar and Hughes, 1984). What are the findings that we can learn from this study?

1. There must be a clear and tangible link between the behaviour and its consequence if the association between the two is to be learnt.
2. Consequences must be immediate to be effective – this fact cannot be stressed too much. Failing to appreciate this principle may be the reason for the many failures in the use of this approach. We can devise procedures to make consequences immediate, as in the above example.
3. Consequences need to be learnt. They gradually affect the future probability of behaviour. Each pupil is different in the amount of time he/she takes to learn the consequence. The behaviour may re-occur from time to time. In the above study the teacher gained the confidence to continue from the daily recording which showed a gradual decrease in inappropriate behaviour.

These findings apply to all consequences. Later we will look at different types of consequences.

Other interesting findings emerged from this study:

1. The amount of detention was directly related to the number of disruptive incidents. For pupils, this seemed far more just, it was preferred to the procedure to being verbally rebuked.
2. The approach enabled an individual assessment and provision for each child. This is a requirement of the 1981 Education Act.
3. As pupils could clearly see the consequence of their peers' misbehaviour, they learned from it (cf. 'learning by observation', Whaley and Malott, 1971).
4. As the overall rate of disruptive behaviour in the class decreased it gave the teacher time to attend to appropriate behaviour. Some pupils, who were not disruptive, asked for their names to be put on the board; one deliberately misbehaved to get that attention.

Punishment: decreasing and suppressing behaviour

Basically the teacher was using a 'punishment' procedure – not as a form of retribution, but, as in behavioural terms, as a means of reducing the future probability of a behaviour (see e.g. Fox, 1982). Many of the effects of punishment are not so obvious. We may summarise the findings here as follows:

1. Punishment decreases or suppresses the future probability of behaviour. People who are suppressed may become depressed.
2. The behaviour recovers when punishment stops. Not only will it recover to its previous level, but for a while the behaviour may occur at a higher level than before. Punishment does not eradicate behaviour; it may also fail to suppress the total rate of misbehaviour. This can be seen across classrooms, where the same pupils may behave appropriately in one class but atrociously in the next. This may be a reason why teachers who do not use punishment object to its apparently effective use by other teachers: suppress the behaviour in one context or at one time and it will emerge at another.
3. Punishment does not teach the pupil how to behave appropriately, it merely suppresses behaviour.
4. The intensity of punishment needs to be increased to maintain its effect over time – people adapt.
5. Physically and psychologically painful events may elicit aggression, which may take many forms. When the pupil is verbally rebuked in the classroom, he/she may verbally retaliate.
6. Punishment may affect appropriate behaviour. Children fearful of misbehaving may also become fearful of making mistakes in their work and not make the effort. Punishment may create anxiety; children lose the will to explore and learn, both by success and error.
7. Punishment maintains negative statements such as 'I don't like this subject . . . this teacher . . . this school'.

We can, then, define a punishment only by its effect. We must measure that effect to be sure.

Guidelines on the use of punishment

The history of civilisation is, in part, one of finding less punitive ways of controlling behaviour. Corporal punishment is now banned in schools.

The problem is that the reformers offer few alternative methods; and it may be the responsibility of teachers to provide pupils with 'normal' life experience. In the somewhat more protective environment of schools there may be the case for exposing pupils to punishment as preparation for later life; thus we should:

1. positively encourage the pupil to make an apology, give a full account of the incident and assure people that the incident will probably not be repeated;
2. clearly link the misbehaviour to the punishment;
3. tell the pupil the exact duration and form of the punishment;
4. ensure the minimum and effective use of punishment, by rigorously evaluating the effect;
5. counsel pupils as to how they should have behaved, so that in future they may learn how to avoid the punishment;
6. not pursue the incident, once the punishment has been served.

Social behaviour is very complex. Punishment is never the only consequence of behaviour. Used in conjunction with other procedures, punishment may be more effective and contribute less side-effects than punishment alone.

Reinforcement: increasing and maintaining behaviour

A reward is a pleasant event given for appropriate behaviour. It may (but not necessarily) be intended to increase the probability that the person will behave in a similar way again. A reward may be delivered hours or days after the appropriate behaviour. In increasing and maintaining a behaviour, we may say we are strengthening or reinforcing it; a reinforcer is defined by its effect of increasing and maintaining the probability that the behaviour will occur again. To be most effective, a reinforcer must be delivered immediately. Reinforcers may be positive or negative; rewards are usually positive. We shall look at both types.

A teacher in a special school for delinquent and disruptive pupils was expected to operate a points system. The pupils earned points for good behaviour. The behaviours were clearly defined and advertised. A set number of points was allocated for each behaviour. The pupils exchanged their points for a variety of tangible rewards at certain times in the day. These rewards, often called back-ups, included sweets, soft drinks, access to TV games, late nights and trips off the centre.

At the end of each lesson the teacher decided how many points the pupil earned for each target behaviour, the points earned being recorded on the pupil's personal card that he carried at all times. This is a fairly typical points system. We may ask if it was a positive or negative system? Was it a reinforcement system? (Scherer and Brown, 1984).

There are three ways of answering the first question: by the adult's subjective view, the pupil's subjective view and the objective view, one gained by action research. According to the adults who operated the system, it was one where the pupils started each session with no points, and earned points up to a stated maximum for each clearly defined appropriate behaviour. This seemed positive, fair and just; a questionnaire of pupils showed they agreed that it was fair and just, but disagreed that it was positive. The pupils described the system as one in which a number of points were promised but then some or all points were taken away for misbehaviour. This seemed negative or punative. Who was correct?

We have noted that punishment tends to elicit aggressive behaviour. During several lessons the pupils' behaviour was observed. The results showed that during the points delivery at the end of the lesson aggressive behaviour occurred in the form of destroying the card, marching out of the lesson, kicking over chairs, threatening and actually hitting the teacher. The pupils also seemed to want to avoid the teacher's award of points by refusing to accept back the card, destroying the card or failing to hand it in and forging the teacher's points and signature.

The system was then changed. Teachers were told that they could give as many points as they felt pupils deserved. Instead of a maximum from which the pupils lost points, they now earned points as decided on by the teacher. The rate of aggressive and avoidance behaviour dropped dramatically. The original system was therefore a negative, punitive one.

Reinforcers must be given immediately. In this example the points were given at the end of the lesson, up to an hour later. The system may be more correctly described as one of bribery and unfulfilled promises. Despite its failings and the side-effects, the pupils reported still that they felt the system was 'just'.

Maintaining escape and avoidance: negative reinforcement

A boy is punished for cigarette smoking in the playground. For a while his smoking stops in school. However, his deprivation of nicotine and/

or peer group acceptance increases. Soon he discovers that he can avoid the punishment by smoking behind the toilets. The behaviour has not changed, only its place; the form of punishment has not changed, but its function has.

Negative reinforcement maintains escape and avoidance behaviour; it is an efficient and pervasive form of social control. If you successfully avoid the punishment, you can never be sure the punishment is no longer there. So the successful punisher who teaches avoidance only infrequently has to punish; the person who is avoiding the punishment has to test the situation by misbehaving. Change the circumstances a little and the testing starts. This is what pupils do to every new teacher, whether probationer or head of department.

Negative reinforcement has three advantages over punishment. First, it does not suppress behaviour; it thereby may not cause depression. Second, it may not elicit aggressive behaviour. Third, it is effective in bringing order out of chaos. Order brings with it predictability, stability and security, it avoids the stress of chaos for both teacher and pupils. It has social credibility and respectability, while negative reinforcement only teaches compliance; in the order it creates, it allows the possibility that positive teaching can occur. The main disadvantage of negative reinforcement is that it maintains avoidance behaviour. Unless we teach the appropriate way to avoid, then we should not be surprised by the way pupils may haphazardly learn. Examples of avoidance behaviour in school are many: lying, to prevent being associated with a misbehaviour; blaming one's actions on another; truancy, from registration because you don't have full school uniform, from particular lessons because you are frightened of getting a low mark in a test, because the teacher always nags, from school because it is unpleasant or boring, or from a conflict because it avoids the consequence; disruptive behaviour, which prevents the teacher setting work or tests, or marking and showing up your poor result in front of the whole class, telling parents or gaining detentions for not learning; not making an effort in class, saying 'I can't do it', for then you don't get marked wrong: cheating, copying others' work, and so avoiding a poor mark; and stealing, to gain a desired event without denial or personal cost.

Negative reinforcement drives behaviour 'underground' to occur behind our backs. The disadvantage of negative reinforcement is that the pupil may not only learn to avoid the inappropriate behaviour, but also to avoid the person who delivers the punishment and the other behaviours required by the punisher.

Maintaining approach and achievement behaviour

To gain a positive reinforcer, the person must first approach or be in the presence of the person who delivers the reinforcer. Rewards may act as positive reinforcers, in that they maintain approach and achievement behaviour. While rewards are generally pleasant events, reinforcers are not necessarily so. In the study by Becker (1971) the pupils gained the attention of the teacher by getting out of their seats, even though the resulting attention was in the form of a rebuke. Positive reinforcers may also maintain inappropriate behaviour, as in the above case where the teacher's attention inadvertently maintained the pupils' behaviour in leaving their seats. Positive reinforcers are not necessarily bribes. A bribe is given to encourage dishonest behaviour, or behaviour that is against the receiver's own interests. A teacher would not act to reinforce dishonest behaviour.

A reinforcer is defined only by its effects, that of increasing and maintaining behaviour, not by the feelings induced in people. Reinforcers may lose their effect. Just as people adapt to punishment, they can become satiated. Events may be reinforcers in one circumstance, but not in others. Teachers' attention may increase appropriate behaviour when delivered privately, but have the opposite effect when delivered in the presence of peers.

Points systems

The points system outlined above was adapted for use with positive reinforcement (Scherer, Shirodkar and Hughes, 1984). Ten classroom rules were defined and advertised. Rules alone have little effect unless they are backed up by consequences. This is illustrated every day on the motorway where speed limits and hazard warning are ignored unless there is a police car about. When the pupils entered the classroom, their names were put on the blackboard. Points were put on the blackboard for arriving on time, quietly getting work out and waiting for the teacher to commence. As the lesson progressed the teacher awarded points for attending to the presentation and the set work, putting their hand up to ask questions and waiting for the teacher to be free to assist. As he went around the class, the teacher marked the work and awarded points for the quality of work and effort shown by the pupil. At all times, the teacher clearly stated, for the whole class to hear, what behaviour the pupil had shown that achieved the points, which were recorded on the blackboard. The advantages of this system may be enumerated, as follows:

1. The teacher was attending to appropriate behaviour that achieved points. This is encompassed in the saying 'Catch 'em being good'.
2. Pupils could not emit both appropriate and inappropriate behaviour at the same time. Increasing appropriate behaviour has the simultaneous effect of decreasing the opportunity to engage in inappropriate behaviour.
3. Positive reinforcement maintains approach and achievement. The pupils had to come to the lesson, fulfil the rules and complete the work to gain the points.
4. Positive reinforcement has a generalised effect, other behaviours may also increase, such as a willingness to learn by trial and error, to say when the work was difficult.
5. Positive reinforcement tends to maintain positive statements such as 'I like this subject . . . teacher . . . lesson . . . school'.
6. The pupils wanted to be involved in the system, recording points earned on the blackboard themselves and honestly stating when they had not earned points. They did not need to cheat, there were plenty of opportunities to earn points and honest behaviour was also reinforced. Participating in the management of the system that controls one's own behaviour may be the first step towards self-control.

Points systems are increasingly adopted as procedures for meeting disruptive behaviour. They make a suitable start, but points systems often degenerate into ineffective negative systems. They do so because it is easy for the teacher to forget to give the points, and simply 'dish them all out' at the end of the lesson without at least describing the behaviour that achieved the points. Where the teacher keeps the record, delivery of points often comes during the coffee break just before records are returned to the headteacher. The pupil will then be oblivious to why or what he has earned. Negative points systems often become an unpleasant experience for pupil and teacher alike.

Token economies

The difference between a points system and a token system is that in the latter tangible tokens are delivered. Points systems are often adopted because they appear to have less problems than token systems. What are these problems?

During the lesson a tangible token is given to a child whenever desirable behaviour is observed; these take many forms from stars to paper coins, coloured disks or actual coins, and they have long existed in education, including stars and that lead on to gold stars and classwork marks that lead to a class position. They may later achieve approval from teachers and parents. Token systems have long existed too in special caring contexts, special schools, children's homes, subnormal and psychiatric hospitals, etc.

The social learning opportunities of tokens include the following:

1. *Tokens can be lost.* So can money, it pays to look after your possessions.
2. *Tokens can be found.* In life we encourage people to hand found items to the authorities. The finder may get a reward, or may be able legitimately to receive the item if it is unclaimed. Taking the same approach to tokens may teach honesty. Some things may be 'found' under dubious circumstances, leaving people wondering if they were stolen. This may be very difficult to prove in absence of proof. The 'finder' can be encouraged to hand it in and gain adult and peer approval for so doing. An intractable problem may be resolved in a positive manner. The 'finder' has not directly gained, but has been given an avenue to correct his behaviour without losing face among peers.
3. *Tokens can be forged or damaged.* Money is made deliberately difficult to forge. Badly written cheques or dubious banknotes are not accepted. Damaged currency is returned with an explanation to the authorities. The same applies to tokens.
4. *Tokens can be stolen.* Tokens have the advantage over money that they can be individually marked for individual children; however, this may deny a valuable learning opportunity. What happens in life? A person accused of having stolen goods is judged by 12 good peers. A superb opportunity to learn about our legal system under the guidance of caring adults. If a pupil steals, it tells us that he lacks the skills to gain the object by legitimate means. The act of theft will prompt us to teach him those skills. In life we are taught not to keep our valuables under the mattress. Open a token bank. Allow pupils to save for major items. Give an interest rate. Teach pupils about banking systems and the value of savings. In life, apart from very low and very high income earners, nearly all adults spend 80–90% of their income per annum. If pupils are not spending at the same ratio, they are being denied spending opportunities. Establish a tax system for 'community' purchases.
5. *Tokens can be gained by extortion.* So can money. Extortion happens all

too often in our schools and involves dinner tickets, books, pens, caps and ties. Extortion is an example of cheating the system. Cheating is a behaviour maintained by a negative or punitive consequences. The pupil finds the effort of earning the tokens too great or beyond his means. We can teach more appropriate means. Extortion is a form of bullying. We could bring the bullies to task and punish their behaviour. This will merely ensure that the bullying occurs behind our backs. We can, however, teach the victims how to respond to bullying.

6. *People with tokens can be fined for misbehaviour.* If we really want to, but then that's life!

It is managerially more convenient to avoid the problems of token economies by using points systems or old-fashioned punishment systems. In so doing, we deny ourselves the opportunity to teach children a number of necessary social skills. A major problem for schools is the shortage of finances for running token systems.

Delivering consequences

Immediate delivery

A major ineffectiveness of rewards and punishments is that they are received too long after the behaviour that initiates them. Life is littered with events that 'bridge' the time gap. Smiles, nods of congratulation and verbal approval are all events that occur both immediately after achievement and when the delayed rewards are received. Frowns, rebukes and shaking head similarly occur both immediately after misbehaviour and when punishment is delivered. These events – smiles, verbal approval, frowns and rebukes – gain the same properties as the reinforcement and punishment that they signal are to follow. With such conditioned consequences, the association between signal and consequence must be learnt.

Teaching the value of tokens and points

At the sweet shop the child asks for sweets. Mother gives the child some coins. These pieces of metal are strange and meaningless to the child. She lifts the child up, the child tells the shopkeeper what sweets she/he wants and then exchanges the coins for them. The coins acquire meaning, they can be exchanged for a desired event. Soon the child learns another fact, that the amount of the desired event that can be had is limited by the number or value of the coins. In the early stages of a child's experience with tokens the teacher may give the token and immediately allow an exchange. Gradually the time between receipt of the token and exchange can be extended. Often, even with older pupils, it is worth teaching about the system by freely giving the pupil an initial balance of tokens and encouraging exchange. If the exchange was good, the pupil will want to earn more.

The meaning or value of a token lies in exchange. Tokens are exchanged for 'backups', and will be valueless unless the backups are desired. All too often, adults see backups only as sweets. Ask children what they want to buy. To delinquent adolescents we sold conkers on string at five tokens each. The conkers littered the staff car-park, it was three weeks before these young men found they could collect the conkers for themselves. They flooded the 'market' with conkers and killed the fad. Often what is desired is what is in short supply and currently fashionable.

If you are going to run a token shop, stock it with a wide variety of things. Do not let adults throw away items. Put them on the shelf, at a price – it is amazing what young minds will be fascinated by. Occasionally run a sale or auction to dispose of items. Often you will find the item will gain a greater price in auction. School token shops can be run on a shoe-string.

The more frequent the opportunity to exchange, the quicker the learning of the value of tokens. Token shops need to be open before and after school and at every break. Classroom token cupboards should be open at the end of each lesson. (Including some commercial items on the shelves may encourage pupils to come to school rather than delay in the local sweet shop or wander along dangerous roads at lunchtime.) Token shops can be profitable. The pupil shop assistants may be paid or encouraged to donate the profits to a school fund.

Even without a school system, teachers may run their own system in class with a variety of backups. One teacher faced considerable problems with four pupils. In exchange for appropriate behaviour he arranged for three to go to the adjacent college with vouchers for their midday meal where they could play pool. The fourth arranged to spend her lunchtimes helping the domestic science teacher to clear up and prepare. Very soon the pupils' attention to work increased to 90 per cent. He then persuaded the pupils to record their own progress, occasionally making his own checks. Their attention remained at 80 per cent (Scherer, Shirodkar and Hughes, 1984).

With a little imagination and effort, a school token or points system can become a valuable self-managing, self-funding resource for teaching the financial system of life, social skills and providing teachers with a positive method of maintaining appropriate behaviour in class. The problem for many emotionally and behaviourally disturbed pupils is that they have learnt the wrong signals from adults. Inconsistent adults may smile or laugh when criticising or punishing, or look stern when congratulating. Token systems can be a successful method of teaching the normal relationship between smiles, frowns and their consequences. Smiles and verbal approval are given in conjunction with the token. After a while, the token is gradually phased out.

Extinguishing behaviour

The only way to get rid of a behaviour is to extinguish it – i.e. stopping the reinforcer from occurring. Extinction is a frustrating, aversive experience. We are denied what we are used to gaining. We experience extinction when we are ignored, and observe it when a child has a temper tantrum. The positive advice is to try harder, or a different approach. Without such positive advice, extinction may have many of the undesirable side-effects of punishment, including aggression. The adult who keeps turning a car engine until the battery is dead, or presses the light switch several times before checking the bulb are demonstrating extinction. Try again, a little harder each time. Mutter, curse or kick the coffee machine, or take it out on someone adjacent!

Intermittent delivery involves a period of extinction. Failing to gain the reinforcement, the pupil tries harder. When the reinforcement occurs, the pupil has learnt to work harder or longer for each reinforcer. Inadvertent, intermittent reinforcement can be seen in temper tantrums. The child kicks up a fuss which is punishing for Mum. Eventually she avoids the punishment by giving in. On the next occasion she may be more resilient. The child tries harder. Mum gives in and an even greater temper tantrum is learnt. The same can be seen in class where a child puts up his hand to answer a question, shouting 'Sir, sir!' At first the teacher ignores this disruptive behaviour, but eventually for peace and quiet takes the pupil's answer.

The skill of ignoring

In the Becker (1971) study, above, the teacher ignored the pupils leaving their seats. This extinguished the behaviour. Ignoring is very difficult, in practice; it requires considerable perseverance. Ignoring only works when a pupil gains your attention by the misbehaviour.

The first problem is that we are taught to attend to and correct pupils' behaviour. Parents and teachers are expected to demonstrate competence in their management of children's behaviour. They may be more likely to attend in the presence of a colleague, senior teacher or inspector. However, the child or pupil then learns that by kicking up a fuss when another adult is around, they may be more likely to gain what they want. The problem is then aggravated. Attending to behaviour is not necessarily demonstrating competence. The parent or teacher needs to feel confident that those around understand that ignoring the behaviour does not mean that the adult is uncaring or irresponsible. The skilful teacher will ignore the child, but keep a distant eye on the child nevertheless. Others around become aware that the teacher is aware.

The second problem is that some behaviour, especially that which has been intermittently reinforced, is highly resistant to extinction. In one study a child repeated the behaviour over 1,000 times before he stopped (Lovass, 1972). This is clearly unacceptable and something else must be tried. A third problem is that there are some behaviours that we cannot ignore, as when a child is endangering himself or others.

Time out

First, let us state one or two things that 'time out' is *not*. Time out is not new. It is as old as the first parent who said 'bed!' to the misbehaving child, or the teacher who said 'stand outside'. Second, time out is not solitary confinement. Unfortunately, people using solitary confinement looked for a 'scientific validity' for their actions. The danger of using a bedroom or classroom for time out is that it associates the room with an unpleasant experience. Children will want to avoid the room in future when it is time for lessons or bed. Finally, time out is not necessarily an aversive procedure.

Time out is a period of time when the child is denied access to the reinforcer maintaining his behaviour. It is particularly useful when the reinforcer is the attention of peers – or we simply do not know what is. The principle may be used in many ways, sending a child to stand outside, sit in a different part of the room away from others or simply ask-. ing the child to stand up, arms folded. It is more difficult to misbehave with adjacent peers when you are standing up. Time out can be a positive experience. Give the child a job that can only be done on his/her own. Send the child on an errand. TIPS (Dawson, 1988) suggests a form of errand they call 'bouncing'. The teacher gives the child a message that is nonsense. The adult receiving the message recognises the nonsense, asks him to wait a moment, then gives a nonsense reply and sends him back. Skilful teachers often use a similar procedure by asking a talkative pupil to come to the front and bring his work. When he does the teacher keeps the child waiting for a moment, comments on the work done and then sends the pupil back.

How do we explain time out?

Time out is extinction, but instead of removing the reinforcer, we remove the pupil. On return, we can expect the behaviour to recover as the reinforcer, perhaps peer attention, is still there. If the behaviour does not recover, then there are two possible explanations. First, the reinforcer has disappeared in the meantime. Second, the experience of time out was aversive. To avoid further experience of time out, the child behaves appropriately. Time out may then be both extinction and the punishing effects of extinction. If this is so, the same guidelines that applied to punishment, above, should apply to the formal use of time out:

1. Tell the child why he is on time out.
2. Tell the child the duration of time out.
3. Keep it to a minimum.
4. Tell the child he can then return if he has stopped misbehaving.
5. Congratulate the child for completing the time out appropriately.
6. Tell him what he should now do to avoid further time out, and how you will help him.

If you are going to use time out, it may be advantageous to practice the skill beforehand. Without waiting for a misbehaviour, ask the child to undertake the exercise, congratulating him/her for so doing. It is then less likely to be perceived as punishment, and you will be more confident about its use with a given child.

There is one major advantage of time out, it gives a cooling off period for pupil and teacher, avoiding confrontation. There is a pitfall, children may misbehave to be placed on time out and thereby escape from the situation they are in, be it the work or the teasing of peers. There is no harm in allowing people to escape, as long as we understand that is what is happening and we can attend to the problem later.

Using more than one consequence at a time

Life is rarely so simple that there is only one consequence of a behaviour at one time. When a pupil is punished, two consequences occur: first, the reinforcing consequence that is maintaining the behaviour; and second, the punishing consequence. When both are in operation, they are competing against each other for control over the behaviour. Seen this way, it is not surprising that once the punishment stops, the behaviour spontaneously recovers. It is also not surprising that punishment is less effective than other procedures. The teacher who keeps a distant eye on a child being ignored is both extinguishing (no attention) and punishing the behaviour (disapproving eye). A variation of using more than one consequence at a time is attending to more than one behaviour at a time. The bouncing procedure not only uses time out, but positive reinforcement for compliance with teachers' requests. The teacher who asks a talkative pupil to come to the front and then positively attend to the work he has completed is using time out and positive reinforcement for work.

Punishment is usually far more effective if the inappropriate behaviour is punished and at the reinforcer the pupil is seeking is given for an appropriate behaviour. For instance, the child calling out can be told, 'Behave that way and I will ignore you. Put your hand up and I will attend to you'. Make sure you do attend sooner than later or the pupil's appropriate behaviour will extinguish and revert to calling out.

Conclusions

The basic principles are relatively few and simple. The number of events that may reinforce or punish behaviour and their relationship to behaviour are infinitely complex. In this chapter we have only just begun to touch on their complexity. Using consequences is the longest established method of changing behaviour. The use is far older than the study of consequences itself.

How you use consequences depends on what you want. If you want a quiet and orderly classroom, use punishment and negative reinforcement. Choose your battleground early, one that you can win and is relatively unimportant. Then go in hard but teach the pupils how they can quickly escape and in future avoid. Occasionally read the riot act. You will gain quiet, docile and obedient pupils. You run the risk of an occasional aggressive outburst. Don't think the astute observer, especially inspectors, will be fooled. They will be aware of the outcome of your strategy; pupils who learn slowly, will not experiment, are anxious about failure, may avoid your class, do not learn self-control and may be very disruptive in the classrooms of colleagues. However, you will be respected by colleagues who respect order, and voices will rarely be raised against you in public. Your pupils may respect you and be polite in passing you in the corridor.

If you want a lively, demanding class where pupils achieve, then use positive reinforcement. Seek out and praise appropriate behaviour and ignore inappropriate behaviour. Colleagues may doubt your control at times, but they will admire the output, effort and achievement of your pupils. Your pupils will often seek you out, stay late at school and make efforts in class and with homework.

These are both ideal types and rarely exist in reality. Sometimes the die is cast for you, especially in the early days of your career or in a new school. Then you quickly need to establish order from chaos and survive the testing-out period. Establish the boundaries of acceptable behaviour by punishment and then gradually move to more positive methods. Even in the private world of the classroom, it is difficult to sail against the wind. If you use positive methods in a predominantly punitive school, your pupils will run riot as the traditional controls relax. If you use negative methods in a predominantly positive school, the pupils will skilfully and subtly run rings around you. Perhaps it is best to assess the needs and the best consequence or combination of consequences for each pupil, be prepared to experiment, and regularly review your approach with each pupil.

Whatever you do, if you want a consequence to have effect, deliver it immediately and clearly. State exactly what the behaviour was that earned it. Use a combination of consequences. Be consistent over time, so that pupils can learn the inevitability of that consequence for that behaviour. Apply the principles creatively. Punishers decrease and suppress behaviour and have a number of undesirable side-effects. Reinforcers increase and maintain behaviour. Negative reinforcers maintain escape and avoidance. Positive reinforcers maintain approach and achievement.

Finally, consider the opportunities of an inexpensive, powerful and positive method of maintaining behaviour that simultaneously teaches a number of social skills and facts about life: the token economy.

References

BECKER, W.C. (1971) *Parents are Teachers* (Champaign, Ill.: Research Press).

DAWSON, P.L. (1988) *Teacher Information Packs (TIPS)* (London: Macmillan Education).

FOX, R.M. (1982) *Increasing Behaviours, Decreasing Behaviours* (Champaign, Ill.: Research Press).

LOVASS, I.O. (1972) *Behaviour Modification: Teaching Language to Psychotic Children* (New York: Appleton-Century-Crofts).

MASTERSON, J. (1988) 'Interview with B.F. Skinner', *Psychologist*, 1, 140-1.

SCHERER, M. and BROWN, B. (1984) 'Time out an alternative to rooms', *Behav. Anal. with Children*, 8, 127-33.

SCHERER, M., SHIRODKAR, H. and HUGHES, R. (1984) 'Reducing disruptive behaviours: a brief report of three successful procedures', *Behav. Anal. with Children*, 8, 52-7.

WHALEY, D.L. and MALOTT, R.W. (1971) *Elementary Principles of Behaviour* (New York: Crofts).

Chapter 11

Using Behavioural Contracts in the Classroom

Peter Gurney

Introduction

Thus far in this book we have discussed behavioural principles and procedures which may be used in the classroom to develop and maintain appropriate behaviour. Many of these procedures have sought actively to encourage pupils to take greater responsibility for their own behaviour, and this is particularly true for behavioural contracts. In this chapter we examine the practical issues and elements involved in the contracting process, together with some theoretical points and guidance on how to make a start. Throughout the chapter the procedures will be exemplified by the case of John. (He is a real pupil but his name has been changed to preserve anonymity.)

John was fourteen years old and attended a city comprehensive school where he received remedial help in the basic subjects. He had been the source of some concern within the school for several months in terms of his disruptive behaviours, which while not violently aggressive, had undermined teachers' discipline and contributed to a deterioration in the concentration and work of a number of his peers. Miss Weeks, the remedial support teacher, tried a simple reward programme but because of inconsistencies between staff it was found ineffective. Miss Weeks was a competent teacher and the curriculum was a reasonable one for those pupils who had special educational needs. John's behaviour was likely to continue since it was supported by the rewards he gained from the teacher's negative reactions and from his peers in terms of their amusement and his increased status.

Another positive reinforcement programme, even a well-designed one, might well have failed again. The teacher had tried everything, as had the head of year and the deputy head in charge of pastoral care. What could be done? Behavioural contracting was one possible solution, and in the end John and Miss Weeks and some subject teachers wrote the following contract which they all signed:

Abbey Comprehensive

A personal contract between a senior pupil and a teacher

1. *Class Behaviour*

   I .. *John Smith* .... undertake to sit quietly and properly in my place, talking only with permission and avoiding being rude or silly. I will try to be patient, especially if being told off, and not allow myself to be provoked.

2. *Work*

   I will make every effort with the work given me during the lesson and will do homework set to the best of my ability.

3. *Appearance*

   I will make every effort to steadily improve my general appearance, dress, grooming, etc. I will have pen, pencil, ruler and any other equipment needed with me.

   I understand that I can earn up to 5 points for each of the sections above, giving a possible total for each lesson of 15 points.

   If I gain over . . .*75%* . . of all possible points my rewards will be .. *a Thursday morning visit with Miss Weeks to the town centre to visit places of interest* ....

   ....

....
Pupil's Signature   Date

....
Teacher i/c Signature   Date

Teacher Contract

   I undertake to award points to the above for each lesson based on behaviour, work, appearance. I also undertake to give encouragement and to help .*John*. succeed in his programme.

   Duration. This contract will run for one week from .. *Monday, 12th January* .. and will be reviewed on .. *Friday, 16th January.*

   Disputes. Any problems arising in the course of the contract should be referred to the Year Tutor who will arrange for a meeting on the same day.

....

....
Subject Teachers' Signatures   Date

The contract ran for 7 weeks with three versions, the two later ones nominating an 80 and 85 per cent level respectively. John earned his reward each week at a level exceeding the nominated percentage level and participated in the half-day visit. The reward was one chosen by John and agreed by his teachers but had previously been his right as part of the timetable. The privilege had been withdrawn the previous term because of his very disruptive behaviour. John now had to earn this privilege.

As a consultant, I would have wanted more precision in the target behaviours. The behaviours nominated here were agreed between John and his teachers, however, and they were confident that it was fair and workable. It was important to carry out an additional check on the behaviour change using a different measure, in this case observing the percentage of on-task behaviour by using the student as an in-dependent observer. Since on-task behaviour had been observed during baseline prior to the contract consultation it was simply a matter of random sampling the several lessons, in this case on different days over five different occasions. The results were as follows:

Percentage of John's on-task behaviour:

pre-contract baseline	contract period
41%	82%

Clearly, the contract had helped John to change his behaviour sub-stantially, showing the same order of dramatic shift as shown by the teachers' points system. This was an example of a pupil–staff contract, run with consultancy help. It shows that contracts can operate consistently in a comprehensive school where a number of different subject teachers are involved. The independent observation gives con-fidence that the contract was successful.

John's contract contains a number of features which will be dis-cussed later in some detail. These include voluntary agreement by both teacher and pupil to change their own behaviour, the adoption of a consequence, or reinforcer, suggested by the pupil, careful negotiation and re-negotiation during the contract period, monitoring and evaluation throughout, together with planning for maintenance and generalisation.

The discussion which follows is divided into the following sections:

- What is a behavioural contract?
- Stages involved in the behavioural contracting process.
- Further example of a behavioural contract.

- Essential features of the behavioural contract.
- Conclusions.

What is a behavioural contract?

What is contracting? Homme *et al.* (1970) define it as an agreement under which the teacher promises rewards in return for the desired learning behaviour by the child. Axelrod (1977), in similar fashion, states that:

> A . . . contract is an agreement between a teacher and a student stating that upon the student's reaching a certain goal, the teacher will reward the student with an event, activity or object that he likes. (p. 60)

Both definitions are inadequate, however, and do no more than define a behaviour modification programme which can simply be imposed by the teacher. No mention is made of reciprocal change in the behaviour of parents and teachers.

A full contract involves a partnership between teacher and child (perhaps others) in which both agree to change their behaviour in exchange for agreed consequences by the other. (For example, Mrs Jones, the class teacher, will avoid making sarcastic comments on Terry's behaviour if he pays more attention in class; Terry will earn short periods of free time by producing neater written work in English.)

We can then regard behavioural contracting in education as both a process and a product. The process involves a negotiation between 'equals' in an attempt to change the environment and behaviour of *both* the teacher and the pupil on a reciprocal basis. The product is a written agreement which all parties sign and which gives details of desired behaviour change, rewards, penalties and duration, with clear procedures for data collection, disputes and re-negotiations. This we may call a 'reciprocal behaviour change contract'. It is this aspect of reciprocity which appears most fundamental to me and is the vital characteristic of behavioural contracting in its most powerful form.

Behavioural contracts are guided by the principles outlined in this book and many of the procedures described form components of contracting. Behavioural contracting could therefore be described as a higher-level strategy. By placing a greater onus on children in the decision-making process, greater responsibility and self-regulating behaviour can be encouraged. Reciprocal agreement by *both* teacher and pupil to change their behaviour is an essential ingredient and negotiation should take place on an 'equal partnership' basis, or at least aim to approach that ideal.

In every case, we need to obtain the willing cooperation of the pupil and also involve the parents whenever possible. At the very least, the parents should be brought in to give their consent and to be better informed. Ideally, they should be actively involved in the programme in some form, perhaps by giving rewards at home for successful performance in a school contract. Reciprocal behaviour contracting is a particularly useful procedure with children of secondary school age because it puts the pupil on a greater partnership footing with the teacher. Behavioural contracts can be used alongside other procedures such as those suggested by Scherer in his chapter.

Stages involved in the behavioural contracting process

This section will examine the practical steps involved in carrying out reciprocal behaviour contracting in an ordinary school setting, namely alerting, identifying the problem consultation, negotiation, implementation, evaluation, maintenance and generalisation.

Alerting

A wide variety of problem behaviours in school can be helped by behaviour contracting. They might range from truancy to being disruptive in class. Several factors are of importance in determining what comes to the attention of staff in the form of a problem. First, the status and personality of the teacher who is referring the problem is a factor. Some teachers have a lower frustration threshold than others. Cheeky behaviour, or taking advantage, might be dealt with easily by one teacher but regarded as a more serious problem by another.

Second, altered expectations or increased awareness by staff is important. The behaviour of a pupil who is always in trouble 'conditions' the staff to expect him to be difficult and, as a discipline control device, they will keep a closer eye on him, noting in consequence a higher frequency of misdemeanours than in other equally disruptive children. They may come to perceive all disruptive behaviour as a deliberate challenge to authority, whether this is the pupil's intention or not. Increased awareness, monitoring and altered expectation not only provide an unbalanced picture of pupil's problem behaviour, but also makes it very difficult for him to change. Not only will he lose the rewards associated with such behaviour, but he would find his teachers' negative attitudes towards him very resistant to change. As with John, putting pupils 'on report' changes teachers' attitudes towards them.

Sometimes the most dramatic or outrageous behaviour of the pupil will be noted and discussed with change in mind. Other behaviours which are more serious problems both for him and for the school may be ignored. In John's case, the wearing of outdoor clothing in the classroom became an important issue yet, in itself, this is relatively trivial. In selecting a problem behaviour for contracting, the teacher needs to list all the problems in order of seriousness from the school's point of view. The most viable one on which to work may not be at the top of the list. This list will form part of the agenda for discussion with the pupil in the negotiation stage.

Identifying the problem

Teachers need to check their own views of the pupil's problem behaviours, or those of other members of staff, before discussion with the pupil. This ideally takes two forms: (a) general observation of one or more behaviours by bringing in an independent observer or maintaining a general frequency log of incidents, together with brief descriptions which can be completed by the class, or subject teacher; (b) collecting data more systematically on one or more specific behaviours which have proved to be a problem from the general observations (either in frequency or degree).

In this case, the behaviour will need to be operationalised and a viable observation system selected. There will be a need, during the observation process, to examine *the behaviour of all the teachers involved*. If the pupil's problem affects only one member of staff, then there is a need to invite one of their colleagues to come into the lesson as an independent observer. If a group of teachers is involved, use may be made of the head of year, deputy head or a visiting student as the observer. We have stressed earlier that the network of relationships linked to the pupil with problem behaviour is crucial. Particular lessons, or particular teachers, may appear to be crucially associated with higher frequencies of the difficult behaviour. These key teachers will need to be drawn into the contracting process as well as the pupil whose behaviour is a problem!

The next step of informal discussion with the pupil should be undertaken by the pupil's key teacher who has already established some kind of relationship. If this is not the case, a third party or 'mediator' (as De Risi and Butz, 1975, term it) may be needed to undertake the task on the teacher's behalf. It could be the head of year or head of pastoral care if either is sufficiently experienced in contracting, a counsellor, or an educational psychologist. In the end, it is the classroom teacher who needs the skills, so using a skilled third person should be regarded as an opportunity for school-based, in-service training (INSET) for staff, as well as a behaviour change programme for the pupil. Minimum requirements will be a person who is prepared to try to like the pupil; is committed to help by the contracting approach; is, or will come to be, liked by the pupil; and one who will be persistent and consistent. The informal discussion has several purposes. First, it aims to probe the pupil's perception of his behaviour. The function of the questioning is to discover in what areas the pupil considers he has problems, how serious he considers them to be and what may be his priority rank order, in terms of changing them. Second, it seeks to create an atmosphere of trust and develop a relationship. Many children with problem behaviours are highly suspicious of teachers and their motives, so it is important to be open and truthful. When combined with a willingness to help the pupil in what he may also regard as a crucial and difficult area, being honest will help the teacher on the way to some sort of relationship, however tenuous. In the case of John, his relationship with Miss Weeks had deteriorated in the current school year because of his disruptive behaviour. It was clear that the preliminary discussions, assisted by the consultant, initiated a gradual improvement.

It is important for the teacher not to enter into discussion with any preconceived ideas or assumptions about the pupil's behaviour, the reasons for it and, particularly, the pupil's intentions. The aim is to become 'aware of the pupils' viewpoints concerning their own behaviour and what they consider to be the explanations. In addition, the teacher should begin to encourage the pupil to be aware of the views of teachers and school of his/her problem and its severity.

Remember that the teacher will be presenting an opportunity for the child to modify his own behaviour and that of others who work with him. It is important to maximise this learning by drawing attention to these features: 'Not only will this contract help you to change your behaviour, Jean, but it will give you ideas on how you can negotiate a contract with others, perhaps with your parents.' Unless these important 'higher-order principles' are actively taught and actively practised in relevant situations, they will probably not be learned and certainly not used. John was encouraged to examine the possibility of a behavioural contract with his parents over home chores and late nights.

Consultation

This is a vital stage in the preparation of a contract. The teacher's knowledge of the network of persons (teachers, parents, professionals), together with the child's opinions, will suggest who should be consulted and which of these persons will directly participate. It is important to know whether they are willing to modify their own behaviour in some respects, in response to change on the pupil's part. Which of them will volunteer to act as observers, to collect data and maintain records? In some cases, the peers of the pupil may usefully be involved. Where the school staff is not familiar with this approach, the consultation will be carried out by the person mainly responsible for preparing the contract, an experienced professional such as a counsellor, or an educational psychologist. Ideally – certainly in the longer term – it will be the classroom teacher or form tutor who is in full-time contact with, or mainly responsible for, the child who should take the initiative for the contract.

It is important that the teacher's requests for information elicit a positive response from his/her colleagues. The inquiry should first ask for strengths and good points of behaviour before asking about inappropriate behaviour. A response should also be sought on what degree of like/dislike exists in the informants towards the pupil in question, what they are prepared to do and what constructive suggestions can be made for the contract, particularly in relation to a list of potential rewards. The data from observations will also form a part of the information needed for the consultation.

Negotiation

Once the consultation stage has been completed satisfactorily, an interview should be arranged with the child by the teacher or the mediator with the purpose of negotiating at least the broad features of the contract. If an outside mediator is involved he/she may consider it easier to see the child separately from the staff to discuss which teacher behaviours should be increased and decreased by the contract. The desired increase of a teacher behaviour may be the main reward for the pupil but a list of other reinforcers needs to be drawn up, discussed and narrowed down. John sought a more positive approach on the part of his teachers, manifested in greater help and encouragement.

Implementation and monitoring of procedures

Close monitoring is required in the first stage of the contract which should be on a daily basis. It is vital to check that all data collection is going ahead as planned, that the giving of rewards is consistent and automatic as scheduled in the contract and not being withheld at the whim of a member of staff or because of forgetfulness. The responsible teacher or the mediator should also make sure that the general terms of the contract are being observed – e.g. that the disputes procedure is being followed quickly and correctly. Periodic reliability checks should be made on the observational data, where possible, and to make sure that staff and pupil continue to agree about definitions of the target behaviour. If a team of staff is involved, as in a comprehensive school, then the coordinator of the contract work will undertake the close daily monitoring, namely the form tutor, head of year, head of house, deputy head (pastoral care) or a counsellor.

Evaluation of the behavioural contract effectiveness

The drawing up of each contract stage will be a time for evaluation, both to assess effectiveness of the previous stage and to influence the conditions in the new contract. Clearly, some experience and skill is required to carry this out. If the teacher is the main 'contractor' or 'coordinator', and without experience, then continuing advice should be sought at these crucial stages from inside the school or, if necessary, by eliciting help from an interested educational psychologist or other professional who is experienced in implementing contracts. The contract demands must be a challenge, yet not so difficult that failure becomes probable.

At the conclusion of the whole contract it may well be that a final or 'terminal' reward is given; this should be appropriate both in nature and magnitude. In John's case, the weekend trip might well be considered of too great a consequence but it worked well for him.

Maintenance and generalisation

In the post-contract stage, some pupils will want to begin a new contract aimed at other behaviours, while others will want to work on a self-contract. It is important that there is not a sudden break with the structure of the previous days governed by the contract. What we want to avoid is: (a) pupil behaviour reverting to pre-contract levels; and (b) staff falling back into their old ways of interacting with the pupil.

With a sudden disappearance of the contract rewards, the pupil's behaviour may deteriorate. One possible procedure to avoid the consequence is to invite the pupil to join a new curriculum or community project within the school for which he/she is given a particular responsibility. Another is that some informal monitoring could be occasionally arranged to check that staff positivity is continuing at post-contract level. Third, a deliberate post-contract programme could be set up in which the pupil will receive random and occasional specific rewards for maintaining the higher frequency of appropriate behaviour. This will gradually fade out the contract. The expectation is that the behaviour will now be maintained by natural consequences in the environment: we need to check that this is happening in practice! Fourth, the pupil could be asked to assist another pupil with a contract and become a part of the helping team.

This situation will bring continuing pressure to maintain his behaviour as an example, but at the same time, he will be gaining extra attention as a responsible school member. In addition, he will be practising the higher-order skills employed in the contracting process, making it more likely that they will be retained and generalised. John was given a 'post-contract' no longer involving points but yielding privileges as a consequence. In addition, he was given responsibility by making him a member of his School Council and he also acted as a peer-manager for another pupil's contract.

Further example of a behavioural contract

This section provides an additional example of a behavioural contract. Michael was fourteen years old and attended a comprehensive school in the south-west of England. Michael's school records had for some months shown his work to be unsatisfactory in terms of a low output and an erratic standard. His form tutor felt that he lacked confidence in his own academic ability and was therefore underachieving. His subject tutors found him likeable but defensive, and also felt him to be wasting his abilities by being too easily distracted.

Michael's year tutor, having had some experience of behavioural methods, discussed the possibility of a contract with him. Michael welcomed the help and clearly wanted to change his behaviour. It was finally agreed between Michael, the year tutor and the relevant subject teachers that he would contract to improve his performance and attitude in Science, French and Design Technology (assessed by points awarded on a merit card) and to increase his attention behaviour to 80 per cent (assessed by the year tutor as an independent observer in a random selection of lessons). Michael's baseline percentage of attention behaviour had been 55 per cent. Specified behaviours were operationalised, as far as possible; Michael's parents were informed and the following contract drawn up after consultation:

Learning Contract No. 1

This is an agreement between Michael Jones and Mr Brown. The contract begins on Friday, 5 February, ending on Tuesday, 23 February. It will be reviewed on Friday, 12 February. The terms of the agreement are:

Michael agrees:
  (a) to increase his attention behaviour to 80%
  (b) to work without being distracted
  (c) to improve his general attitude to work
  (d) to increase his overall performance in French, Science and Design Technology.

Mr Brown agrees that:
If Michael earns 65 or more points (out of a possible of 80) in a week, Mr Brown will award him a Certificate of Merit.

If Michael achieves an average of 80% or over on attention behaviour in a week, Mr Brown will provide him with an extra period of Art activity.

signed ....
(Michael Jones)

signed ....
(Mr Brown, Year Tutor)

The contracting was highly successful, achieving 95 per cent attention to task behaviour in Contract 3 at the end of the term and 85 points (out of a 100) in four subjects (Mathematics having been added). Michael then received an agreed final reward of a visit to a naval base arranged by his parents.

A number of points merit further comment here:

  (a) Attitudes are difficult to measure but all parties considered them important and they were rated on an agreed 5-point scale.

(b) To earn the same rewards (chosen by Michael), successive contracts demanded and secured a greater effort by him.

(c) The parents were involved and were responsible for the final reward, which was related to proposed career choice.

(d) No attempt was made at the outset to improve learning behaviour in *all* subjects, but only some (where most cooperation was guaranteed or behaviour difficulties greater). An additional subject was added later, however.

(e) Michael wanted help and was glad to receive it. As noted earlier, one must never assume that a pupil likes, or intends, to behave in the way that he does.

(f) Note that at fourteen years of age a Merit Card is still a high-priority reward for Michael, and also extra time spent on Art. Teachers sometimes assume that Merit Cards are not motivating and miss the potential reward of providing extra time in a favourite school subject.

Essential features of the behavioural contract

Here there are a number of elements to consider, including duration, behaviours, rewards, penalties, bonus clauses, dispute procedures, data-gathering arrangements, re-negotiation structure and form of wording. Each will now, in turn, be discussed briefly.

1. *Duration*. An initial contract can extend over a period of days, a week being useful because it is a natural cycle and not too long. While contracts might run from, say, one week to a whole term, we have found it helpful to have a review involving re-negotiation after weeks 1, 2, 4, 6 and 8, for example.

2. *Behaviours*. Behaviours need to be operationally defined in specific terms and they must be accessible by observation – e.g. stealing from shops is not easy to check and standing around would inhibit it! Observers can then reliably collect data, and the pupil can recognise improvement, even though it may only be a small difference from baseline. In a contract pupils are more likely to question definitions and data-collecting procedures and to have their own view. A deeper personal involvement encourages the pupil to assume more responsibility for personal behaviour than previously. As discussed earlier, the agreed behaviour should be func-

tional; it should be considered important in the school setting, both by teachers and pupil, and appear amenable to change.

3. *Consequences for achievement*. The pupil is seeking to identify for himself, under guidance from the teacher, consequences which will function as powerful reinforcers – i.e. increase desired behaviour substantially. The pupil should be asked to list several possibilities because there could be difficulties with a first choice – e.g. too massive, or would have to be delayed for too long.

4. *Penalties*. While hard evidence is difficult to find, it is the opinion of many of us who have used contracts that some form of penalty clause is useful in increasing the likelihood of success. Two points need to be made, however. First, a contract penalty is decided by the *pupil*, or by him/her in consultation with others. Second, no penalty should be massive in terms of wiping away a really substantial amount of a reward already earned. It is better to consider a delay in giving the reward, or a short period of neutral time in which no earning can take place.

5. *Bonus clauses*. Bonus clauses are a way of recognising a short-term substantial effort or a prolonged successful effort over time. It may take the form of additional amounts of the existing reward or a different, more unusual, reward – e.g. a visit to the zoo with parents. John was able to participate in a weekend trip at the end of term.

6. *Disputes*. The good contract recognises the possibility of dispute and plans for it by making the procedure clear – i.e. who is to be brought together, when and where, how the meeting will be conducted, who can initiate the whole procedure and who will arbitrate.

7. *Evaluating progress*. Hopefully, some methods are already in existence, in which case it is a question of adapting them to the particular target behaviour(s) of this contract. If not, the first contract will have to constitute a training programme for staff and pupils. It is important, where possible, to take data on the inappropriate behaviour before the consultation process begins (and the pupil is aware of any proposals for a contract). Data collection should continue during the consultation stage and the drawing up of the contract to detect any changes.

A number of different methods of data collection are possible and appropriate for either the class or subject teacher, or an independent observer. These range from checklists to various forms of random sampling (see assessment section). Ideally, reliability checks should be carried out periodically throughout the contract period and this will clearly require an additional observer. It will help to have this kind of data available in the event of a dispute which may arise about the observation and data-collection results. The priorities, however, are (i) to help the pupil change, and (ii) to learn from the contracting process. Reliability must take third place to these considerations but still remains important.

8. *Re-negotiation structure*. It is helpful for the pupil to know that a stage of his/her contract has a definitely limited life and that there is the opportunity to review it in a neutral fashion at the end of this period. Some disputes are avoided in the short term by this procedure and may be set aside until the time for re-negotiation arrives. A neutral venue needs to be nominated and decisions made about who will be present, who is to lead the discussion (in the case of self-managed contracts this will be the pupil who is consulting his/her advisers!) and the procedure by which the contract can be amended for the next stage.

9. *Form of wording*. It is vital that the contract is clear to all the parties involved – i.e. sufficiently detailed and easily understood. This applies most particularly to the pupil. The person writing the contract, whether teacher or mediator, should phrase it in every-day language, perhaps even using the pupil's own words. The wording should be put in a positive form throughout and include the elements discussed earlier. The behaviour changes agreed by the teacher(s) and the pupil should be clearly specified, together with a time limit for the first contract and a date for its re-negotiation.

When all parties are satisfied with the wording and the starting date has been settled, everyone directly involved will sign the contract and date it. There is little research to support the power of signing a pupil contract, but most professionals involved with behavioural contracting agree that it represents a powerful extra commitment and an additional factor which contributes to potential success. A checklist of essential features is placed at the end of the chapter.

Conclusions

This chapter has set out to describe the powerful procedure of reciprocal behaviour changes contracting as a flexible and individual form of help, both for children with special needs and other pupils with problem behaviour in the ordinary school. It is time-consuming but infinitely rewarding: it becomes more economical when a large number of staff are familiar with the approach. Teachers can expect use of it to produce a wider spread of change than simply that of the target behaviour. Additional changes in pupil behaviour may involve a more positive attitude to school and authority, a greater interest in learning and improved relationships. In the teacher we may also detect improved attitudes and relationships, a more experimental approach to teaching, increased job satisfaction and greater confidence. Reciprocal behaviour change contracting, in essence, is an individual approach and each written contract should be 'tailor-made' for the pupil involved. Despite what has been said earlier about easily understood statements, I have acted as a consultant in a behavioural contract for Debbie, a fifteen-year-old elective mute, in which the contract terms read like a medieval charter. Debbie understood it and found it highly motivating; the contract was very successful.

It is vital to make every contract an opportunity for INSET, preferably on the action research model. Similarly, each contract is an opportunity for pupils to learn the contracting skills, as well as to be helped in behaviour change. As Quinto and McKenna (1977) point out, 'Pupils need to realise that they are in reality and certainly in the longer term, producing something for themselves and not for the teacher'.

Appendix: Reciprocal behaviour change contracting

A checklist of essential elements in a written reciprocal behaviour contract would include the following:

1. Title;
2. Contract no.;
3. Name of pupil;
4. Name(s) of teacher(s), peers, parents and other professionals who will directly participate;
5. Name of consultant/mediator (where appropriate);
6. Date of commencement;
7. Duration;
8. Finish date;
9. Target behaviour(s);
10. Form of monitoring and data collection;
11. Behaviour changes agreed by pupil;
12. Reciprocal behaviour change agreed by teacher/adults;

13. Consequences (rewards/reinforcers) for pupil achieving target;
14. Bonus clause;
15. Penalty clause(?);
16. Dispute procedure;
17. Arbitrator(s) name(s);
18. Signatures (by all those directly involved);
19. Copies for information to persons concerned.

References

AXELROD, S. (1977) *Behavior Modification for the Classroom Teacher* (New York: McGraw-Hill).

DE RISI, W.J. and BUTZ, G. (1975) *Writing Behavioral Contracts* (Champaign, Ill.: Research Press).

HOMME, L., CSANYI, A.P., GONZALES, M.A., and RECHS, J.R. (1970) *How to Use Contingency Contracting in the Classroom* (Champaign, Ill.: Research Press).

QUINTO, F. and McKENNA, B. (1977) *Alternatives to Standardized Testing* (Washington, DC: National Educational Association).

Chapter 12

Survival Skills for The Comprehensive School*

Roger Burland

Introduction

The time of transition from the primary school to the comprehensive school is an anxious time for most children. Such anxiety could be considerably reduced if children were prepared adequately while in their primary school. Although most comprehensive schools arrange visits for such children which include the imparting of such information about how the school is organised and run, the children are generally lacking in the skills necessary to adapt to such a dissimilar life from that to which they have become accustomed. From the small primary school where they have had one personal teacher, where they are also known by all the other teachers and addressed by their first name, they are thrust into a huge complex, where they are constantly moving, coping with strange titles of form teacher, year heads, heads of lower and upper school, counsellors and probably addressed by their surnames. They are expected to find their way around a huge building, usually without any seemingly logical design, coping with vast numbers of other individuals streaming in many directions. Suddenly from being the oldest in their primary school they become the youngest in the new school. This position can put them in the situation of being a victim to teasing, bullying or being led into wrongdoing. These children are taught by many teachers and because they have limited contact cannot possibly get to know and understand them as their primary school class teacher did. How then, can the child communicate effectively with such a person? Surely more time and effort should be employed to prepare

*This paper was originally published in 'Educational and Child Psychology,' and we are grateful to the Division of Educational and Child Psychology of the British Psychological Society for their kind permission to reproduce it here. (DECP 4:1, 1987, pp. 22–28)

children for what to them can be an alien world and a terrifying experience.

Chelfham Mill School in Barnstaple, north Devon, is a residential unit for 42 maladjusted boys aged between seven and thirteen years. The school has pioneered the use of behavioural techniques in changing behaviour, learning alternative appropriate behaviours and acquiring appropriate academic, social and recreational skills (Burland, 1981, 1984; Burland and Burland, 1981). The main aim is to return children home and to mainstream education. They have been taught in classes with a child–teacher ratio of 1:7 and therefore adjustment to the larger classes of the senior school is even more difficult. Because of this fact and to ensure success after a somewhat chequered career, a scheme to teach the skills necessary to function effectively after transfer has been evolved which takes place over the last year at Chelfham Mill. This scheme could easily be used with all primary-age children, or used in part or total to help children already in the comprehensive school who are experiencing difficulties with their peers or teachers. At Chelfham Mill School the survival project is the culmination of social skill training which commences at an early age using a well-established scheme, 'Steps to Self-Sufficiency' (Burland, Mendham and Brown, 1977). Many of the skills taught are molecular – e.g. maintaining eye contact or shaking hands – and although some children can construct an appropriate social interaction from such individual skills, with experience it has been shown that many require to learn a complete social strategy. Such strategy teaching plays a large part in the survival skills acquisition.

Understanding and knowledge of the comprehensive school

Many comprehensive schools arrange visits for the primary schools in their catchment area during the summer term. At Chelfham the children visit a local comprehensive school much earlier in their last year. It is very important for them to have experience of what the senior school is like (size, numbers, organisation, etc.) to put their survival skills programme into perspective and to be meaningful. Before the visit, the boys practise note-taking on facts about the school and positions of staff and their titles, and pertinent question-asking. After visits, class discussion and project work draws together information and observations. This is particularly useful, for the boys come from different parts of the country and will be attending such day visits to the schools to which they will return, hence it gives them a 'dry run' at the exercise.

The basic requirements to be an OK person

From questioning many comprehensive school teachers, it appears that there are four main requirements of a pupil to be considered basically acceptable to a teacher:

- to be punctual for lessons;
- to be clean and tidy;
- to complete assignments on time;
- to have the right books and equipment for each lesson.

Thus during their preparation for leaving boys are reinforced for good time-keeping. Their timetable requires them to attend many lessons in different situations with different staff, and incudes PE lessons, where they have to change and shower afterwards. This practice is invaluable in learning how to organise effective movement, predict distance and time intervals. They also have to carry all their books and equipment with them, so that by the end of the year this becomes second nature. During this year they are set homework, which is doubly effective in learning the skills of packing the schoolbag efficiently in the morning, as well as organisation of homework. At first, they are helped by residential staff who remind them to do their homework and suggest suitable times and situations where they can do it. Later they are expected to be quite independent in these respects. Their class teacher first praised good performance to establish the appropriate behaviours, but later used only sanctions for inadequate performance to simulate comprehensive school conditions.

Usually the above skills are learned after discussion, demonstration and practice with acknowledgement and praise to reinforce the skill acquisition. Occasionally individuals need special programmes to help them (e.g. one boy frequently mislaid his pen, which was frustrating to his teacher and himself). A simple programme was devised where the teacher could ask him to produce it at any time, and if successful, he was given a ticket which he could save to purchase certain class privileges. This established greater care in looking after his pen and also generalised to other equipment

Strategies of social interaction between child and teacher

It is of vital importance in situations where teachers are busy and a child is competing with others for the little unprogrammed time a teacher has available in a day for that child to be able to interact efficiently. It is helpful if he has provided in the past a positive experience for a teacher. Thus if he has fulfilled the requirements of the previous section and is seen to be punctual, tidy and reliable, he has provided a good basis for such an experience. Beyond this is his social behaviour in the past to that teacher, and the following subskills should have been part of that behaviour.

Use of greetings

When encountering a teacher in a casual situation for the first time in a day – e.g. meeting when entering the school gates, 'Hello, Sir', 'Good morning, Mr Green', accompanied by a smile, is appropriate. (The only other appropriate time then in the day for formal interaction such as this is in a 'goodbye, Sir' situation.)

Usually a smile is sufficient positive recognition of another's presence and leavers at Chelfham are encouraged to do this. It is pointed out that this is probably only necessary when the child meets a teacher face to face or passes in a quiet corridor. In busy situations, such as main thoroughfares during lesson change-over, it is more appropriate to ignore staff (who are probably moving quickly with head down or eyes in long focus anyway, to enable them to cope with getting from A to B in a short time without having to acknowledge every child and adult they know).

Politeness

In their basic social skills training all boys at Chelfham are taught and constantly reinforced for polite behaviour. Thus the basic 'please' and 'thank you' become second nature. It is important to point out and practice these words in all situations. Some children do not realise it is appropriate to use them when seeking a teacher's help with schoolwork and after help has been given. Other acts, such as opening doors, stepping aside to let a teacher pass, offering help in cleaning up and fetching and carrying, are other examples of polite and considerate behaviour.

At this point, it is important to draw attention to a crucial part of the training of leavers at Chelfham Mill School. Old boys still attending comprehensive schools are brought in to lead discussions on the skills necessary to survive. They provide information, deal with questions and comment on demonstration of skills by leavers. When they have known the leavers personally, it is particularly helpful as they are able to comment on their strengths and weaknesses.

Praise, recognition and compliments

Boys at Chelfham Mill are encouraged to praise their peers from an early age, as well as eventually to self-reinforce themselves realistically. Because of the extensive use of praise by staff as part of the total therapeutic process, the boys are well used to its form and effect. The leavers have usually been in positions where they have been required to praise younger peers in helping them with academic work or in learning social skills. Thus pointing out that they can praise and compliment their teachers is a fairly natural transition for them to make.

Acknowledgement of help would seem to be the easiest way to compliment a teacher. For instance, when a teacher has explained how to do a maths problem such acknowledgement can be given by the child saying, 'That's really clear now', 'I've never understood these until now', etc. Other compliments can be given more directly by remarks such as 'That was a really interesting lesson' or 'Can you tell me if there is a book to read, so I could learn more about this?'

If a child has engaged the above skills with reasonable success, he will have provided teachers with positive experiences and they will be more ready to receive him socially, listen and help. This will only be achieved if he then can contribute the appropriate skills of approach and interaction.

Social approach

This skill is taught from an early age at Chelfham and leavers have the main task of adapting it to situations in the senior school. The components of effective social approach are as follows.

Choosing the appropriate moment. This involves ensuring the teacher is available for interaction – i.e. not teaching, talking to a colleague, rushing out of the rain, etc. – and that he evokes a relaxed, friendly mood – i.e. not looking worried, angry or harassed.

Using the correct introduction. This should include an initial smile (allowing for the fact that the interaction does not contain bad news or an apology (see below) and a suitable verbal opening, such as 'Excuse me, Mr

Brown, I wonder if you could spare me a moment?' If he is then invited to continue the child would need to speak clearly and get to the point as quickly as possible. He should always stop if the teacher begins to speak but be ready to correct any wrong impression the teacher may have formed. This can best be achieved by using such remarks as 'I'm sorry, I have not made myself clear' or 'I see what you mean, Sir, but . . . ' (During the interaction the child would ensure the following are followed.)

Using appropriate eye contact. It is always important that initial eye contact is used. Throughout the interaction eye contact should be engaged and disengaged, to emphasise important verbal points. Eye contact should take place between 50 and 60 per cent of the time. Too much eye contact can give the wrong impression, such as when one of our old boys reported back that he had been accused of insolence by a teacher. He said, 'I really gave him good eye contact all the time just as I had been taught here!'

Posture. The body should be relatively still and placed far enough away from the other person to allow for comfortable eye contact but easy listening. The arms and hands can be used to underline verbal statements, but such movements should be relaxed and not sudden. The feet should be still, only moving to relax muscles. The skills already outlined are used in the majority of social interactions but one important exception is when apologizing.

Apologizing. The main aim here is that the apology is effective, and that it is accepted and possible retribution is minimal. Thus, when apologizing, a submissive pose should be adopted, wherein the head is bowed and hands held behind the back or clasped at the front of the body. The child waits for an invitation to speak, but does this as quickly as possible, as it is important to commence the introduction with the words 'I wish to apologize'. This enables the receiver of the apology to relax somewhat as he knows that the interaction is proceeding in a way that he would wish. Then the important point for the child to get over is that the event will not recur by making such comments as 'I will be more careful next time' or 'It won't happen again, Sir'. Such comments may be accompanied by a raising of the eyes and firm eye contact by the end of the sentence. This skill is not taught to get a child out of trouble, but to allow him if he wishes to apologize to do so effectively.

All the above skills are taught in groups, with boys undertaking behaviour rehearsal of the various skills. The rehearsal is videoed, so that each child can see his own performance. Others in the group comment on performance, criticize but also praise and suggest where improvements can be made. Often a child will say 'I can't do it that way', so alternatives are looked at to suit his style and personality. After such sessions, practice takes place *in vivo* with teachers prompting children and reinforcing good performance. Monitoring of the use of skills is undertaken when boys are with teachers not personally involved with the skills teaching programme.

Interactions with peers

Similar training is undertaken in teaching social strategies to effect interactions with peers. The old boys' experiences are particularly useful in indicating which alternative strategy may work or not for an individual in any particular situation.

Avoiding bullying and teasing

To avoid bullying and teasing, a child must not obviously present as a potential victim. He must neither reward the bullies or teasers by his behaviour consequential on their actions. Thus if confronted by peers who are likely to tease or bully, he should not avoid them or move away unless he can do this without being noticed. It is far better to keep moving on course with head erect and eye contact made with the potential adversaries. A fearful look should be avoided, and this is best achieved by alternative facial expression – i.e. smiling or whistling. Movement should be purposeful, and if peers need to be passed, a short verbal acknowledgement should be given such as 'Hi', 'All right?', etc. Any initial taunt or intimidating action should be ignored as though not noticed. If such actions proceed, then countermeasures should be taken.

The joke response would seem from experience to be quite effective. Thus if a child is called names which are usually quite predictable, he should have ready various answers. 'Hey, squirt, when you going to grow a bit?' could be countered by 'I'm standing in a hole'. To be realistic, taunting would probably be of a crude nature and may call for crude repartee. In a physical attack an over-dramatization of a comical nature could result in a cessation – i.e. sinking to the knees crying 'Mercy, mercy', or the joke again, 'I'm a black belt in snakes and ladders – watch it'. Again, some children may be able to treat attackers with disdain: 'OK, feel better now?'. Essentially, however difficult, cowering or crying should be avoided because it reinforces the bully or teaser.

Avoiding being led into trouble

At times, peers may suggest activities which are against school rules. Sometimes it is found difficult to say 'no', but if prepared with a practised strategy a child is more ready to do so. It is important to be assertive with a tempter. Full eye contact should always be used and verbal interaction should be strong and to the point. Thus, if a child is asked to miss afternoon school and go to the amusements arcade, he should counter by saying, 'You know it's against the rules. It's stupid because the owner will only ring up school and then we're in trouble. I'm not doing it.' Essentially the child is saying, 'I'm not afraid to do it, but it is foolish and not worth doing it', thus remaining assertive.

Being popular with peers

We have already made various points about how not to be unpopular and, in some ways, 'being not unpopular' is perhaps a more realistic aim. A paper by Scott and Edelstein (1981) seemed interesting and worth applying in our leavers' programme. Essentially they found that students saying positive things about others were found to be as popular as students who said positive things about themselves. The latter group engaged in 'other-enhancement' where the object is to communicate 'I like you and find you interesting'. The other-enhancer asks many questions, follows them up with further inquiries and gives positive feedback to the receiver. He also encourages the receiver to talk. The former group engaged in 'self-enhancement', where the communication was 'I like myself and I enjoy life'. The self-enhancer talks about his interests in positive terms and expresses positive opinions about many things. He does not encourage the receiver to talk, but does not engage in blatant egotistical statements.

Thus leavers were trained in both other- and self-enhancement. They found self-enhancement more difficult, it is not easy to be modest yet positive about one's own achievements or positive qualities without seeming to boast. It is important for any child to follow his peers' attitudes and behaviour, otherwise he is an outsider. The overall skill, however, is knowing how far to go and definitely when to draw the line.

Skill training and practice of strategies have the main advantage of making a child aware of his own potential in controlling his environment. It is to be hoped that he would not have learned strategies like recipes from a cookery book but will have learned principles which can be adapted to different situations. The skills and strategies have only been applied to a small sample of children and follow-up can only provide anecdotal information on success or failure. A more scientific approach would be necessary for effective evaluation, and studies with children re-integrating to mainstream education compared with children leaving ordinary primary school would be valuable. Children have demonstrated how they enjoy learning these social skills and can very well see the point of them.

References

BURLAND, J.R. (1981) 'A brief overview of behaviour modification at Chelfham Mill School', in: *The Behaviourist in the Classroom*. Ed. Wheldall, R. Educational Review Offset Publications No. 1, Birmingham.

BURLAND, J.R. (1984) 'The token economy and contracting in the closed community', in: *Behaviourism and Learning Theory in Education*. Ed. Fontana, D.(Edinburgh:Scottish Academic Press).

BURLAND, J.R. and BURLAND, P.M. (1981) 'SPOT. Special Programme of Training for parents and children: the development and evaluation of a behavioural programme for maladjusted children operated by parents in the home environment', *International Journal of Behavioural Social Work and Abstracts*, 1, 2, 87–107.

BURLAND, J.R., MENDHAM, R.P. and BROWN, T.W. (1977) *Steps to Self-Sufficiency – Social and Self Help Skills Training (4th edn)*, Chelfham Mill School (Barnstaple: Viaduct Productions).

SCOTT, W.O.N. and EDELSTEIN, B.A. (1981) 'The social competence of two interaction strategies: an analogue evaluation', *Behaviour Therapy*, 12, 482–92.

Chapter 13

Behavioural Systems Projects in Junior and Secondary Schools

Irvine Gersch

Introduction

Rutter and colleagues (1979), and Reynolds (1985), have clearly shown that factors within the school are vitally important to our understanding of behaviour problems. There has been other research showing how teaching methods, disciplinary systems, teacher behaviour and the conditions at school related to children's behaviour problems (summarised by Docking, 1980). There is now wide acceptance of the fact that schools themselves make a difference to pupils' progress and behaviour. Two sets of approaches have much to offer those of us engaged in helping children and teachers in the secondary school, namely systems analysis and behavioural approaches.

This chapter describes two projects, one in a secondary school and one in a junior school. These are examples and illustrations of the sort of work that can take place with a whole-school staff, but it should be stressed that each school needs to develop its own system and procedures which feel right and 'comfortable', and which fit. There are no 'quick-fit' or easy solutions and the *process* of arriving at change is as important as the nature of the change itself.

The systems and behavioural approaches – in outline

Burden (1978, 1981) has argued and shown that an understanding and application of systems theory can provide the psychologist with a good basis to work in schools. Burden's argument goes as follows:

1. One can only understand an individual's problems, given an understanding of the context within which he/she lives and works.

2. Often it will be the system which needs to change rather than the individual.
3. A psychologist needs to become an effective systems analyst and systems engineer if he/she is going to be of value to schools.

Burden (1981) goes on to explain that a system comprises a number of components. For example, a school system might involve the roles of members of staff, the departmental organisation, the streaming procedures, disciplinary rules, the way pastoral care is organised, and so on. The aim of the approach is to analyse the system as a whole and to intervene by altering the system.

The grid below, 'Levels of analysis, assessment and intervention', illustrates two extreme levels of work. In the real world we would rarely find one end of the continuum operating alone, but the table is intended to make clear the dichotomy albeit artificially; the boxes contain examples of some factors, methods and possible interventions.

Behavioural methods are more familiar, and involve reinforcement, specifying behavioural targets, specifying a consistent staff response, and examining the rules, rewards and sanctions in school.

LEVELS OF ANALYSIS, ASSESSMENT AND INTERVENTION

	INDIVIDUAL CHILD LEVEL	SYSTEMS LEVEL
FACTORS ASSESSED	*e.g.* Personality IQ Child's behaviour Attainments	*e.g.* Roles Procedures Staff organisation Hierarchy Pastoral care system
METHODS OF ASSESSMENT	*e.g.* Testing the child Observation of child Interviewing child	*e.g.* Discussions with staff Spending time in the school Surveys Observations
INTERVENTION	*e.g.* Remedial help for child Special school for child Treatment for child	*e.g.* Change the system, or a bit of it

Both of the projects which follow were carried out by the school's educational psychologist (myself), working with the whole-school staff, after careful negotiation, planning and role clarification with the headteachers concerned. The role taken by the psychologist as organisational consultant includes coordinating the process of change, suggesting ideas, working with groups of staff, providing research evidence and evaluating outcomes.

The secondary school project

The rate of suspension in the secondary school was high, and frequently followed a specific pattern: disruptive behaviour in lessons, lateness, failure to complete homework, answering back, not concentrating, producing poor work and showing negative attitudes. The school itself had excellent resources but was located in an area where one might expect more than average problems. Many of the children had known special educational needs and it was not possible, nor indeed desirable, to cater for all of these outside school through special school placements. The headteacher was willing to allow free and open discussion with staff about the existing systems. Finally, staff indicated an interest in looking at their current practice, with a view to change, but were naturally sceptical.

Step I: The first shot

Following a discussion on 'Control and Discipline in School', the staff split into groups and discussed: (a) rules, (b) rewards and (c) sanctions being presently used, and suggested improvements. These were to become the three areas in which new subsystems would be introduced.

Step II: The working party

A working party was then established which subsequently reported back to an open staff meeting. It was agreed that a democratic principle would be established, that policy changes would be discussed, voted upon and, if the majority agreed, then the revised system would prevail. The headteacher, however, retained the right of veto.

Step III: The working party reports back

The working party carried out research in the school, met frequently and finally suggested:

(a) a further workshop on curriculum development (which was later convened);
(b) more contact with parents;
(c) a merit system;
(d) a review of school rules;
(e) a survey of existing punishments;
(f) that the whole staff work together.

Step IV: The rules

Since all the school rules were not known to all staff, the working party sought to bring the rules up to date. All the children were asked to compile important rules and to indicate those of which they approved or disapproved. A new set of draft rules was produced, debated and worded carefully, in behavioural terms, and finally distributed to all concerned. From there on, these rules were to be included in the staff and children's handbooks, and used as a basis for form tutors to discuss regularly with their pupils.

Step V: The merit system

A survey of staff and children revealed that insufficient rewards were being employed in school, and letters home would be a potent reinforcer for children. A merit system was agreed as follows:

1. Every teacher would give out a total of 10 points, each week, typically by awarding 1 point to an individual pupil, immediately following desirable behaviour.
2. These points (or indeed fractions of points) would be recorded in the child's own booklet and in the staffroom.
3. Once a child obtained 10 points, he/she would receive a Merit Certificate to take home. The certificate would state why the points had been awarded.
4. For practical purposes, it was agreed that each teacher could operate an 'overdraft' of 3 points per week, provided that they still gave an average of 10 per week.
5. Initially some teachers resisted the idea of giving reward points. However, it was agreed that a consistent staff commitment was required and that there was a need to set a minimum and maximum number of points awarded each week, in order to establish a stable 'currency'.

6. Headteacher's special bonuses were to be awarded to children for desirable behaviour observed around the school.
7. It was accepted that points would be awarded for effort, desirable behaviour and individual improvements in work rather than for outstanding work alone, so that every child had a chance to receive points.
8. Interestingly, at first many teachers felt that it would be too difficult to award 10 points each week; after an experimental period, however, it soon became clear that more points were needed; some teachers awarded fractions of points, in order to give more opportunities for rewarding children, and the number of points to be awarded by every teacher was raised, eventually to 15 per week.
9. Attempts have now been made to introduce differential Merit Certificates: an ordinary Merit Certificate after 10 points, but after 3 Merit Certificates, a child would receive a gold certificate.
10. Many teachers reported positive gains in the children's classroom behaviour, and the merit system has become firmly established in the school.

Step VI: Sanctions

The working party suggested a new system, rather than a simple list of sanctions, with a team support network, whereby any teacher experiencing difficulty with a child exhibiting behaviour problems could enlist the help of a colleague. Eventually this was coupled with a clear reporting system, involving the form tutor being given specific information by a subject teacher (on a set form), and then the head of year calling a meeting with staff, child and parents if the problem persisted.

Of all the systems, this was the most difficult to sustain, perhaps because of the difficulty of finding time to report. None the less, it was planned that more contact between tutor and head of year would be encouraged and a formal system of recording information was agreed. A form, or 'incident report', was devised.

Coordinating the project. A school system is a growing, developing and changing network. The working party turned into a 'maintenance team' to review and change the system as time went on. Three years later all subsystems (the rules, merit and sanctions systems) were observed to be firmly established as accepted parts of the school.

Evaluation and conclusions. It is hard to evaluate a project like the one described, and indeed no statistical evidence is to hand; the following points, however, may be made about the project:

1. It heightened staff awareness of what could be done by teachers in school.
2. It aided staff morale and strength through working together as a team and arriving at joint decisions about actions which could be carried out consistently. Nobody feels happy about working on a scheme alone, or having minimal impact.
3. Children were reported to enjoy the merit system, and cases of improved behaviour and attitudes were also reported. The headteacher felt that many pupils had gained self-confidence through the award of Merit Certificates.
4. The number of referrals to the School Psychological Service decreased, and when children were referred, it was much easier to work with teaching staff.
5. The project makes the point that only to deal directly with individual children when problems arise is ineffective and, perhaps worse, collusive, in allowing us to point the finger at the child, when we need to look at the system. There are, of course, still times when it is necessary to focus on pupil change too.
6. The psychologist was invited to take on a new, challenging and exciting role. During staff meetings there was a need to discuss research evidence, clarify ideas, help design mini research projects in school, help evaluate changes, make suggestions, give advice, support and encouragement, though not to dictate.
7. Arends and Arends (1977) stressed the importance of schools finding their own solutions, and the whole process of discussion being helpful. Using a democratic approach, one avoids the game of 'knock down the expert', whereby 'failure' is attributed to any party.
8. Several teachers changed their views about the use of reinforcement, behavioural shaping and other aspects of behavioural approaches and, most commonly, about the value of rewards.
9. Such was the interest generated in the detailed treatment programmes applicable to maladjusted children that a request

was made by staff to help set up and run social skills training courses for pupils, within school. As a result, approaches were made to the headteacher of a school for maladjusted pupils, who agreed to offer the services of a specialist teacher to run a treatment group. Eventually the teacher withdrew and acted purely on a consultative basis. The social skills training course has become a routine part of the pastoral care curriculum, for selected pupils, and is run by several interested teachers who work in consultation with the school counsellor and psychologist.

A junior school project

I have described a systems project in a secondary school. This section describes a primary school project. Primary schools, have their distinct systems and sets of subsystems. The programme described here had several negotiated stages, agreed with the headteacher, including:

1. negotiating procedures for change;
2. identifying problems;
3. meeting the whole school staff to discuss the processes leading to change, and giving a talk to staff;
4. setting up working parties which would meet regularly over a set period of time;
5. arranging full decision-making staff meetings to consider proposals put forward by working parties;
6. evaluation of the outcomes.

Negotiations

In order to bring about any change to an organisation, there needs to be an accepted agreement by the visiting consultants and those within the organisation that change is required and that the procedures adopted are acceptable.

It was agreed that decisions would be made at special staff meetings, and that working parties of teachers would be employed to deal with specific areas. The first session in the programme was to be entitled 'problem identification' in which the consultants (being two educational psychologists – myself and Christine Cargill) would meet with the whole-school staff to identify areas of concern.

Problem identification

Staff were encouraged to list difficult pupil behaviour in as precise a way as possible, to describe the location where such behaviours occurred, the triggers to such behaviours, who was involved in behavioural incidents, typical outcomes and the normal teacher-action. It was agreed to adopt an experimental approach, in which any recommendations and changes put into effect would be evaluated and future amendments made if required. The aims of the programme were explicit:

1. to have a clear understanding of the behaviour required of children;
2. to help increase that behaviour;
3. to discuss and share new systems of behaviour management.
4. to arrive at a clear and agreed system of management.

During the first session, 'Problem identification' school staff produced a long list of pupil behaviours which were causing concern; these were grouped together and analysed under three main headings:

1. school work and working on-task;
2. anti-social behaviour/social behaviour;
3. following school rules.

Working parties

Each working party was to focus on one of the above topics; each was given a brief to finalise their proposals in written form, feed back their recommendations to a full staff meeting and carry out any research with pupils which they felt was required. A decision-making staff meeting was arranged some two months later, enabling staff to debate the proposals, to decide upon which ones to support and to make decisions about the remaining proposals. It was agreed that all recommendations would be passed to the headteacher for enactment and he had the right of 'veto'.

Although there were three main areas of concern about pupil behaviour, five areas were identified by the working parties:

(a) preparation of a merit system within school;
(b) the production of a staff handbook;
(c) a review and publication of school rules;
(d) a review of the social skills components of the curriculum;
(e) a review of the curriculum.

Outcomes

Eight major outcomes arose, as follows:

1. A re-organisation of the school day.
2. A new set of school rules.
3. Production of a merit system.
4. Agreed procedures for teachers dealing with disruptive behaviour.
5. Efforts to increase parent involvement in school activities, particularly assemblies.
6. A review of the curriculum.
7. Discussion of a social curriculum.
8. Agreement to produce a staff handbook.

Re-organisation of the school day

Almost immediately it became apparent that some degree of disruptive pupil behaviour was occasioned by the timing of assembly, placement of crisp stalls, distribution of dinner tickets and other school organisational demands. For example, assemblies occurred just before playtime and towards the end of assembly, prior to the children being dismissed for play, a crisp stand was set up, much to the interest of the children. Once in sight, children positioned themselves to be first to the crisp stand. This meant that as soon as assembly ended there was a rush to the back of the hall where it was situated, with much noise and pushing.

It appeared that several children had to leave the class in the morning in order to go to the office to get their dinner tickets, and this caused classroom disruption. Staff also felt that pupils coming in from the playground often arrived late, disrupting the start of the lessons.

It was agreed that the timing of the assembly should be reconsidered and that more staff should be present. At the end of each playtime, it was agreed that children should be lined up by their teachers, and accompanied to their classes in an orderly way. It was also agreed that the crisp stand should be placed elsewhere (out of sight) and that dinner money should be collected inside the classroom.

Comments were also made about pupils' disruptive behaviour during lunchtimes, when they were supervised by midday assistants. Midday assistants are left with the daunting task of supervising a large number of pupils, with minimal support. One suggestion was that there should be greater communication between midday assistants and teaching staff, and midday assistants were brought into the merit system (see below).

A new set of school rules

School staff agreed that it was vital for there to be a consistent set of agreed school rules, written up and publicised for all children and parents. After lengthy discussion, 10 school rules were formulated and discussed with pupils. It was felt that the discussion about school rules was as important as the final outcome, and it was agreed that these rules might be amended, on review.

Production of a merit system

The working party produced a system of rewards involving children earning 'smiley faces', which would lead to a merit mark and with 15 merit marks leading to a certificate. There were bronze, silver and gold certificates, awarded progressively as more certificates were earned.

It was agreed that every teacher should give 20 'smiles' a day, and an allocation of 'smiles' was given to all non-teaching staff (including the caretaker, midday assistants, secretaries and special welfare assistant). Charts were drawn up and displayed in each classroom and ways of recording agreed. Staff also agreed to give book tokens at prize day to any pupil who had obtained a gold certificate.

Procedures for teachers dealing with disruptive behaviour

Staff decided on a hierarchy of teacher responses which they felt would be useful:

(a) verbal disapproval – teacher reminding children what was expected of them;
(b) ignoring difficult and attention-seeking behaviour, when · appropriate;
(c) social skills training;
(d) use of behavioural charts;
(e) home–school book – parental contact;
(f) prohibiting pleasant activities;
(g) detentions at playtimes;
(h) sending a child out of class to another member of staff.

When problems persisted, it was felt that staff should consider having a case discussion with other members of staff to discuss the child's special educational needs (e.g. learning, emotional, behavioural or social) with a view to planning a clear course of action or approach to meet those needs. Regular (fortnightly) lunchtime meetings with staff to discuss children causing concern were also envisaged.

Within the hierarchy of teacher responses it was suggested that when problems persisted, school staff should write to parents, identifying the problem asking for parental assistance and inviting them in to help, in a constructive way. A home–school book or behavioural chart was also considered. It is of note that a special welfare assistant attached to the School Psychological Service was available in school to assist with behavioural and other programmes. The final sanction available to schools was that of a 'cooling off' period or formal suspension, although it should be acknowledged that formal suspensions in a junior school are extremely rare, and indeed discouraged in all but the most exceptional and probably dangerous situations.

Curriculum review

School staff came to the conclusion that a review of the curriculum was required, and that it would be helpful if a whole-school approach was agreed. This was ongoing at the time of writing.

Social curriculum and social training

One working party was specifically devoted to producing ideas about ways of improving children's social behaviour in school, and after discussion staff did feel that they would like a social behaviour project to become a regular timetabled part of school life. It was agreed that 'role play' might form an important part of the programme and that teachers in the same year should meet in order to coordinate social skills projects. Some teachers were more interested in the use of drama in social skills training than others, but all felt that some discussion about pupils' behaviour would be of assistance in the classroom.

Parental involvement

Mention was made by several staff that more positive contact was possible with parents. As a first step, parents were more actively encouraged to attend assemblies, often to see their own children perform, and it was also accepted that 'positive letters home' could be a useful addition to the merit system.

Agreement to produce a staff handbook

Given the vast amount of information and suggestions involved in the programme described, it was felt that there was a need to summarise much of it into a handbook for staff.

Evaluation

The project was evaluated some 16 months after its introduction. The evaluation consisted of two elements. First a trainee educational psychologist carried out individual interviews with the headteacher, members of the teaching staff, school secretary, midday assistants and other non-teaching staff. Seven parents and five children were interviewed. Second, a questionnaire was distributed to all members of the teaching and non-teaching staff at the school, and the results were analysed.

Interviews with staff, pupils and parents

The main findings were that a change in systems within the school had had a marked effect on the attitudes, feeling and general atmosphere in the school. Staff were reported as feeling happier and there seemed to have been an increase in staff morale. The children reported that the teachers behaved in a 'nicer way' and their peers seemed less prone to arguing and fighting. The teachers felt that the re-organisation of the school day resulted in children arriving in classes at the same time, in a more orderly way at the beginning of lessons, and that less difficulties occurred as a result. Most welcomed the newly revised set of rules, but some new members of staff were not always aware of the detailed set of rules, and some pupils felt that they could have been consulted more directly and given a greater chance to express what they felt.

The merit system was definitely seen as being the most important change, by staff, children and parents; all felt that this was a useful way to encourage desirable behaviour, although there was some criticism of the system by midday assistants. This may have been due to the fact that more guidance and help was required for the system to be used at lunchtime. All staff reported that they were looking for positive behaviour to encourage and the system helped them.

Most teachers felt that the hierarchy of teacher responses or guidelines of actions were being used, but they did not necessarily perceive it as a simple system. Children were surprisingly clear about what would happen if they misbehaved, and of the stages they would go through.

They could further identify the kinds of behaviour that would warrant different levels of punishment and teacher action. It seemed as though the system was working effectively and served to give the children a degree of security in being able to anticipate the consequences of mis-demeanours, thereby reducing uncertainty. The report concluded that the new system 'offers a unified, structured approach to discipline and the recognition of desirable behaviour'.

The questionnaire survey

Every teaching member of staff, the special welfare assistant, secretaries and caretaker were invited to respond to a written questionnaire. Staff were invited to comment about changes in pupil behaviour and atti-tudes since the operation of the new system. Some 87 per cent of staff felt that the new systems had been helpful, to some degree, in improving pupil behaviour and attitude to work; about a fifth stated that the systems had been 'very helpful', more than a third said 'helpful', and a further quarter said 'a little helpful'. There was no substantial difference in the report with regard to 'pupil behaviour' or 'attitude' to work. Only one member of staff felt that new systems had had no effect.

A final question invited staff to indicate whether or not they thought the programme had been worthwhile; 100 per cent of the staff responded positively. Each respondent felt that the programme and the process had been worth while; they felt that some significant alter-ations had occurred within the school, and the process of staff working together to solve problems had been an important factor in raising staff morale and contributing to positive changes in pupil behaviour.

Conclusions

By way of conclusion, it would seem helpful to highlight a number of important points which arise from the projects.

1. The projects emphasise the importance of staff working together, making joint decisions and generating ideas. It is all too easy to underestimate the degree of expertise which lies within school staffs; considerable information and ideas for change can be gleaned from both staff and pupils, and although outside consultants can be of assistance, care is needed to ensure that the expert advice available from those *within* schools does not get overlooked or under-estimated.

DIAGRAMMATIC SUMMARY OF CONCERNS, AREAS REVIEWED
AND OUTCOMES

PROBLEMS CAUSING CONCERN:

1 Schoolwork and working on-task
2 Anti-social behaviour
3 Following school rules

WORKING PARTIES TO INVESTIGATE, SURVEY AND
SUGGEST PROPOSALS TO IMPROVE:

1 Schoolwork
2 Social behaviour
3 Rule following behaviour, through review of school
procedures

POTENTIAL OUTCOMES IDENTIFIED:

1 Preparation of a merit system within school
2 Production of staff handbook
3 A review (and publication) of school rules
4 A review of social skills components of curriculum
5 A review of curriculum

OUTCOMES:

1 A re-organisation of school day
2 A new set of school rules
3 Production of merit system
4 Agreed procedures for teachers dealing with disruptive
behaviour
5 Efforts to increase parental involvement
6 Curriculum review
7 Review of social curriculum
8 Production of staff handbook

Fig 15   Diagrammatic summary of concerns, areas reviewed and outcomes

2. There is increasing evidence that teaching is a stressful job and that there are several antidotes to stress, including teamwork and the use of consultants (Dunham, 1983).

3. The projects involved educational psychologists working as organisational consultants, in a wider way than is conventional, where the focus is on the single child.

4. Although there were positive outcomes, staff were united in feeling that a number of pupils still remained as so-called 'hard-core', who continued to present significant problems. A school system project would be unlikely to eradicate *all* pupil behavioural difficulties in school; indeed the aim is to alter the backcloth and context with regard to behaviour problems. However, there is no doubt that a merit system and use of special welfare assistant time in school can be used creatively to help pupils whose behaviour continues to cause concern. The hierarchy of teacher responses also reveals ultimately *which* pupils warrant greater attention.

5. It should be stressed that every school is different, and other outcomes might be expected to occur in other schools; however, similar democratic procedures and working parties could, of course, be used generally.

6. It is possible to level a criticism of the projects, in that there was greater room for consultation with pupils and parents; and although such consultation was done to some extent; more was possible.

7. Of merit in the junior project was the involvement of the caretaker, school secretary, special welfare assistant and midday assistants. They are all significant adults in the lives of children at school and are often left out of school systems changes.

8. Burden (1981) writes that, using a systems approach over six years, some projects have been successful in implementing change, but most have received the approval of teachers for psychologists to work in this way. He says that every project was exciting, exhausting and worthwhile and this was also our experience.

9. Finally, it is perhaps worth stressing that when schools are concerned about general pupil behaviour, it is worth while tapping the expertise of whole-school staffs, identifying patterns of such behaviour and looking towards what can be done within the school as a *whole*, rather than focusing on individual pupils. What is clear is that the power of a whole-school staff working together, analysing problems, brainstorming ideas and suggestions, and making decisions together and evaluating outcomes of any changes made, should not be underestimated. I am currently evaluating a whole-school proj-

ect, involving working groups of pupils as well as teachers, and it is felt that this is an important area worthy of development. Certainly, for real change to be effective and not to be blocked, the involvement of all the staff in the process is essential and offers exciting possibilities.

References

ARENDS, R. and ARENDS, H. (1977) *Systems Change Strategies in Education Settings* (London: Human Sciences Press).

BURDEN, R.L. (1978) 'Schools systems analysis: a project centred approach', in *Reconstructing Educational Psychology* Ed. Gillham, W. (London: Croom Helm).

BURDEN, R.L. (1981) 'The educational psychologist as instigator and agent of change in schools: some guidelines for successful practice', in: *Reconstructing Psychological Practice* Eds McPherson and Sutton, A. (London: Croom Helm).

DOCKING, J.W. (1980) *Control and Discipline in Schools* (New York: Harper and Row).

DUNHAM, J. (1983) 'Coping with stress in school', *Special Education: Forward Trends*, 10, 2, 6-9.

GERSCH, I.S. (1984) 'Behaviour modification and systems analysis in the secondary school: combining two approaches', *Quarterly Journal of the Association for Behavioural Approaches with Children*, 8, 3,pp. 83-91.

REYNOLDS, D. (ed.) (1985) *Studying School Effectiveness* (Brighton: Falmer Press).

RUTTER, M., MAUGHAN, B., MORTIMORE, P. and OUSTON, J. (1979) *Fifteen Thousand Hours: Secondary Schools and their Effect on Children* (London. Open Books).

Acknowledgements

I wish to acknowledge the work of Ms Cargill (Educational Psychologist), school staff, and pupils in the schools concerned as well as the help of my colleague, Martin Shearn (Senior Educational Psychologist). The views expressed in the chapter, however, remain my own responsibility and do not necessarily reflect those of the LEA or schools in which the projects took place.

Parts of this chapter were first published in the 'Quarterly Journal of the Association for Behavioural Approaches with Children' (1984) 8, 3, pp. 83–91; and in 'Educational and Child Psychology' (1986) 3, 2, 61–70.

We are grateful to the Division of Educational and Child Psychology of the British Psychological Society and the Association for Behavioural Approaches with Children, for giving us permission to reproduce the relevant parts here.

SECTION D

Partnerships in Meeting Disruptive Behaviour

Chapter 14

Partnership between Educational Psychologists and Teachers

Don Hills

Introduction

To use a military analogy, teachers and educational psychologists quite often meet either on or near the scene of battle in meeting disruptive behaviour. Most commonly, educational psychologists are akin to support troops called in to discuss tactics, supply refreshment and, hopefully, to help bring peace to a troubled region! Discussing tactics may involve suggesting guidelines to help prevent battles arising in the first place; supplying refreshment may mean to offer help during the heat of a particular battle; and helping to bring about peace will probably involve taking an active part in the negotiations bringing a cessation to the hostilities. The essence of the partnership is that it is the teacher who is in the fray, needing practical help and guidance. In my experience, most teachers do not really want the psychologist to 'take over' – they look for understanding of the issue, help in resolving the immediate problem and realistic suggestions for avoiding trouble in the future. To mix the metaphors, it is a partnership between the doer and the enabler, the actor and the 'coach' or the general practitioner and the consultant.

The basis for partnership

At the outset, it should be remembered that teachers and psychologists share a minimum of two important experiences: training as a teacher, and experience in the classroom. They often share other experiences – e.g. a first degree in psychology, or a postgraduate qualification in some aspect of child special needs. What differentiates them is that the psychologist must embark on a specialised postgraduate training (usually to Masters degree standard) in the practise of educational psychology; normally he/she will then resign their teaching post to devote themselves full-time to LEA service as a trained psychologist. This parting of the ways has obvious implications for the development of professional skills. The teacher will go on to (hopefully) become highly skilled in the art (or, perhaps, science?) of teaching which presumably involves an ability to help, guide and enable each child to develop socially, emotionally and cognitively into that humane, well-rounded human being so beloved of books on educational philosophy.

And what of the psychologist? Since that parting of the ways referred to above, he/she will presumably have achieved most of the skills referred to in the Association of Educational Psychologists' recent pamphlet entitled *EPs – Their Work and Implications for Training* (obtainable from AEP, 3 Sunderland Road, Durham). Briefly, these skills are summarised under four main headings: (a) *communication* – e.g. establishing effective rapport with children, teachers, parents and other professional colleagues, and the preparation of clear and practical guidelines and reports; (b) *gathering information* – e.g. providing guidance on the social, emotional and cognitive development of children in particular home and community contexts, as well as the uncovering of individual child characteristics through effective assessment techniques; (c) *effecting change* – e.g. helping to plan practical intervention strategies at an individual or group level based on accurate observation and relevant knowledge of the child; and (d) *evaluation* – e.g. determining whether strategies have really 'worked' in the sense of all-round child wellbeing, not simply the achievement of short-term objectives.

What do teachers expect of psychologists? Very little research has been carried out. In the Hampshire Education Department's publication, *An Evaluation of a School Psychological Service* (March 1979), nine secondary school heads, ten senior pastoral care teachers (usually deputy heads), 32 middle school heads and 29 first school heads were asked what skills discriminated the psychologist's contribution from those of other specialist visitors to the school (e.g. advisers, education welfare officers, and social workers). Skills agreed on by at least 20 per cent of these 80 senior staff were: (i) diagnostic skills, the relation of cause and effect; (ii) the skill to make recommendations, practical advice for the classroom, and to know which possible treatment will meet the child's needs; (iii) skills in testing and interpretation; (iv) ability to consider all factors and their interaction when assessing problems and provide an independent unbiased view based on objective measurement and observation; (v) breadth and depth of experience with children with special needs and their development, maturity of the psychologist and knowing all schools in the area well; (vi) knowledge of available resources and possible teamwork contacts with other services; (vii) skills in interviewing and relating to parents especially and other adults. Relating to strangers quickly and getting 'good' information; (viii) ability to relate to teachers and work successfully with them, communicating psychological skills to them, and communication skills – verbal and written – with other adults; (ix) to have knowledge of schools and teaching by being trained teachers; and (x) up-to-date psychological knowledge, especially regarding child development, and thereafter.

A comparison of these senior teachers' expectations regarding psychologists with those of the AEP, referred to earlier, shows a reasonable measure of agreement, with the teachers giving slightly more weight to work with individual children and psychologists a little more weight to advisory work with those caring for children. However, agreement about the particular skills of psychologists is clearly strong enough to promote a good working relationship between teachers and psychologists. Assuming a similar agreement about the particular skills of teachers, then the only remaining factor ensuring a positive partnership is the effectiveness of both sets of professionals in joint planning and action.

A partnership in meeting disruptive behaviour

The partnership needs to extend to both senses of the word 'meeting' – i.e. having direct experience and helping to provide solutions. My own view is that psychologists should, on occasion, be prepared to experience the difficulties encountered by teachers either through direct observation or, if mutually agreeable, taking a difficult class for a short period in order to gain a truly emphatic understanding of disruptive behaviour. Interviewing the child individually and meeting the parents can further aid such understanding, as can getting to know the teacher's personal style and approach. There is no doubt that the well-known phenomenon of a 'personality clash' does sometimes happen, and if a particular teacher is possibly unwittingly actually provoking the disruptive behaviour, then this needs to be sensitively pointed out in the spirit of partnership. By the same token, if the psychologist's advice lacks reality, practicality or humanity, then this too needs to be fed back to him/her by the teacher.

There remains the controversial question as to whether the psychologist should 'take on the child for treatment'. When I first trained as an educational psychologist, we were considered as 'treatment experts'. These days it is recognised that teachers and parents are the main 'treaters' of children and that the psychologist's main job is to help them do that job well. It must be said, however, that many psychologists do take on therapeutic work with individual children.

There are other psychologists who feel they can contribute most to the partnership by working at the macro rather than the micro level – i.e. by helping to change the organisation of the school as a pastoral system such that positive behaviour is maximised and disruptive behaviour is minimised. Where this form of joint working is possible, then clearly there exists a marvellous opportunity for a 'partnership in prevention'. This approach is at the heart of the PAD (Preventative Approaches to Disruption) materials and is also implicit in many other published programmes of guidance – e.g. TIPS, BATPAC and SNAP.

Partnership in action

Perhaps the reader is a teacher who is asking how the principles of partnership advocated so far can work effectively in his/her school and classroom? Imagine, then, I am your local 'educational psychologist' and you want to discuss your worries about some aspect of disruptive behaviour. What kind of support and advice can I offer? I suggest that we first try to look at the behaviour in context before actually seeking a solutions for I believe that looking at the conditions in which the disturbing behaviour arises is an essential prerequisite to finding a solution.

It may be that your particular worries are shared by other colleagues in your school and that a whole-school approach can be worked out, perhaps, along the lines suggested by Irvine Gersch in this book (Chapter 13). Or you may be fortunate enough to have a school support team available locally with both specialist teacher and psychologist expertise on hand. Where a school policy on conduct exists, it clearly helps to act as the initial backdrop for discussions between teacher and the psychologist. Let us suppose, however, that we have considered the general context in which a particular pupil's behaviour is occurring and now wish to examine more specifically what can be done in terms of support in your helping the pupil.

In the area in which I work we have devised a general approach to assessment and intervention called Diagnostic Teaching, which advocates a period of reflection and observation prior to any intervention (change in teacher approach). In many cases, the early phases of reflection and observation have proved sufficient to help the teacher re-assess exactly what is happening in the teacher–pupil interaction within the classroom context and the problem magically disappears! What seems to happen in these cases is that a greater understanding of the pupil's needs and strengths, combined with what the teacher has to offer, brings about a different perspective in which nagging worries dissolve. Where an intervention programme is carried through, a period of reflective evaluation is suggested in order to decide what exactly has happened. In our approach to Diagostic Teaching, then, we have the four phases of reflection, observation, intervention and evaluation. Figures 16–19 give a brief indication of the materials we use. These are supplemented by notes and individual discussion (sometimes one-to-one, sometimes in a teacher support group), but notice that the recording sheets have been devised with an emphasis on simplicity and economy. We sought to encourage maximum flexibility within the general structure, preferring to use open-ended boxes for teachers' responses rather than, for example, long checklists which tend to cramp creative thinking and prove tedious in use.

Let us suppose you have filled in the Child Profile (Figure 16). We now have a 'snapshot' of your pupil in the various areas of attainment, behaviour and cognition giving us a kind of 'ABC' of how he/she presents currently within the classroom. As your psychologist, it helps me enormously to have this brief, one-page teacher's eye view of the child setting behaviour within a general context of ability and attainment and pointing to assets as well as problems. It allows both of us to reflect upon the needs of the child and gives a useful pointer as to whether any specific observations now need to be carried out.

The notes accompanying Figure 17 suggest various kinds of observation which can be attempted, with a reminder to include other relevant evidence from parents and the wider community. It is here that my training as a psychologist may be helpful in advising about particular kinds of observation, given the conditions pertaining in your classroom. You may find it helpful for me to be involved in observation, depending on the age of the child.

As suggested in the notes accompanying Figure 18 all the previous work in observation and reflection should now prove invaluable in planning a suitable intervention programme. In my experience, teachers are often keen to work out their own programme using the psychologist as consultant. While we take joint responsibility for the programme, it is you, as teacher, who bears the brunt of the work.

A key part of any programme designed to help disruptive children is

---

CHILD PROFILE   *Confidential*

Please fill in some brief comments in the appropriate spaces below. If you have any specific information (e.g. test results) please give it, but the main aim is a 'snapshot' of the child's functioning in the various areas at the moment.

Name of child: *Date of Birth:*   *School:*

Home address: *Tel:*

                                          Parents notified: YES/NO*
                                          *(Please delete as appropriate)

ATTAINMENTS

Language	a) *Spoken expression*	b) *Understanding*
Reading	a) *Accuracy*	b) *Comprehension*
Creative writing and spelling		
Writing and drawing	a) *Handwriting*	b) *Drawing*
Gross motor skills		
Number	a) *Concepts*	b) *Application*

BEHAVIOUR

Motivation	a) *Towards school in general*	b) *Towards 'work'*
Self-concept		
Attitude towards others	a) *Towards other children*	b) *Towards adults*
Social skills		

COGNITION

General ability	
Specific abilities	

IN GENERAL – What are the child's main assets and problems at the moment?

Main assets	Main problems

Date: *Signed:*   *Position:*

Fig 16   Child Profile

OBSERVATION SCHEDULE

From the Child Profile, you now need to extract the main assets and problems and ask how strong or weak they really are. If appropriate you can administer certain attainment tests, but remember these can be unreliable with some special needs children. Another way of observing the strengths and weaknesses in more detail is by carrying out a series of 'mini-teaching' experiments to discover which approach the child responds to best. Yet another way is to observe the child's behaviour in the normal day-to-day activities so that you can set up a 'baseline' or benchmark from which future progress can be judged. This latter approach is particularly appropriate for those learning and/or behavioural problems where you need to know in more detail how the child is responding in normal classroom situations. If the behaviour in question is occurring frequently you can use sampling techniques. For less noticeable behaviour you may need the help of another to act as observer, or to free you to do so.

We recommend that the period of observation be at least a week so that fluctuations in response by the child can be accounted for. We also recommend that you describe the behaviour in question as objectively as possible, e.g. for academic behaviours such as reading – 'read Book 3 with an 80% success rate' (not merely 'he read well' or 'he tried hard'). For non-academic behaviours such as aggression – 'he kicked John twice in a five minute observation session' (not merely 'he was nasty to John'). The general aim of the observations is to gain a clear view of the assets and problems of the child in terms of frequency and intensity. Please summarise the results of your observations in the Schedule below, and remember to include other relevant evidence, e.g. information from parents and the wider community.

Name of child: *Date of birth:*   *School:*   *Teacher:*

1   *MAIN ASSETS*

Behaviour in question	*Type of observation*	*Date started*	*Date finished*
(a)			
(b)			
(c)			
2 *MAIN PROBLEMS*			
(a)			
(b)			
(c)			

(Go on to another sheet if necessary)

Fig 17   Observation Schedule

PROGRAMME DETAILS

Completion of the Observational Schedule should help you decide what sort of intervention plan (or 'programme') to set up. It may be that your observations have shown that the child was making more progress than you had previously thought – in which case only minor alterations to the existing teaching programme will be necessary. Alternatively the observations may reveal that major changes are needed. Either way, you set out clear objectives to be achieved within a specified period of time (say, half a term). The behavioural objectives can relate to learning activities, attitudinal or motivational improvements, behavioural changes – or a combination thereof – but be sure to specify precisely what you are after, e.g. 'Billy will read Books 4 & 5 with a 95% success rate', or 'Tony will reduce his aggressive behaviour (previously specified) from 10 to no more than 2 incidents a day on average', or 'Mary will increase her span of concentration on a particular task from 5 min to 15 min'.

The types of intervention are legion and can relate to improving assets, reducing problems, using the assets to help reduce problems, etc. The important thing is to build up feelings in the child of confidence and success based on your observations of his particular strengths and weaknesses. Have a carefully designed programme of activities aimed at achieving the objectives by a series of learning steps (or 'targets') small enough to promote success with time enough for effective reinforcement. By all means, tap into published programmes if they *really* suit your child, but be prepared to work to a programme devised entirely by yourself. Be prepared also to work along with parents and other significant figures in the community who know the child. Once you have sorted out your objectives and the hoped-for means of achieving them, fill in the appropriate spaces below.

Name of child: *Date of birth:*   *School:*   *Teacher:*

OBJECTIVES	*TYPE OF INTERVENTION*	*Date started*	*Date finished*
1			
2			
3			

(Go on to another sheet if necessary)

Fig 18   Programme Details

the promotion of success which, as suggested in the figure, can be accomplished by such strategies as improving assets and thereby reducing problems. Teachers and psychologist need to work at what will most boost the confidence of the disruptive child, who may cover feelings of despair and frustration with aggressive, attention-seeking behaviour. Sometimes improvements in behaviour are quickly observed with improvement in educational attainment.

The final stage of evaluation is crucial. In addition to judging the success or otherwise of the initial objectives we can also evaluate the *unintended* consequences of the programme (they usually occur!) and, perhaps most important, ask what overall changes have occurred. The Diagnostic Teaching model is holistic and interactionist in outlook, and it is vital to ascertain what has happened outside as well as inside school for the child during the programme, especially if parents have been involved; Figure 19 gives a framework for so doing, and for deciding whether any further programme, modified or otherwise, is necessary.

The reciprocal nature of the partnership

So far we have sought to emphasise the reciprocity of training, outlook and working practice between educational psychologists and teachers. The psychologist's specialist training in communication, gathering information, effecting change and evaluation is put at the disposal of his/her teacher colleague, who offers valuable diagnostic information in the course of daily contact with the child. The expectations stemming from each side of the partnership are often high, and the touchstone of effectiveness is frequently brought into focus when children disrupt and emotions run strongly. In the Diagnostic Teaching model of assessment I have espoused it is the teacher who is the assessor and the psychologist who acts as consultant. Each helps the other in working towards positive change and the responsibility for programme outcomes is joint; and, with increasing age, the child also becomes an active partner with accompanying responsibility for change in a positive direction. Where parents can be engaged, they too become responsible members of the team.

Of necessity, the actual balance of work and accompanying responsibility will vary according to the commitment of the people involved. Supposing, for example, you as a teacher happen to attend my workshop about methods of dealing with disruptive behaviour. You then mention, in passing, the needs of a particular child, and this is used as a

EVALUATION SHEET

Following completion of the programme, look at the Observation Schedule and Programme Details sheets to see what changes there have been in the listed behaviours. Were the objectives achieved, and if so *how* well? If they were not achieved, how badly? Put relevant comments in the appropriate column below. Then look back at the Child Profile Sheet and note any other changes in the child's functioning so that you can gain a broad view of any significant changes. The programme may have produced unintended or unexpected consequences and it is important that these are evaluated before deciding upon future action. Taking all of the changes, and their interactions, into account, it is now time to ask the key questions – is your child *generally* more happy, more motivated, more successful, at school and at home? Note these points briefly below in the 'General Comments' box, and when you have decided on your next course of action (e.g. continue programme, stop programme, set up a modified programme, refer on to Special Needs Support Service) enter brief comments in the 'Future Action' box.

Name of Child: *Date of Birth:*   *School:*   *Teacher:*

1. *Evaluation of programme results* (see notes)

OBJECTIVES	ACHIEVED (TICK)	NOT ACHIEVED (TICK)	COMMENTS
1			
2			
3			

2. *Evaluation of wider issues* (see notes)

GENERAL COMMENTS	FUTURE ACTION

(Go on to another sheet if necessary)

Fig 19   Evaluation Sheet

focus for group discussion about approaches to that kind of problem. If the matter is taken further through assessment under the Education Act (1981) procedures, then you may well look for guidance about specialist provision. Nevertheless, even where specialist provision is effected, it may be important to the child that you do not 'wash your hands' of him/her. They may have gone into full-time, special school placement but your continuing interest, as the previous teacher, in their progress could be vitally important in maintaining or even building up their self-esteem. Teamwork to the end!

Finally, I wish to emphasise that establishing good relationships between educational psychologists and teachers as partners is an intensely individual one, bringing into play the strengths of both sides. The use of Diagnostic Teaching, mentioned in this chapter as a focus for partnership in assessment, arose from the joint concerns of a number of colleagues in north Devon to find a basic tool for communication and action. It was evaluated and modified through use in both teacher support groups and in work with individual children. Readers of this book will need to establish their own approaches and forms of partnership based on local conditions, particularly the skills of colleagues (whether psychologists or teachers), or indeed any other personnel able to help in meeting the needs of disruptive children.

Acknowledgements

I wish to thank my patient colleagues in the North Devon Special Needs Support team for allowing me to bend their ears on so many occasions, and for the excellent practical advice given by them and other colleagues in the Devon Education Service when drafting this chapter. And special thanks to my secretary Jean Jones, for her unfailing support.

References

AINSCOW, M. and MUNCEY, J. (1984) *Special Needs Action Programme (SNAP)* (Cardiff: Drake Educational Associates).

ASSOCIATION OF EDUCATIONAL PSYCHOLOGISTS (1986) 'Educational psychologists – and their work and implications for training', AEP, Durham.

CHISHOLM, B., KEARNEY, D., KNIGHT, G., LITTLE, H., MORRIS, S. and TWEDDLE, D. (1986) *Preventative Approaches to Disruption (PADS)* (London: Macmillan Education).

DAWSON, P.L. (1988) *Teacher Information Pack (TIPS)* (London: Macmillan Education).

HAMPSHIRE EDUCATION DEPARTMENT (1979) 'An evaluation of a school psychological service', Hampshire Education Department, Castle Hill, Winchester.

WHELDALL, K. and MERETT, F. (1987) *Behavioural Approaches to Teaching Pack (BATPACK)* (Birmingham: Positive Products).

Chapter 15

Involving Parents in Behaviour Management: A Whole-School Approach

Sheila Wolfendale

Introduction

This chapter sets out to sketch the broader perspective of parental involvement, examining the rationale and some key concepts, thus providing the context in which involving parents in policy and practice of behaviour management is set. A model is then proposed which amounts to a school-based, 'systems' approach, enabling educators to formulate procedures for involving parents at a number of levels. How fully to 'allow' parents to participate in decision-making is considered to be a matter for each school and governing body to determine. Each level is illustrted by emerging practice in this relatively new area. The chapter concludes with a look at the feasibility of these ideas and requisite professional development, and draws attention to a number of texts which could provide the basis for developing strategies.

Working with parents as clients or partners

While there are now numerous examples of parents being *involved* in education and the learning progress of their children, there are as yet no models or working examples of parents being *equal* participants in these enterprises in mainstream education. Portage (Bishop, Copley and Porter, 1986; Cameron, 1986) is held to be the best illustration we have at present of parent–professsional cooperation, in which parents play an equal part.

Mittler and McConachie (1983) outline a definition of partnership with parents which involves a full sharing knowledge, skills and experience. They perceive a commitment to partnership as resting on the assumption that children will learn and develop better if parents and professionals are working together on a basis of equality than if either is working in isolation.

Wolfendale (1983) identifies parents as partners when they are active and central in decision-making; have equal strengths and 'equivalent expertise'; contribute to as well as receive services; and share responsibility, so that they and professionals are mutually accountable.

Whether or not partnership in these terms is desirable or realistic, developments to date demonstrate how effective working links between parents, teachers and other professionals can be.

Developments in parental involvement

Events have moved rapidly in the last 15–18 years on a number of educational fronts. In the mainstream where the parental presence is increasingly manifest, especially in primary schools with parents coming into school to hear reading and to help in the school–community 'interface'. In some schemes, the learning and social needs of parents are met in schools, including pre-school, where an increasing number of nurseries and children's centres are designated as Family Centres in which parents are welcomed and encouraged to stay and participate (Wolfendale, 1983).

Two areas of parental involvement which represent major growth areas are parental involvement in reading and special needs, brief résumés of which are given below of 'proven' exemplars of home–school and parent–professional collaboration.

Parental involvement in children's reading

This is a burgeoning area and its take-up and parameters have been chronicled (Topping and Wolfendale, 1985) (included in this book, which constitutes a review as well as a planning guideline, are descriptions of seminal projects – e.g. Haringey; the Hackney PACT, Griffiths and Hamilton, 1984; and paired reading, Morgan, 1986).

Special educational needs and parental involvement

In recent years an increasing number of parents of young physically and/or mentally handicapped (severe learning difficulties) children have become directly involved in assessment and diagnosis, acting as teachers of their own children, as in Portage (see above) (and Newson and Hipgrave, 1982; Mittler and McConachie, 1983; Wolfendale, 1983;

Cunningham and Davis, 1985, for accounts of collaborative work between parents, teachers and others). Parental involvement along these lines is based on a set of premisses:

- that parents are experts on their own children;
- their skills complement professional skills;
- they can impart vital information and make informed observations about their own child;
- they have the right to be involved and should contribute to decision-making.

It is, in part, upon such premisses that the extension to parents' rights in the 1981 Education Act rests. The (DES) Department of Education and Science Circular 1/83 accompanying the Act spells out the philosophy: 'assessment should be seen as a partnership between teachers, other professionals and parents, in a joint endeavour and to discover and understand the nature of the difficulties and needs of individual children' (para.6).

Behaviour problems : involving parents in a whole-school approach

Children's behaviour and emotional problems is uncharted territory. Guidance and therapy with families have long been the province of clinicians in child guidance and psychological services and there are thousands of case files to attest to this approach.

The exclusivity of the therapeutic model (with its associated medical overtones) began to diminish during the 1970s due to a number of developments, such as increased pastoral provision in schools; the creation of units, centres, sanctuaries which offer parents as well as child counselling (on a drop-in or appointment basis); and growth in counselling courses for staff in education and social services. The adoption of family therapy and behaviour management programmes in clinics has helped to reduce mystique about 'therapy magic' and clarified the processes by which problems can be identified, articulated and prioritised for action.

Applied behavioural analysis is a preferred problem-solving framework for many 'away from home' settings in which disruptive behaviour is 'treated', but the inclusion of parents in school-based programmes is still not commonplace. In North America there are numerous manuals for parents, teachers, counsellors. In the UK there are few texts which could be used as a basis for conjoint parent–teacher (and child) use; front runners among those available include Westmacott and Cameron (1981), Wheldall, Wheldall and Winter (1983) and Herbert (1985). Westmacott and Cameron offer a carefully prepared framework for tackling behaviour problems 'to enable parents, teachers and others to arrive at a strategy for self-help', and Herbert offers a 'practical guide to parents in caring for their children'. Burland and Burland (1981) describe a special programme of training for parents and children, in which parents are key agents for effecting and maintaining behaviour change, and their children are equally actively involved in a joint endeavour with staff at the children's residential school.

The danger of excluding parents from these provisions is to perpetuate the divide between home and school (Wolfendale, 1983).

Evolving strategies

It is possible to devise strategies for involving parents on some basic assumptions which could constitute a positive baseline for action, such as:

- parents care about their children's welfare and well-being;
- parents want to bring about behaviour change if this is in their child's best interest;
- parents want to cooperate;
- parents will respond to invitations to participate;
- parents can make a contribution.

The examples given earlier of current work attest to the validity of these assumptions.

The strategies presented below are in the form of planning guidelines, which can be translated by teachers and schools wishing to apply them into aims and objectives appropriate to the situation. We give the possible overall aims below in summary form, then reiterate, in turn, at each level.

Summary of aims:

1. To appraise existing provision and its bearing on and relevance to disruptive behaviour in school and/or reported at home.
2. To review the workings of the school system with a view to incorporating parents.

3. To identify professional skills for working with parents and to provide INSET.
4. To examine critically how existing provision can be used and extended to involve parents and children in intervention approaches to disruptive behaviour.

To aid planning, the tasks and strategies identified and listed here are conceptualised on several levels:

I   :   Current provision.
II   :   The school system.
III   :   School-focused INSET.
IV   :   Direct work with parents and children.

Level I: Current provision

Aim: to appraise existing provision and its bearing on and relevance to disruptive behaviour in school and/or reported at home.

Relevant current provision includes:

- Curriculum arrangements for children with behaviour difficulties and those who are disruptive or disaffected.
- Social curriculum – e.g. clubs, societies organised by staff or pupils.
- Pastoral arrangements for support and guidance to pupils by key staff.
- Provision of units and sanctuaries.
- System of discipline and sanctions within the school.
- Internal communication and incident-reporting system.
- Current policy and arrangements for involving parents – e.g. involvement in reading programmes.

Level II: The school system

Aim: to review the workings of the school system with a view to incorporating parents.

The system and its workings that could best apply to parental participation include:

- Open evenings and current forums for seeing parents.
- Parent governors and their access to and information about school.
- Potential of the PTA for extending the dialogue.

- Designated liaison teachers, with a brief for contacting parents, other agencies.
- Involving parents in critical incidents, suspension procedures, referral, assessments, receipt of written reports.
- Information about school sent to parents and others.

Level III: School-focused INSET

Aim: to identify professional skills required for working with parents and provide INSET.

Considerable expertise will already exist but it may need to be extended to more staff. 'In-house' training does not preclude LEA and centre-based in-service; the rationale for school-focused in-service is that it can be tailor-made to fit unique school circumstances. School staff can be involved in a tutoring capacity, as can e.g. educational psychologists, social workers and others. Depending upon the topic area identified or prioritised, a number of formats could be employed, including:

- Small group/departmental working parties, discussion groups.
- Staff workshops.
- Large/small skills training groups.

Concepts could include:

- Concepts and ideology of parental involvement.
- Review of parental involvement.
- Identifying areas of disruptive or worrying behaviour amenable to parental participation.
- Viable forms of parental involvement.
- Identification of skills required for working with parents, making home visits.

Level IV: Direct work with parents and children

Aim: to examine critically how existing provision can be used and extended to involve parents and children in intervention approaches to disruptive behaviour.

While previous levels can validly constitute 'ends' in themselves, they are also means to an end, namely realisation of the aim for direct work with parents. The implemented programmes will be the core of a policy that involves parents in strategies for dealing with disruptive behaviour.

The model(s) of school-focused INSET, outlined above, would not preclude joint skills training workshops for parents and teachers (and children?) which then form part of the intervention. Such joint workshops could then become more than a straight training forum; their 'by-products' would include increased mutual knowledge and understanding, shared aspirations and agreed targets. Staff and parent training in parental involvement in reading effectively utilises participant techniques such as video feedback, role play and modelling exercises, with plenty of practice at each skill stage (Topping and Wolfendale, 1985). Some possibilities for joint endeavours include:

- Behaviour causes concern at school and home; joint programme is agreed and participants concur on the use of baseline measures, length and type of behaviour management programme, and means of reviewing and evaluating progress. An explicit contract may suit all parties.
- The curriculum can be used as a vehicle for bringing about behaviour (as well as learning) change, as in the adoption of parental involvement in reading; in general literacy and numeracy work; in some parent–child projects and fact-finding exercises; and in an extension of active tutorial work.
- Establishment of regular discussion and review meetings to which parents contribute their 'equivalent expertise' and are involved in planning and reviewing provision for disruptive and problem behaviour. One spin-off from this forum is that the spotlight ceases to focus on an individual child, and parents are enabled to take a broader perspective of 'problems' within the school context.

Applications : practice and possibilities

Some work has been and is being tried out, which corresponds to levels III and IV postulated above. For example, Coulby and Harper (1985) describe parents' problem-solving groups, involving professionals too, at which parents were enabled to present pressing problems of immediate concern and were able in the group to discuss solutions which they could try out over the following days; the authors conclude:

> The immediacy of the feedback and the close support that the group generated produced some substantial practical changes for

some parents. The focus was on day to day behaviour difficulties (p.151)

The Oldham Psychological Service has explored teachers' and parents' views over collaboration in pastoral care and dealing with behaviour problems. The educational psychologists and teachers are providing in-service for teachers on how they involve parents in the schools' pastoral care system, in a secondary school, and have produced materials to accompany the in-service. Paul Marciniak (1986), during his training year as an educational psychologist, was on placement in Oldham and undertook a study based in one secondary school that aimed to examine the viability of levels III and IV within the model proposed in this chapter. He used a mixed interview and questionnaire methodology to explore teachers' and parents' views on closer cooperation on problem behaviour. Results indicated general consensus between parents and teachers on the appropriate strategies to adopt, with agreement also that both agencies should work together on problems located in home and school. Marciniak concludes that the work that had already been started by educational psychologists and teachers, mentioned at the beginning of this paragraph, could therefore fruitfully be extended.

Based on his own work, McConkey (1985) provides a rationale, ideas and practical possibilities for organising and running parents' groups. He considers many ways and means of forming working relationships between and among group participants, using different media as course aids. Although McConkey's many ideas and suggestions were not necessarily specifically aimed at managing problem behaviour, they could be applicable within the frameworks suggested in this chapter at levels III and IV.

Lovitt (1984) provides a case study designed to demonstrate the effectiveness of the combined forces of the home and school being brought to bear upon the 'inappropriate behaviour' of a twelve-year-old boy. Using an applied behaviour analysis framework, Walker and Shea (1984) outline a detailed approach to parent training and home–school behaviour management which includes many strategies to increase, decrease behaviour and facilitate home–school communication; their training objectives are:

- to increase the parents' knowledge of the techniques of behaviour modification;
- to increase the parents' skills in the application of behaviour modification techniques in the management of their children's behaviour;

- to provide both the parents and the teacher with a common perspective of child behaviour management and to facilitate cooperative child behaviour management effort. (p.170)

Using instruments such as the Behaviour Log Form, parents are encouraged to record and report upon behaviour within its occurring contexts, as well as upon its antecedents and consequent effects. Measures to facilitate the process of selecting targets are suggested such as the Target Behaviour Kit, and the authors provide a long list of home reinforcers divided into sections, some of which are: 'consumable food reinforcers', 'reinforcing activities in relation to food reinforcers', 'social reinforcers', 'tangible reinforcers' and 'game activity reinforcers'. This chapter is one of the few to date which presents a sound foundation for joint action by home and school.

Topping (1986) observes on the basis of his review into the involvement of parents whose children present behaviour problems, 'generalisation of improved behaviour from home to school does not seem to happen' (p.199). This, and its converse, may be due to the fact that traditionally home and school have not interacted over these seemingly non-educational problems. Consequently, little transferable, generalisable experience exists in devising and maintaining behaviour change programmes equally involving teachers and parents. This chapter is proposing a conceptual framework and a methodology in order to address this omission and to create an expectation that home–school collaboration over behaviour problems, whether occurring at home and/or school, is a prerequisite for problem-solving.

These approaches encompass prevention and 'treatment'. Another area, ripe for action research, is that of joint parent–teacher (as well as other practitioners') assessment of behaviour, adjustment, identification and definition of problems and concerns. One example, that of Parental Profiling (Wolfendale, 1988) could be applicable, where parents construe a written account of 'My child at home' using guidelines and professional support if they need or want this. In their profile they can highlight and expand upon aspects of behaviour, emotional responsiveness, moods that are of concern and within context. Their account can complement teachers' and other people's view on the child and pave the way to joint problem formulation and problem-solving. The Appendix to this chapter contains a Parental Profile of Robin, completed by his parents. Robin was referred to the school psychological service for persistent 'acting out' and aggressive behaviour in

school, and his parents painted a picture of him at home which provided initial data to complement reports from school.

The flowchart in Figure 20 outlines a model of involving parents
directly at level IV within the framework of levels I–III as outlined in
this chapter. The focus and the emphasis of a behaviour change and
management programme may not be equal either on school or home,
depending where the concern and problems are most felt. The model
set out on the left-hand side shows that at all stages communication
between teachers, parents and others involved remains close and all
parties are kept informed at all times. On the right-hand side a worked
example is given of Robin, whose Parental Profile is reproduced in the
Appendix. How his parents, teachers and educational psychologist
dealt jointly with his behaviour difficulties is shown from identification
through to evaluation of the first phase of the intervention, and illustrates the sequential nature of the model.

Further reading

The reference list includes texts that provide practical guidelines for
parental involvement strategies, such as : Rutherford and Edgar (1979)
on interpersonal communication skills and assertiveness; Berger
(1983), which has a Parent Needs Assessment Questionnaire; Herbert
(1981) for parent training and parent groups; Topping (1983), which has
a section on parent training; Wolfendale and Bryans (1989) which offers
a Personal-Descriptive Observation Sheet for use at school, which
could be adapted for use also at home; Westmacott and Cameron
(1981) on observing and recording; Robertson (1981) on teaching techniques; and Cunningham and Davis (1985), who base their approaches
to developing counselling skills on personal construct theory. Wielkowicz
(1986) offers a chapter which encourages the practitioner to appraise
the nature of behaviour problems within home and school contexts as
a precursor to formulating problem-solving strategies – in effect, a mix
of ecological and behavioural frameworks. In like vein, this author
(Wolfendale, 1987) expounds the notion of collective responsibility for
managing behaviour in the primary school and lists areas of relevant
responsibility for teachers, parents, support agencies and explores the
idea of 'key people', who would be identified as having central responsibility for dealing with individual problems.

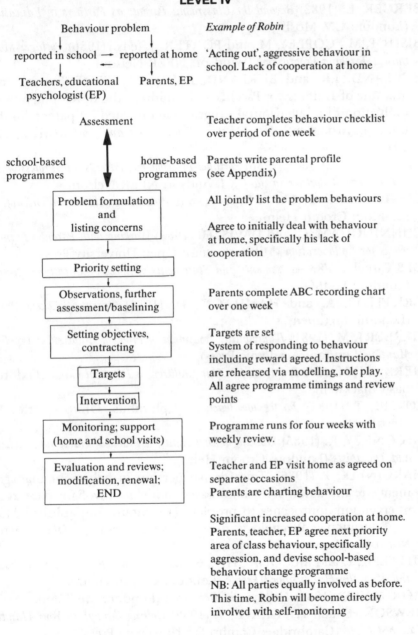

BEHAVIOUR MANAGEMENT: A SCHOOL AND HOME APPROACH AT LEVEL IV

Behaviour problem

Example of Robin

reported in school → reported at home

'Acting out', aggressive behaviour in school. Lack of cooperation at home

Teachers, educational psychologist (EP)

Parents, EP

Assessment

Teacher completes behaviour checklist over period of one week

school-based programmes

home-based programmes

Parents write parental profile (see Appendix)

Problem formulation and listing concerns

All jointly list the problem behaviours

Agree to initially deal with behaviour at home, specifically his lack of cooperation

Priority setting

Observations, further assessment/baselining

Parents complete ABC recording chart over one week

Setting objectives, contracting

Targets are set
System of responding to behaviour including reward agreed. Instructions are rehearsed via modelling, role play. All agree programme timings and review points

Targets

Intervention

Monitoring; support (home and school visits)

Programme runs for four weeks with weekly review.

Evaluation and reviews; modification, renewal; END

Teacher and EP visit home as agreed on separate occasions
Parents are charting behaviour

Significant increased cooperation at home. Parents, teacher, EP agree next priority area of class behaviour, specifically aggression, and devise school-based behaviour change programme
NB: All parties equally involved as before. This time, Robin will become directly involved with self-monitoring

Fig 20   Behaviour Management: a school and home approach at Level IV

References

BERGER, E. (1983) *Beyond the Classroom: Parents as Partners in Education* (London: C.V. Mosby).

BISHOP, M., COPLEY, M. and PORTER, J. (eds.) (1986) *Portage: More than a Teaching Programme* (Windsor: NFER-Nelson).

BURLAND, J.R. and BURLAND, P.M. (1981) 'SPOT: Special Programme of Training for Parents and Children: the development and evaluation of a behavioural programme operated by parents in the home environment', *Int. J. Behav. Social Work and Abstracts*, 1, 2, 87–107.

CAMERON, R.J. (ed.) (1986) *Portage: Preschoolers, Parents and Professionals – Ten Years of Portage in the UK* (Windsor: NFER-Nelson).

COULBY, D. and HARPER, T. (1985) *Preventing Classroom Disruption* (London: Croom Helm).

CUNNINGHAM, C. and DAVIS, H. (1985) *Working with Parents: Frameworks for Collaboration* (Milton Keynes: Open University Press).

DES Circular 1/83 *Assessments and Statements of Special Educational Needs* (London: HMSO).

GRIFFITHS, A. and HAMILTON, D. (1984) *Parent, Teacher, Child* (London: Methuen).

HERBERT, M. (1981) *Behavioural Treatment of Problem Children, a Practice Manual* (London: Academic Press).

HERBERT, M. (1985) *Caring for Your Children, a Practical Guide* (Oxford: Basil Blackwell).

LOVITT, T. (1984) *Tactics for Teaching* (Columbus, Ohio: Charles E. Merrill).

McCONKEY, R. (1985) *Working with Parents, a Practical Guide for Teachers and Therapists* (London: Croom Helm).

MARCINIAK, P. (1986) 'Towards partnership in behaviour management – examination of a school-based model for involving parents in intervention approaches to problem behaviour', unpublished MSc in Educational Psychology dissertation, Psychology Department, North-East London Polytechnic.

MITTLER, P. and McCONACHIE, H. (eds.) (1983) *Parents, Professionals and Mentally Handicapped People* (London: Croom Helm).

MORGAN, R. (1986) *Helping Children Read* (London: Methuen).

NEWSON, E. and HIPGRAVE, T. (1982) *Getting through to Your Handicapped Child* (Cambridge: Cambridge University Press).

ROBERTSON, J. (1981) *Effective Classroom Control* (London: Hodder and Stoughton).

RUTHERFORD, R. and EDGAR, E. (1979) *Teachers and Parents, a Guide to Interaction and Cooperation* (Boston, Mass.: Allyn and Bacon).

TOPPING, K. (1983) *Educational Systems for Disruptive Adolescents* (London: Croom Helm).

TOPPING, K. (1986) *Parents as Educators* (London: Croom Helm).

TOPPING, K. and WOLFENDALE, S. (eds.) (1985) *Parental Involvement in Children's Reading* (London: Croom Helm).

WALKER, J. and SHEA, T. (1984) *Behaviour Management, a Practical Approach for Educators* (St. Louis, Mis.: Times Mirror Mosby).

WESTMACOTT, E.V.C. and CAMERON, R.J. (1981) *Behaviour Can Change* (Basingstoke: Globe Education).

WHELDALL, K., WHELDALL, D. and WINTER, S. (1983) *Seven Supertactics for Superparents* (Windsor: NFER-Nelson).

WIELKIEWICZ, R. (1986) *Behaviour Management in the Schools* (Oxford: Pergamon).

WOLFENDALE, S. (1983) *Parental Participation in Children's Development and Education* (New York: Gordon and Breach).

WOLFENDALE, S. (1988) 'Parental contribution to Assessment', *Developing Horizons No. 10*, National Council for Special Education.

WOLFENDALE, S. (1987) *Primary Schools and Special Needs: Policy, Planning and Provision* (London: Cassell).

WOLFENDALE, S. and BRYANS, T. (1989) *Managing Behaviour : A Framework for Schools*, National Association for Remedial Education, Lichfield, Staffs.

Appendix: Parental Profile

Parental profile of Robin, aged 8½ years (see Wolfendale, 1986, for guidelines).

The early years

Robin was born prematurely, a much-wanted son who has received a lot of love and attention. He liked a lot of cuddling and was given everything he wanted.

What your child is like now

1. Health

Very good overall health, good school attendance. Eats very well, very fit. One night spent in hospital in 1983 as a result of putting a finger out of joint.

2. Physical skills

Enjoys riding his bike, climbing trees. His favourite pastimes are playing with wood and nails – he makes guitars using elastic bands, swords, etc. He would like to use penknives. Robin is happier in the garden, he only stays indoors in the winter, colouring books.

3. Self-help and care

Enjoys playing in the bath, does not wash himself. Tries to comb his hair. Does not tidy his room, sorts his toys out sometimes. Robin is very good with his money, counts it and spends carefully, checks his change and the amount of sweets bought. Goes about on his own, to town centre on his bike and to the nearby park.

4. Speech and language

No problems understanding language, he can describe and explain any situations. He does convey messages from school, except ones concerning himself in trouble.

5. Playing and learning at home

Favourite toys are 'Star Wars' and 'He-men' figures, 'Action Man' (dressing up). Plays with other boys in the garden. Does not like reading, watches some TV when weather is bad.

6. Relationships

Mostly has good relationship with Mum and Dad, squabbles with sisters. Gets on well with other children. He is sometimes cheeky to adults when Mum and Dad are not around. Good with baby sister.

7. Behaviour at home

Does not cooperate, will not do as he is told, even when he has been told before. Sometimes offers help in the house – i.e. carrying things. Does not fit in with routine unless it is a treat for him. Sulks and has temper tantrums, shouts, bawls, slams doors, hits one sister (aged 10).

8. At school

As far as Mum and Dad are aware, he has good relationships with children at school, don't know about teachers except that he is always 'in bother'. Believe that he has made some progress with reading, writing, etc.; but he refuses to work until the last minute. Miss D., the headteacher, has been very patient with Robin, his class teacher had had to have him removed because of his disruptive behaviour.

Your general views

- How do you compare your child with others of the same age?
  Mum and Dad see Robin as the same as others of his age.
- What are your worries, concerns?
  Robin copies older children, is easily led. We are worried about what he will do next, concerned about his problems at school.
- What do you think are your child's special educational needs?
  Robin should be in a class/school where they have more time, and Dad feels he is better with a male teacher.
- How do you think your child sees his difficulties?
  Robin does not appear to realise that his behaviour is a cause of concern.

Chapter 16

Partnership with Pupils

David A. Lane and Fiona Green

> To operate effectively, the school should be at the centre of a network of partnerships. (Adams, 1986)

Education as negotiation

If it was ever true that schools were places where teachers taught and pupils received knowledge written up on the blank slate of their minds, it has certainly ceased to be so today. Schools, as an increasing body of research indicates, are places where realities are negotiated (Hammersley and Woods, 1984). Teachers are 'sussed out' by their pupils, and upon the result depends the level of work produced. Partnership therefore is not an optional extra, but a recognition of the reality that life in school exists by negotiation.

The successful student is one who has negotiated a balance between what the teachers wish to teach and what he/she wishes to learn. The failing student, or the one who presents a challenge (inappropriately 'disruptive') to the school is often the child who has lost faith in that process of negotiation. Such a child may decide that the school will not meet their personal needs, and entering into a partnership with the school therefore becomes irrelevant (Lane, 1990).

As schools set out to meet the needs of children seen as 'special', they embark upon a highly complex task. Yet in attempting to meet the special needs of children, schools face the dilemma of how to identify effectively those needs, without generating the negative effects of labelling the child. It has long been recognised that labelling can actually reinforce a handicapping condition, leaving the child less, not more, able to cope: 'The net effect is often to limit the educational and social opportunities, rather than to enhance them' (Adams, 1986).

Concern has also grown that there is a relationship between labelling and ethnicity (Eggleston, Dunn and Anjali, 1986). A disproportionate number of young people from ethnic minority backgrounds have found themselves categorised as in need of 'special education'. The views of academics, writing from a black perspective, and community pressure groups are finally being heard (Jones, 1980).

Much of special education has been dominated by a paradigm, which placed any difficulty as a deviation from natural occurrence within the individual (Catalano, 1979). Green (1980), for example, in looking at the life histories of pupils who truant clearly demonstrates outcome variables which may have little to do with the actual behaviour of the child, but may have much to do with administrative processes.

Thus, as Galloway *et al.*(1982) and Topping (1983), among others, have pointed out, we have an invention of the 'Disruptive Child', which prevents us from looking for causes of disruption within the school. Unfortunately, many of our approaches to an assessment, including that under the Education Act (1981), tend to perpetuate such myths. Labelling a behaviour as changeworthy is a socially defined process.

The political nature of that process is shrouded in the mists of 'professional objectivity', which are enshrined in the 1982 Act. As Ullman and Krasner (1975) have pointed out, behaviour to be understood must be seen in terms of the act itself, its social context and the observer who is in a position of power.

One of the few ways to change the worst effects of this process is the establishment of a partnership between the observed and the observer. In part, it is possible to diminish the inequality of the power partnership involved, through improving access to information.

Establishing such a partnership often presents some problems for professionals. As studies of client experiences with a variety of professionals (Davis, 1981; Cunningham and Davis, 1985) indicates, there is often a strong sense of dissatisfaction. Clients often feel that their own contribution to decision-making is devalued, or not heard at all. If attention is paid to the client's view, one often gains the impression that professional mismanagement of the referral process is the rule rather than the exception.

This level of dissatisfaction is particularly marked in the area of freedom of information (Cohen, 1982). Client dissatisfaction prompted a change in recent years towards acceptance of partnership. Those working collaboratively have recognised the benefits of mutual sharing of relevant knowledge and skills. Yet the problem for professionals should not be underestimated. As Cunningham and Davis (1985) have indicated, when the professionals view themselves as experts, they take control and elicit such information from the client as they see relevant. A move towards a collaborative or consumer model exposes the professional's vulnerability. The professional has to respect the client's knowledge and competence. Service provision becomes a matter of negotiation in such a model; this cannot happen without mutual respect and a free flow of information:

> One implication of this is that professional power is not entirely determined by their professional status, but by their effectiveness in establishing the negotiating processes and helping to find solutions. It follows that the professional in this model is more vulnerable. The defences of superiority, indispensability and infallibility are not so easily maintained. (*ibid.*)

Both of us, starting our journeys from different points, arrived at the same place in 1973, with a commitment to open files. Fiona Green ran a truancy unit, the Open Class, which operated on a partnership basis. David Lane, working as a school counsellor, referred pupils to that unit, and continued the association when a year later he was appointed to establish the Islington Educational Guidance Centre; in 1975, Fiona Green joined him at the same centre. Two trends, one with origins in the Free School movement (F.G.) and the other in behavioural psychology (D.L.) were merged in a lively and productive partnership. We shared in our independent development of open files, the Open Class and the Islington Educational Guidance Centre a sense of the value of partnership. The aim, as we saw it, was to improve the relationship between the individual and important people and places in their lives, not to adjust them to fit inappropriate demands.

Open files: a basis for partnership

If a partnership is to operate, the information on which a decision is to be made must be shared. The open file provides a basis for partnership (Cohen, 1982).

The recent adoption by the Inner London Education Authority (ILEA) of school files open to parents, and psychological reports open to clients, gives recognition to the rights of clients to know the basis on which proposals are made.

When the present authors were first developing open files in the early 1970s, the level of resistance was great, yet it is now more or less accepted practice; however, merely opening a file does not ensure a partnership. A partnership approach requires a different conception of the purpose of a file. It becomes not a receptacle where reports about the child or family are kept, but an active profile of achievement (ILEA, 1986).

Our approach to the file was to see it as a working document of achievements, not problems to be solved. Opening a file meant that inaccurate information on a child could be challenged and discussed, and that standard welfare, social and psychological reports which contained global information were not used. Rather each piece of information had to justify its existence in explaining why a specific problem existed (Lane, 1978). Each party to an intervention programme knew the basis on which action was being taken, and the child became a valued partner.

The concept of an open file fits very well with an approach to education which emphasises a shared purpose and a negotiated contract. In emphasising the concept that schools exist by negotiation, it is not argued that in most schools this is necessarily a planned process. Most of it is not.

Where decisions in a school rest in a few hands, there is a limit on the process of negotiation; in such a context, an open file makes little difference. The ethos of a school is set, in part, by the distribution of power within the school, and the extent to which pupils, parents and teachers see senior management as listening and supportive, as well as effective. Partnership can be part of that process (Lane, 1973), with the open file as a central focus. The level of satisfaction expressed by parents with their child's schooling seems to decline with age, and pupil satisfaction measured in terms of disruption and non-attendance shows marked increase in the final years (Hargreaves, 1986; Galloway *et al.*, 1982).

The level of conflict or attendance can be seen in terms of the success or failure of the process of negotiation. The task of the school is to ensure that its clients value what is offered, and afford it sufficient priority to choose it, rather than competing needs. The contract which emerges determines the level of cooperation obtained. The use of such a theoretical position which emphasises contractual negotiation within the framework of exchange theory (reciprocal exchange of values) provides a useful format for a partnership to analyse a school situation and plan interventions (Lane, 1972, 1975).

A well managed company in industry, it has been argued (Peters and Waterman, 1982), is one which has a shared purpose that everyone in the company knows and *is proud to practise*. The same applies to the well-run school – it has an ethos which all are proud to share. As Hargreaves (1986) has pointed out, the ethos lies in the people in the school. Open files and the child as a partner are neither necessary nor sufficient to ensure that the child and parent see themselves as partners in the creation of a school ethos, but they can be useful as a starting-point. Used creatively, they can become a profile for partnership and thereby generate a sense of purpose which the various members of the community which is the school are proud to share.

The open class: a truancy project

Official responses to truancy have failed to recognise basic fundamental issues. The main one has to do with the role of the school, the service it provides not only in terms of the quality of the education offered, but also in terms of the need for sensitive handling of the many social and family problems brought into school. These problems may prevent children from learning effectively, but – more than that, they may create a 'pull' away from school and encourage 'survival' adaptations which make the school a less attractive and a less relevant place. This is compounded by the inability of the family with overwhelming financial and emotional problems to get the children to school regularly because they see the school as the lowest of their priorities at home.

In a situation where one or more family members are seriously ill, for example, particularly when it is a parent, a child will stop attending school for fear that the parent's condition will worsen, or that she will die while the child is away at school. Even if they do get away, they rarely do well because of the level of anxiety and upset while at school. Busy teachers with large classes will often not recognise these problems, so will deal with them insensitively or inappropriately.

Action taken by Education Welfare Officers (EWO) also depends on a great many variables: methods of working, the caseload in any particular week; the attitude of the child's school and family; and perception of duties and the nature of the role, all of which are crucial to the action adopted (Green, 1980).

It is against this background that the York Way Open Class (MacInnes, 1974; Turner, 1974) was set up to work with truants – girls from one comprehensive school in north London. It was jointly funded and staffed by the education department and social services. Social and psychological problems were managed by staff with a wide variety of skills. We had in common a child-centred philosophy and a belief in self-regulation. Parents were involved in the setting-up process, and soon girls who had previously not attended school for periods of up to 3 years began to attend full-time.

The reasons for its success (for children attended continuously) lay in the main in the fact that they were directly involved in negotiating their own contracts of work and were parties in the establishment of the week learning programme, and the management of time, money and resources. Each child took a turn at the different roles they had identified as necessary to effective learning such that each had a good grasp of all the skill necessary after a period of a year. Children would meet to discuss issues over coffee each morning; individual problems often came up and were sympathetically and supportively handled by the group, staff and children alike. Everything involving each child's educational welfare was negotiated by child and external agencies, who were often invited into meetings. For example, if a family was experiencing particular financial problems and the child wanted to follow an education course that required financial support, the social worker or EWO would come in and discuss ways of obtaining a grant towards that course, so speeding up the process. Many problems that occupied a large amount of the EWO's time were ameliorated in this way, which left time for the child to learn and for the agencies to concentrate on other cases.

Partnership at the class extended to the parents. All parents were closely involved in the creation of the class at its inception. One parent even came to work at the class initially on a voluntary, and later, a paid basis. They learnt to become supportive of their children's emerging autonomy, while they designed complementary programmes of work in the home. They were involved in maintaining their children's progress, and actively engaged in putting forward innovative ideas on the direction of the Centre's work, when they attended the monthly progress reviews alongside their children. Such collaboration between pupils, parents and staff was exciting and acted as a stimulus to the Centre. The monthly review also acted as a forum in which inter-family disputes or difficulties could be aired openly and worked through. This employed the skills of the relevant agencies; involved cooperation with the child; provided feedback to the larger group in terms of how it affected the group; and generated respect for confidentiality on specific issues. Thus the Open Class became the centre of a network of partnerships. Children requested formal lessons; they were never imposed, and towards the end of their time they also asked to be entered for exams, which they passed.

Apart from the academic lessons, the girls had experience of making films, writing plays, painting and cooking, and they had residential experience away from home in Yorkshire and Devon, becoming involved in the Dartington ROSLA projects. Many of these girls would probably have been received into care – at considerable cost to the community – and their problems would have remained unsolved had it not been for the Centre's involvement. A four-year follow-up study of a sample of 27 girls who attended one of these classes was undertaken. The expressed degree of contentment with their lives and the stability of employment patterns or settled relationships, and their low level of delinquency as compared with a control group drawn from the same secondary school, was notable.

The Islington Educational Guidance Centre

The Islington Educational Guidance Centre was established to provide short-term intervention for children aged 3–16 years, who were referred for severe conduct disorders. The formal point of referral was intended to be the individual child; however, in practice, the individual never represented the primary focus of the work. Our research had established the importance of looking at the individual in the context of the school system. The Centre's policy was therefore based on assumptions derived from the research, the services provided arising out of those assumptions. The central assumption was that it was not enough simply to look at characteristics within the individual for explanations of behaviour labelled 'anti-social', but rather it was necessary to look at the response of the child to the environment, and its response in return. Thus that environment became the main focus for attention.

The referrals received by the Centre might originate from a number of sources – i.e. teachers, psychologists, educational welfare officers, child guidance, etc. – and take a variety of forms. A teacher might ask for help with a child who is disruptive in class, or a head of department might seek help with a whole class which was proving difficult. A headteacher might be looking for advice to set up a programme to deal with problems in the playground at breaktime. A Child Guidance Clinic might want to establish a joint family–school intervention, or a psychologist might be seeking a behavioural assessment of a group of children to support other data obtained. A group of teachers/probation officers, etc. might be seeking a training input. To meet these needs, the Centre provides the following services:

1. Advice, analysis and intervention directly within the school or other setting, in close partnership with those directly involved.
2. The Centre may also carry out a joint teaching programme in the school with the family, or part-time individuals or agencies.
3. Following intervention at (1) or (2), above, follow-up support would be provided for as long as was needed to ensure that gains were maintained and new objectives which arose met.
4. Training and ongoing supervision of practitioners in a variety of settings would be available as necessary.
5. A counselling service for pupils and practitioners would be provided when no alternative sources were available.

The success of the programme developed at the Centre depends upon the combined efforts of the schools, the children, the families, other agencies and the centre, in pooling resources and skills to meet complex problems and the use of validated techniques of analysis and intervention. The importance of that partnership has been established at the experimental, theoretical and practical level (Lane, 1978).

There are three key ways in which that partnership is made explicit:

1. Through the use of open files.
2. Through the use of a negotiated assessment system.
3. Through combining (1) and (2), above.

Thus, at each stage, the information on which decisions are made is shared; and only that information which can justify its existence as a contribution to solving real world problems is retained (Lane, 1974, 1978). Traditional 'global' psychological, social and educational reports are rejected.

The analysis of a problematic situation: a five-phase process

1. The definition phase

When faced with a 'problem' situation, what might the practitioner do? The answer is any one of a number of things – all of which might work. Some of these might lead to deviance amplification, and some to a solution, but frequently the result is a process that labels the child as the focus of the difficulty and excludes the possibility of the child and parent cooperating with the professional.

Where does one start? One starts with a description by someone of a situation they consider to be a problem – 'The worst class I have ever taught – somebody must do something about it'. Contained within that statement are two elements: the behaviour which is causing concern, and the objective of the referring agent. Both the behaviour and the objective need to be clarified.

A start can be made with the behaviour. What is it that the class, or members of it, actually do? Those behaviours have to be operationally defined, so that a naive observer could sit in the class and reliably record the occurrence of any given instance of the behaviour.

The question then becomes: 'Why is that behaviour a problem?' For example, does it interfere with a specific piece of learning or does it disturb others, and to whom is it a problem? If one can determine that the behaviour is a problem, and to whom, it might prove possible to clarify objectives.

To define objectives, it is necessary to determine the actors involved in any situation, and those who are not involved, but who might have a legitimate interest in the situation. All of those involved may have objectives they are trying to achieve, and the clarification of those possibly diverse objectives must be undertaken. The reality is that those actors include the child, and partnership must therefore begin with the recognition of those objectives. The child's perception of the situation has to take its place alongside other views. Unfortunately, that cannot be achieved if the child is described in global terms – e.g. lazy, aggressive, provocative, etc.; the child will simply react with denial, rationalisation, and so on. The child has been relegated to the role of the defendant in a trial. If, however, the emphasis is on a clear definition of actual behaviour, prepared by the teachers and the child, a level of agreement becomes possible. On the basis of that agreement about behaviour, negotiation of objectives can take place.

If this preliminary discussion reveals the existence of an agreed problem definition and a set of objectives which can be usefully analysed, a process of assessment can follow.

2. The assessment phase

The purpose of assessment is to gather necessary information and test hypotheses in order to arrive at a formulation of the problem. The emphasis is on necessary, reliable and refutable information, not every conceivable bit of information which might be available.

There are a number of ways in which a situation might be assessed, the choice being determined by the nature of the problem, its setting and the objectives of those involved. Involving the child in the assessment phase, at the very least, adds a valuable observer, but at best it provides a perspective which is unavailable in any other way.

This does not mean that teacher and child have the same role, rather that they have complementary roles and, at times, the teacher may need to be more dominant. The roles played will vary over time. But the child (and parent) does have access to a broader perspective on the behaviour of concern in a variety of settings. Recognising that there are some setting in which problems occur, and others in which they do not, provides a starting-point. Understanding the difference between these settings often leads to potential explanations.

3. The formulation phase

Once all the information is obtained, the process of formulation can begin. The aim is to provide an explanation which demonstrates why given behaviours occur. On the basis of the formulation, predictions are possible about the likely impact of any changes introduced into the situation. The formulation is not just one person's explanation; it has been established through a cooperative process of information-gathering and hypothesis-testing. It has then been further discussed and refined, and any suggestions for intervention talked through, so that eventually one arrives at an agreement. The agreement consists of the formulation, intervention options, a definition of each participant's role, the objectives to be met and the end-product. As Cunningham and Davis (1985) point out, 'Ideally, the process of negotiation should lead to mutually agreed solutions'.

4. The intervention phase

In the intervention phase, the particular actions which are to be undertaken are specified and a contract between the parties is entered into. The contract is run and monitored to see that it works as predicted. The ongoing process of evaluation is critical and enables the formulation to be tested, and if necessary, altered. When 'negotiation' has taken place, it reduces the likelihood of failure, because all parties have a stake in the outcome – they have shared responsibility.

5. *The follow-up phase*

This is the key phase to ensure that gains are maintained and that new objectives are met, and that reflection on the whole process takes place for future benefit. A formal process of review must follow every intervention and, periodically, groups of interventions. Otherwise poor techniques will not be eliminated and necessary changes in the school structures will not be clarified. Poor practices continue far too long in most settings, because they are not periodically challenged. This particularly applies to high-profile problems which generate crisis reactions, rather than whole-school policies (Tattum and Lane, 1988). Involving the child (and parent) in this process, based on shared objectives and open files, generates an effective partnership and realistic change.

Attempting partnership: an example

An example has been chosen (which is in some respects unsatisfactory) to illustrate that sometimes even an attempt at partnership can generate effective change. The material, due to shortage of space, only partly reports the complexity of the case.

Andrew was a ten-year-old boy attending a primary school and was referred to Islington Educational Guidance Centre. The referral described him as: 'A very violent and aggressive boy, who loses his temper with very little provocation.' His attitude to female staff was also seen as problematic, since in the words of the teacher, 'He treated them as inferiors'.

In terms of the earlier discussion, such a definition is useless. You cannot start a partnership with a child by accusing him of being an aggressive person. Instead the teacher was asked to provide and record details of actual incidents, encouraging him to report exactly what happened, not interpretations of why it happened. This material was discussed with the child and his parent, and Andrew was asked to make similar records. These were compared.

In looking at the incidents, Andrew was prepared to agree that he did act in the way described. A consideration of the objectives of the various parties produced a wide divergence.

The referring teacher saw himself as strong and able to control Andrew, whereas female staff failed to exercise strict discipline. However, that was seen as being Andrew's problem, and he had to learn to accept this control. The parent (father) expressed the view that he was strong and able to control Andrew, that females were weak, but that was their problem. They had to learn to exercise firm control. The headteacher agreed with the class teacher, but felt that Andrew should be excluded and special schooling found.

Andrew felt that his behaviour was perfectly justified. It was apparent that Andrew was faced with a group of male adults who held views on women very similar to those which were the subject of the complaint against him. No agreement on objectives was possible, at this stage, but agreement on specific (though not all) aspects of the behaviour was obtained. As a way round the difficulty, a new objective was suggested, that was 'to investigate the settings in which the behaviours were more or less likely to occur'. Father agreed to this, but did not wish to make a record; but both Andrew and the class teacher were prepared to record (a simple tick on a chart) each time a defined incident occurred and the setting for it (time, place, personnel). It should be noted that the school was not asked to ignore behaviour they saw as inappropriate during this period. They reacted in the usual way, applying such consequences as were seen to be appropriate. Subsequently a functional analysis was attempted (recording events which immediately preceded and followed any incident), again based on records produced by the child, teacher and headteacher. The agreed role of the Islington Educational Guidance Centre was to facilitate their data collection and discussion of it.

The record indicated that most incidents occurred either in that teacher's class or when he was on playground duty; only rarely did difficulties occur with a woman teacher. Discussion of the material with Andrew revealed that he did not 'lose his temper and strike out', as had been suggested, but rather he made a deliberate decision to hit some people in certain settings, in response to specific types of provocation. This pattern was discussed with the child, teacher and father. The father, in the light of this information, was no longer prepared to agree that the behaviour was a problem and emphasised that 'his son should stand up for himself, if provoked'. The class teacher expressed the view that the boy was 'on a power trip', and that any work he attempted would be undermined.

A formulation was possible, and this was attempted; a number of factors were noted, three of which are discussed here:

1. Andrew could predict when he would behave in the specified way (hitting out, etc.), justified the behaviour to himself and was encouraged in that belief by his father.
2. The response of the school to an incident resulted in his

removal from an aversive situation (where he was being provoked) to one where the situation was talked through (the
head's office). The 'verbal repartee' with the head that was
involved was something Andrew quite enjoyed.

3. Males in positions of power consistently reinforced the view
that women were inferior.

It was possible, after much discussion, to produce an agreement that
factors 1 and 2, above, might be relevant and could be altered. No
agreement was possible on factor 3 and the 'validity' of the finding was
questioned by the teacher, even though it was based on the teacher's
and Andrew's own record.

Intervention strategies were established, which included:

1. A set of alternative behaviours for Andrew to use when he anti-
cipated being provoked, or was provoked.
2. A set of alternative strategies which the school could use in
dealing with such incidents.
3. An agreed set of 'cues' to be exchanged between the parties to
indicate impending action.

The interventions were agreed. This was possible because a specific
outcome within a defined timescale was included, that is something
was being done.

The follow-up indicated a substantial reduction in the number of
incidents. However, in spite of the evidence of the objective record, the
school still saw him as a problem. A Bristol Social Adjustment Guide
(BSAG) (Stott, 1971) had been administered originally and it was
repeated. This indicated that the child was less hostile (i.e. more trust-
ing of adults), but more inconsequential (impulsive, distractable, etc.) It
was not clear if he had actually become more impulsive, or whether the
reduction in other problems had enabled the school to focus on different ones.

The child and teachers were asked to look at the material and,
between them, discuss how the strategies could be improved. They
decided that the 'cueing' system could be tightened up, so that the
teachers became aware of Andrew's concerns, and he of the teachers',
at an earlier stage in any incident. A further follow-up indicated satisfaction by all parties. A closer association between the child's and
teacher's perspective had been accomplished.

The BSAG score changed from 27 to 7, behaviours giving rise to concern. The school felt that at the final level (7), the difficulties were

containable within the framework or normal school discipline. A further follow-up at the end of Andrew's primary school career indicated that matters remained satisfactory.

It was apparent throughout that obtaining agreement between the parties would be difficult since they held diverging views. However, by concentrating on actual incidents rather than explanatory fictions, and by involving the respective parties in data collection and only proceeding on those aspects of the situation on which agreement was possible, step by step, a partnership was evolved. Each party, including the child, became responsible for the success of the partnership.

Conclusions

We have argued that partnership in education is not a luxury, but a recognition of the reality that school life exists by negotiation. Those practitioners who have developed partnership approaches with clients testify to their value (Lane, 1988).

Our work over many years has demonstrated that children, even those who many would regard as being least able to cooperate with adults, can become effective partners in their own education.

References

ADAMS, F. (1986) *Special Education* (Harlow: Councils and Education Press).

CATALANO, R. (1979) 'Health, behaviour and the community' (Oxford: Pergamon).

COHEN, R. (1982) *Whose File Is it Anyway?* (London: National Council for Civil Liberties).

CUNNINGHAM, C. and DAVIS, H. (1985) *Partnership with Parents* (Milton Keynes: Open University Press).

DAVIS, M. (1981) *The Essential Social Worker* (Oxford: Pergamon).

EGGLESTON, J., DUNN, D. and ANJALI, M. (1986) *Education for Some* (Trent: Trentham Books).

GALLOWAY, D., BALL, T., BLOOMFIELD, D. and SEGAL, R. (1982) *Schools and Disruptive Pupils* (London: Longman).

GREEN, F. (1980) 'Becoming a truant: the social administrative process applied to pupils absent from school', unpublished Masters thesis, Cranfield.

HAMMERSLEY, M. and WOODS, P. (1984) *Life in School* (Milton Keynes: Open University Press).

HARGREAVES, D. (1986) *ILEA Truancy Conference* (London: ILEA).

ILEA (1986) *Profiling in Schools* (London: ILEA).

JONES, R. (1980) *Black Psychology* (New York: Harper and Row).

LANE, D.A. (1972) *Contact Therapy*, Islington Educational Guidance Centre, London.

LANE, D.A. (1973) 'The problem or order,' *Remedial Education*, 8,3, 9–11.

LANE, D.A. (1974) *The Analysis of Complex Cases. Islington Educational Guidance Centre* (London: ILEA).

LANE, D.A. (1975) *Dependency: Techniques of Prevention*, Monograph, IEGC/King's Fund Centre, London.

LANE, D.A. (1978) *The Impossible Child* (London: ILEA), Vols 1 and 2.

LANE, D.A. (1990) *The Impossible Child, or the Lost Entrepreneur* (Trent: Trentham Books).

LANE, D.A. and TATTUM, D. (1988) *Supporting the Child in School* (London: Professional Development Foundation), Vols 1 and 2.

MACINNES, C. (1974) 'The open way', *Times Educational Supplement*, 2 August.

PETERS, T.S. and WATERMAN, R.H. (1982) *In Search of Excellence: Lessons from America's Best-run Companies* (New York: Harper and Row).

STOTT, D.M. (1971) *The Social Adjustment of Children* (London: University of London Press).

TATTUM, D. and LANE, D.A. (1988) *Bullying in Schools* (Trent: Trentham Books).

TOPPING, K.J. (1983) *Educational Systems for Disruptive Adolescents* (London: Croom Helm).

TURNER, B. (1974) *Truancy* (London: Ward Lock).

ULLMAN, L.P. and KRASNER, L. (1975) *A Psychological Approach to Abnormal Behaviour* (Englewood Cliffs, NJ: Prentice-Hall).

Conclusion

Irvine Gersch

By way of conclusion it will be helpful to underline and highlight a few themes from the book.

The variety of contributions testifies to the fact that there are many possibilities when dealing with challenging behaviour. There is much, however, from behavioural science and methodology which is of use to practitioners. Partnerships with professionals, parents and children are key principles.

Many of the contributors demonstrate that when problems arise it is a clear and careful assessment which must be the first step. Plans for behavioural change should then be constructed carefully and in consultation with all concerned. Due regard must be paid to the ethical implications of changing someone's behaviour and to the special circumstances of children. Any changes need to be monitored closely and evaluated in objective terms.

We hope that those reading this book will find some of the ideas and projects useful. Even so, there is no substitute for individual solutions of individual problems. When it comes to challenging behaviour we should all beware of quickfit, all-encompassing solutions. No two situations, schools, children or indeed practitioners are going to be the same. Hence ideas will need to be adapted and modified. We hope that our book will be used in the same way: as a trigger and stimulus rather than a textbook of solutions.

Index